Law School

2nd Edition

by Tracy L. Simmons, JD, MA

for dummies®

A Wiley Brand

Law School For Dummies®, 2nd Edition

Published by: **John Wiley & Sons, Inc.**, 111 River Street, Hoboken, NJ 07030-5774, www.wiley.com

For general information on our other products and services, please contact our Customer Care Department within the U.S. at 877-762-2974, outside the U.S. at 317-572-3993, or fax 317-572-4002. For technical support, please visit https://hub.wiley.com/community/support/dummies.

Wiley publishes in a variety of print and electronic formats and by print-on-demand. Some material included with standard print versions of this book may not be included in e-books or in print-on-demand. If this book refers to media that is not included in the version you purchased, you may download this material at http://booksupport.wiley.com. For more information about Wiley products, visit www.wiley.com.

Library of Congress Control Number is available from the publisher.

ISBN 978-1-394-29419-0 (pbk); ISBN 978-1-394-29420-6 (ebk); ISBN 978-1-394-29421-3 (ebk)

Contents at a Glance

Table of Contents

Introduction

Welcome to the wide, wonderful, and sometimes wacky world of law school! The book you hold in your hands will come in handy even more than that 10-pound casebook you just bought (or will soon buy). That's because it's a reference guide for those who want the inside scoop on getting into law school, staying sane while you're there, and graduating with the job of your dreams. Everything you need to know to survive and thrive in law school is right here in this book. And what's a piddly investment compared to $100,000 to 200,000 in student loans, right?

This book fits three (or four) years of blood, sweat, and tears into 27 chapters. I funnel all the important information you really need to know into this book so you can get started as quickly as possible on your path to successful law studentdom.

Why do I feel I have the qualifications to relate this information to you? That's easy. Although I graduated from law school in 1999, I have worked in law school admissions, financial aid, diversity initiatives, and student affairs since the fall of that year.

I can't think of any applicant I've worked with as an admissions dean, consultant, and mentor who didn't bring intelligence, wit, and willingness to get things done with them to the table, so I know you aren't a dummy. Heck, you surely can't be, because you've done well enough in college and on the LSAT or GRE that you're either seriously thinking about or already in law school. You've proven to yourself that you have the mental moxie and drive to make it in a competitive academic environment. All you have to do is embrace the strategies of law school success I outline here. Look out, world!

So sit back and follow me into the exhilarating world of law school, content in the knowledge that just reading this book puts you head and shoulders ahead of your law school (or future law school) classmates. Your GPA and résumé will thank you for it!

About This Book

I know that many law school books, blogs, and social media accounts are competing for your attention. When I was applying to law school, I sought as many resources as possible. But the following are several compelling reasons I think you need to choose this book instead:

>> **It's written by someone who's been there, done that.** It feels like only yesterday that I was pulling my hair out over finals, procrastinating on my studies, awaiting the feedback on writing and research memos, and searching for internships. But I've also spent time with current admissions, financial aid, and student affairs professionals and, most importantly, listened to and heard from actual law school applicants and students. That's why you can count on this guide to give you the most up-to-the-minute information you need to get through law school.

>> **It's every law student's book.** This book is aimed at students from every tier of law school, from lowest to highest. It covers issues most relevant to *all* law students, from seasoned students to part-time students to students with accommodations to K-JD students to people with previous careers. This book addresses everyone because today's law school classes are filled with bright, talented students from every undergraduate major, socioeconomic status, age group, and occupation. The bottom line is that this book is for everyone who wants to understand the law school experience better.

>> **It's well-rounded.** This book doesn't assume standard law student protocol (for example, that you're going to opt for a traditional legal career, compete to become a member of the moot court team or law review, or even take the bar exam). Instead, I aim to present *all* your options, particularly the off-the-beaten-path ones that aren't talked about all that much in law school.

>> **It's realistic.** When you're in law school, you hear plenty of myths, such as the ones that say only the top 10 percent of law school graduates get jobs or that you have to land a big firm summer job because everyone else is doing the same. This book cuts through the law school rumor mill and gives you the real truth, straight up.

Use this book as a coach, mentor, friend, cheerleader, prelaw advisor, career counselor, admissions advisor, hiring lawyer, and all-around reference. It's the equivalent of the upperclass student you never thought you'd luck out to know, the one who's willing to lead you by the hand and share battle-tested strategies each and every day.

Foolish Assumptions

In writing this book, I made a few assumptions about who you may be as a reader:

- » You're an absolute beginner with no prior knowledge of how to decide which law school to attend or what applying to law school even takes.

- » You may have heard a few law school horror stories.

- » You already have an acceptance letter in your hot little hands (congratulations!), and you want to know how to choose courses that can benefit you down the road and select the right extracurricular activities for your personality.

- » You aren't necessarily 22 and straight out of college.

- » You don't necessarily go to an Ivy League law school or sit in the top 10 percent of your class.

Icons Used in This Book

If you're at all familiar with *For Dummies* books or you've skimmed through this one while debating whether to buy it, you probably noticed the charming little icons interspersed throughout the margins (why can't casebooks adopt these?). Here's the lowdown on what they mean:

TIP

When I want to reinforce a piece of advice, I use this icon.

REMEMBER

If you remember nothing else from this book, this icon signals an important tidbit to file away in your brain.

WARNING

When I discuss an aspect of law school that can potentially reach out and bite you (an unequivocal tort), I use this icon. I also use it to point out things that may be dangerous to your GPA, social life, or wallet.

Beyond the Book

In addition to what you're reading right now, this book also comes with a free, access-anywhere cheat sheet. To view the cheat sheet, simply go to www.dummies.com and type "Law School For Dummies Cheat Sheet" in the Search box.

Where to Go from Here

By picking up this book, you've taken an important step toward ensuring your success in law school. But where do you start? If you're still considering law school or you're in the midst of applying, start with Part 1. If you've already passed this milestone and you're about to start your almighty first year, go straight to Part 2. And if you're in over your head with all the work you have to do, start with The Part of Tens for a good chuckle. Go ahead and dog-ear the pages to your heart's content. That's what this book is for.

1

Considering Law School

IN THIS PART . . .

Decide whether you're ready for law school.

Get familiar with the law school experience.

Pick the right law schools to apply to.

Work through the application process.

Figure out how to finance your education.

Enjoy pre-orientation and orientation.

Chapter **1**

Exploring the Realities of Law School

Never has being a lawyer been more popular! Law school applications are up significantly, and law school seems to be the "in" thing to do across the country, regardless of whether you're a graduating college senior or a middle-aged career-changer. If you're looking to take that first step on the intellectual journey of a lifetime, now is a prime time for doing it. At first, everything about law school can seem intimidating and intense, but rest assured that this chapter starts you out on the right path by offering an overview of the entire law school experience.

Demystifying the Law School Experience

Many prelaw students are confused about what law school entails because they may not know anyone who is in or has been through the experience. (I surely didn't when I applied.) How does the saying go? You don't know what you don't know. That's definitely true as it relates to law school. It's a big mystery. So in this section, I fill you in on exactly what you can expect as a new 1L (first-year law student).

As part of the admissions process, I encourage you to actually visit a law school classroom in person or virtually if that's offered. That way, you can find out

>> How the faculty or professors engage their students

>> More about the Socratic method (check out the later section "Surviving the Socratic method")

>> How prepared the students are (or aren't)

>> How long the classes are

>> How you should address your faculty members (they're professors, not "teachers")

Ultimately, being prepared, being organized, and getting your mindset right for the journey are key. Just as admissions professionals tell you as you begin your application process!

Preparing for three (or four) years of blood, sweat, and tears

No one denies that law school is a lot of work. You have three years (or four, if you're a part-time or evening law student) of challenging classes, approximately 100 pages of reading every night, and sometimes only a midterm and a final exam that determine your entire grade for each class. On top of the academic load are time-consuming extracurricular activities, such as the law review or a law journal, moot court, and the myriad other organizations you can join. (See Chapter 19 for complete details about law school extracurriculars.)

And in your free time (who said anything about free time?), you're expected to send out résumés and cover letters while prospecting for your 1L and 2L summer jobs (see Chapter 20) and postgraduation permanent job (see Chapters 21, 22, and 23). Sound rough? It can be, but if you're up for it, law school can be one of the most rewarding experiences of your life. This is all you've worked for and dreamed of!

Initially, the law school process can seem so intimidating. You have no clue about how many hours per week you need to study to be a successful law student. You don't know how to take notes in law school. You keep hearing the word *outlining*, but you have no idea what that means or when you should start doing it.

You can also easily underestimate the amount of time you need to spend just reading. Law school reading is different from reading a regular textbook. You're often reading old cases with dense and unfamiliar language. You may take an hour to read a handful of pages because the format is something you aren't used to and the words are unfamiliar to you.

Some students grasp the contracts concepts very quickly, while others struggle with civil procedure. Others walk away with a significant appreciation and understanding for property, while some really have a hard time understanding why an accident is a tort with one set of facts but not a tort with another set of similar facts.

What I can tell you is that all these things vary from one student to another. You'll eventually hit your stride and settle in.

Dealing with the law school setup

If one term describes how the law school experience is set up, it's *high school*. For many ABA (American Bar Association) law schools, all your classes are in one building; you have assigned seats and lockers again, and gossip spreads like wildfire. I'd have to say that "high school" is definitely an apt description.

REMEMBER

Despite its high school vibes, law school is professional school. I'm not saying you won't have fun or like all your professors, classmates, and so on, but your reputation is important. Remember that maintaining a good reputation is easier than rebuilding a tainted one. The respect of your classmates, faculty, and administrators is yours to gain or lose.

REMEMBER

Your law school reputation is important because the legal profession isn't that big. Your classmates may be on a future hiring committee or be opposing counsel in a case important to your career trajectory. Treat people well so they have positive memories of you. It may make a difference one day.

Whether you're starting law school as a full-time student or part-time student, you want to ensure that your life is in order. Doing so means figuring out things like the following:

>> Where you're going to live and how you're going to get to and from class

>> Where you'll get your prescriptions filled

>> What your budget is and whether you should pack lunch versus buying lunch on campus

>> How many cups of coffee you need throughout the day to be a functional human (if you're a coffee drinker)

- **»** What type of environment you need to study in

- **»** Whether you're taking notes on your laptop or handwriting them (which may be determined by what your professor allows)

- **»** How prepared you need to be for classes that start in the morning classes versus classes start later in the afternoon

- **»** How to adjust your study schedule based on which subject(s) you find more challenging and which you find you like and easily digest

You'll receive a ridiculous amount of advice about how to manage law school, your professional persona, and so on. At the end of the day, do what's best for you. Most people have good intentions, but only you know your learning style, how many friends is enough, and who you need mentorship from.

Your first-year law school class is divided into *sections* or *tracks,* and you attend all your classes as a 1L with the same people. That can become trying when your class has several *gunners* (people who constantly raise their hands, usually just to hear themselves talk). In time, however, you may grow to appreciate the comforting feeling of seeing the same faces, especially when it comes time to speak in front of 60 to 100 of them! But most importantly, these folks become lifelong friends. You rarely meet a lawyer who doesn't remember their track/section. These students become members of your family, potential partners, godparents to your kids — and opposing counsel.

Surviving the Socratic method

One of the horror stories you've heard about law school is true: Professors really do call on you in front of the entire class. The intense questioning that professors direct toward students is referred to as the *Socratic method* because Socrates (that famous Greek philosopher dude way back when) apparently liked to clarify the responses of his students by asking them more and more questions rather than by providing answers. The scary part is that the Socratic method is something many law students haven't experienced.

The very thought of the Socratic method petrifies most prospective students because they're so unaccustomed to the idea. No college class that I've ever heard of (or taken) requires you to engage in a one-on-one interrogation session with a professor, sometimes even while you're standing up. I know, I know. Fortunately, by the 2L and 3L years, many professors tend to ease off the Socratic method; they often teach courses in lecture or discussion format. (Chapter 12 explains why.)

REMEMBER

The Socratic method does require you to really know your material; otherwise, you'll be embarrassed in front of the class while stumbling around for even a hint of the right answer. It also forces you to think quickly and challenge your previously held assumptions. It truly tests your understanding of the material in a unique and often scary way.

Though this situation is terrifying for most people, you can and will survive. Preparation is important. Prepare to be wrong; to walk away without a clear-cut, black-and-white answer; to be open-minded; and prepare to have a deep conversation with your professor while your classmates silently cheer you on!

Overall, I think the Socratic experience was a beneficial one for me. Although at the time it may have caused a few ulcers, in hindsight I can see it made me more comfortable about speaking in front of an audience (the class) and being on the mock trial team and more appreciative of the verbal jockeying that lawyers do in the courtroom.

The Socratic method can be frustrating and exhausting. But after you get the hang of it, get to know your professor, and learn how to brief cases, take notes, and outline, you may feel much better. Notice I didn't say you *will* feel better. For many law students, every semester or quarter brings the same anxiety and stress.

The only way through it is to do it.

Developing a lawyer's mindset

The whole point of law school is to train you in the fine art of problem-solving and legal reasoning. You're being prepared to become an advocate, a policy maker, and a changemaker. To do so, you must train your brain to think, write, and talk differently.

Thinking like a lawyer

Lawyers look at problems differently than laypeople. When lawyers hear someone talking about an incident, they listen for the ordering of facts and try to discern the precise issue without getting caught up in insignificant details. This process is what law school is all about.

The concept of *thinking like a lawyer* (see Chapter 12) is a change that comes over you subtly during your first few weeks of law school and more significantly at the end of your first semester or first year. You may be surprised how quickly you begin thinking differently about everyday items, news stories, and issues that arise in front of you during your first couple of weeks of law school.

Some law students swear that it's never happened to them, but your non–law-school friends and family are likely to be better judges of that. Listen closely to their comments after your first year. Are they saying things like "You're so much more analytical or logical than you used to be"? Do you find yourself thinking about everyday situations — like a banana peel lying on the floor of a supermarket — just a little differently than you did before law school? If so, you know that thinking like a lawyer has begun to take hold.

Adding legalese to your vocabulary

Legal writing is very different from everything else you've learned. It's brief. It's factual. It isn't flowery at all. You rarely see adjectives in legal writing.

The transformation to the lawyer's way of writing and speaking is swift for some people. They're surprised at how quickly they begin to pick up on the legalese. For others, those first legal writing assignments are alarming. Be prepared for your legal writing professors to be very critical. Every word, detail, citation, and so on matters, and their job is to make you transform your writing as quickly as possible. They're setting you up for the rest of your career — in law school and as an attorney.

Assessing Whether You Can Make It in Law School

At a minimum, you need to have a love for learning, reading, and writing and a penchant for studying — plenty of studying — to succeed in law school. In addition, successful law students

>> Manage their time effectively

>> Don't succumb to procrastination

>> Are strong writers (or willing to put in the time to improve)

>> Get reading done in a timely manner

>> Prepare for each day's class

>> Juggle multiple tasks simultaneously

>> Sometimes delay gratification (in other words, they put off going out for the evening to spend extra time getting their criminal law outline in better shape)

Similarly, full-timers can put in time on an extracurricular activity like moot court or a law journal (see Chapter 19) without sacrificing the quality of their schoolwork. Extracurricular activities aren't required but come highly recommended because they're great preparation for legal jobs. They're opportunities to network, to take a break from studying, and to socialize.

Can I do it? Do I belong here? These are questions that come up quite frequently throughout the first couple of weeks of law school. I can't tell you that they won't come up at other times as well. The most important thing to remember is your why. Why are you doing this? Why are you working this hard? Staying motivated and keeping your self-talk as positive as possible are important. You want to be confident while also being humble.

Going part time versus full time

Full-time programs for most candidates really look like 60-to-80-hour-per-week jobs. It's that much reading, writing, and thinking. If you need to work full time to support yourself, avoid excessive post-law school debt, or pay tuition, you can consider opting to go to law school in the evenings or part time during the day. Most part-time and evening programs run four years rather than the traditional three, so think about how quickly you want to enter the job market. A few hybrid programs are available, but they're rare.

Part time or full time is a big decision for many candidates. If you have a job you love that will pay for you to attend law school, it seems like a no-brainer. The reality is very few part-time programs are left, though. Fewer than half of ABA law schools offer part-time or evening programs. Also, know that most part-time programs are actually more like three-quarter-time programs. The workload is less for part-timers, but it's still very heavy.

REMEMBER

Part-time law students face challenges that their full-time peers don't. Part-time students need to make sure they have enough time to handle the often-overwhelming responsibilities of school, full-time work, and household and family life. Often, they have their hands too full to participate in some of the traditional extracurricular activities, such as law reviews and journals and moot court. Luckily, schools make opportunities available to part-time and evening students to ensure they don't miss out on co-curricular and/or extra-curricular opportunities.

Over the years, many law schools have found that part-time students do relatively well because they have jobs and /or family obligations that they're trying to balance, so their time management skills are on point. They want to get in and out in three years, be done with this whole school thing, and become an attorney.

The bottom line: Weigh the pros and the cons of going part time or full time for yourself.

Evaluating your study skills

Law school, like most other graduate programs, requires you to really buckle down and study. But studying in law school doesn't mean the kind of last-minute studying that may have worked well for you in college. Studying for law school classes is more of a little-bit-each-day-of-the-semester sort of studying that keeps you up to speed (prevents you from falling behind) and enables you to absorb as much information as possible. The volume and depth of reading in law school is vastly different from what you may be used to. You can't be a passive listener in a law school class. You have to keep up with the lecture, conversation, and discussion in each class.

Many new law students are shocked to discover the things that worked for them in undergrad or even grad school don't work for them in law school. Those that were visual learners realize that they're auditory learners. Others realize they need to write their notes and then type them and then put them into cards or outlines to ensure that they've memorized the rules. If that information is scaring you, take heart; most law schools have academic programs throughout orientation to help you figure out what works best for you.

TIP Doing a little self-assessment and backup planning throughout the summer before school can put you ahead of the game. Be prepared to make some changes. Are you someone who needs to type your notes? How will you adapt if you have a professor who doesn't allow laptops? If you're an auditory learner and your professor doesn't allow you to record their lecture, what's your plan B?

If you don't already have these kinds of study skills, you need to gain them quickly before law school starts; otherwise, you'll find yourself struggling to keep up. Chapters 11 and 13 have some hints on developing successful law school study skills.

WARNING If you suspect that you may have a learning disability, get testing as soon as possible.

Managing the pressure, stress, and highs and lows

For most people the volume of work and the intensity of law school's classroom engagement is very different from that of other programs. Law school is a space where you have to be engaged in class all the time; you don't really get an opportunity to check out. Gaining a good sense of time management before entering law school is your best protection against the debilitating kind of stress that can crop up thanks to the constant pressure of your classes and obligations.

So what do you do when you start feeling overwhelmed? Most schools provide you with a variety of opportunities to cope with stress through counseling sessions and student organization activities or programming.

You'll need tools like stress management and self-care throughout your career as a lawyer.

REMEMBER

Considering Other Important Factors Before Deciding on Law School

Enrolling in law school isn't something that you can do on a whim (or because you don't know what else to do with your college degree). You must take into account whether spending three (or four) years of your life (and a bunch of money) engaged in the study of a discipline that realistically may not land you the job of your dreams right off the bat is really worth it. Here are some points to consider:

>> **What will you do with a law degree?**

>> **How does the debt you'll take on relate to your chosen career path?** You want to be sure you can manage your debt and the lifestyle you envision.

>> **Are you putting yourself in a position where you can maintain the level of study, commitment, and focus you're going to need in your first (and second, third, and maybe fourth) year of law school?** Be sure to assess your mental health, your spiritual health, and your physical capacity.

>> **Are your family members, friends, mentors, and supervisors (if you'll continue working) ready for the fact that you won't be available in the same way for the next three to four years?**

These are just some of the considerations that you may add to your list. Doing your research as a prelaw student is key. Talk to as many people — law students, lawyers, and law professors — involved in the law as you can. Actually go to a law school or two and sit in on some classes. Do you like what you hear? Do some job shadowing and/or informational interviewing (which I cover in Chapters 20 and 21). Find out what your student tour guide likes and dislikes about law school and/or their careers. Only by being armed with as much information as possible can you make a well-informed decision.

TIP

Taking a hard look at your financial situation

Law school is certainly a financial sacrifice, so do the math. The real math.

>> **Have you looked at your current student loan debt?** Many prelaw students don't realize that having a large amount of student loans often precludes new graduates from taking lower-paying jobs they'd really like in favor of the ones that will help with loan repayment.

>> **Have you considered the career paths that you may be interested in and how those may impact your overall lifestyle after you've completed law school?**

>> **Have you saved up enough money to live comfortably for your first year?** Have you paid off as much of your credit card debt as you can?

TIP

Don't live like a lawyer while in law school. Being more frugal now ensures that you can enjoy the fruits of your labor after you begin working as lawyer as opposed to only working to pay off your debt.

>> **Do you have a spouse or partner to consider?** Childcare? Elder care?

>> **Have you reviewed whether the health insurance the university/law school offers meets your needs?**

>> **Are you conducting your own scholarship research?** This task should be part of your school application process. Does the law school offer other scholarships or opportunities to decrease your debt while you're in law school? These may include scholarships in the second, third, and/or fourth year; work-study jobs; or paid research assistance or teaching assistant roles.

REMEMBER

Paying close attention to your overall indebtedness can ultimately impact your career choices. Choose wisely so you can do the work you're most interested in or most passionate about.

Law school is certainly a financial sacrifice, but that sacrifice is mitigated when you're committed to taking advantage of the benefits of a legal education, including potential upward mobility, qualification for a broader range of jobs, and (sometimes) greater income. A legal education is an investment in your future.

Critiquing your reasons for becoming a lawyer

Why do you want to become a lawyer? This point is going to be important when you're up reading the case for the third time at 11 p.m. You know you're going to be called on tomorrow — drilled about the facts, the rules, the analysis — and you still don't quite understand why the ruling came out the way it did. In times like these, you must remember why you're putting your heart and soul into this professional degree.

REMEMBER

Your why is your motivation. Your inspiration. It's what you'll come back to when you start to feel overwhelmed or self-doubt or imposter syndrome sneaks in.

Peeling back the glamour

When you think about why you want to enter the law, base your reasoning on your observations of real lawyers engaged in their typical, everyday, low-profile work and not on high-profile cases that come around only once in a great while.

Because of the way many movies and TV shows portray lawyers, many people think all lawyers live glamorous, jet-setting lives. But the truth is that most lawyers fresh out of school earn what some people with bachelor's degrees make. The National Association for Law Placement (NALP) found that the median starting salary of JDs from the class of 2023 in legal jobs was $90,000. The median law firm salary was $165,000. Also remember to factor in lost earning potential during the three years of school (for full-time students) and tuition and living expenses.

In addition, keep in mind that gigantic law firms aren't where the majority of U.S. lawyers find work. Instead, many lawyers are employed by firms with fewer than ten attorneys, private businesses, public interest organizations, the judiciary and academia, or the government. (Chapter 21 has a rundown of all the settings in which you can practice law.)

That's why you need to make sure that a sky-high salary isn't your only motivation for wanting to enter law school. (Of course, that salary may come eventually, after years in practice.) Identify the other reasons, such as your love of advocacy, desire to truly help people, or interest in a particular practice area, that are driving your decisions.

TIP

Focus on what matters to you. Doing what makes you happy and allows you to sleep at night, along with paying your bills, is the key to job satisfaction.

Identifying who's really behind your decision to go

The decision to attend law school needs to be yours, and yours alone. You don't need to give in because of a persuasive parent, because all your friends are doing it, or because it's a respectable profession in society's eyes. Instead, you must have your own reasons for pursuing a career in the law that have nothing to do with anyone else's opinions. All too many law students are unhappy in law school, mostly because they went into it for the wrong reasons. Make sure you're not one of these people; otherwise, you're in for a long and depressing three (or four) years.

The Law School Experience Year by Year

Traditional programs are three years for full-time students and four years for part-time students. Each program is made up of the first (1Ls), second (2Ls), third (3Ls), and potentially fourth (4Ls) years, each with its own particular characteristics. The 1L curriculum is pretty much the same across the board at all law schools, though some have introduced professionalism courses, legislation courses, and/or tax courses. Some law schools have introduced year-long courses.

First year: They scare you to death

The notion of scaring you to death comes from an old law school saw. It's based on the terror that grips many 1Ls regarding the sheer amount of work they need to do and the fear of being grilled in the Socratic method I cover in the earlier section "Surviving the Socratic method." Getting used to the workload, the professors' interrogations, and infrequent opportunities to measure whether you're truly understanding the materials takes some time and effort. Chapter 8 offers some great hints to help you ease into your first year.

You'll be busier than you ever imagined. The volume of reading and the intense nature of the material can be alarming to many new law students. The language can be challenging. But it can also be fun, energizing, and life-altering in a positive way.

Second year: They work you to death

Busy, busy, busy. Grades are in. Units are counted, and you're now rising 1L. Which means you're now 2L!

Your second year is often considered the hardest because you have many different commitments competing for your valuable time. You'll probably be working on a law journal, law review, moot court, or other co-curricular or extracurricular involvements (see Chapter 19), which takes up most of your spare time. (As I note earlier in the chapter, part-timers have more time limitations, but law schools are finding creative ways to ensure part-time students have access to similar opportunities.)

You've spent the summer interning or clerking, gaining expert experience and applying all you learned in your 1L year. You may have taken summer courses or participated in a study abroad program (or both). You're now also becoming more involved on your campus in any number of ways:

>> Taking on leadership roles for various clubs or organizations

>> Participating in moot court, mock trials, or journals

>> Becoming a research assistant or teaching assistant for your favorite professor

>> Helping bring in the next class by serving in the admissions office as a student ambassador or tour guide

Third year: They bore you to death

The third year is often the easiest, because by then you're an old hand; you know what you need to do to get by, and you may not even care that much about hammering away at your studies when you already have a job offer in hand. At this point, you know what you're doing — how to manage your schedule, which professors require papers versus exams, how to manage your internships along with your coursework along with your personal life. With graduation (see Chapter 25) and the bar exam (see Chapter 24) right around the corner, you may find you want to savor your last year of studenthood before moving out into the real world!

REMEMBER

You still have a lot to consider as a 3L. You're now seeking that job offer and preparing for the bar exam, submitting all your character and fitness items, and thinking about how you're going to pay for your expenses while you're not working during bar exam preparation and the bar exam.

Charting the Law School Course

You pass through many milestones during law school, ranging from the first time you're called on in class to finding a summer job. Each one is important in your development as a future lawyer, and each has its own triumphs and tribulations along the way.

TIP

Pay attention to your milestones, accomplishments, and triumphs. Small wins often lead to major gains. You're developing skills that will advance your career and help your clients. Don't be afraid to celebrate a solid grade on a memo or successfully answering a question in class. It's all part of the process.

Choosing an area of practice

Some but not all law students choose an area of practice, such as tax, intellectual property, social justice, environmental, or corporate law, to informally specialize in during law school. This informal specialization means they take lots of courses in these areas, work summer or part-time jobs in these fields, and generally try to get as much experience as possible. The purpose of doing so is to figure out whether they'd enjoy actually specializing in that area in legal practice. (See Chapter 22 for more information about various practice areas.)

REMEMBER

Throughout the application process, many admissions professionals tell you that you don't have to know what type of law you want to practice. Many of us say you just need to know that you're going to have to work hard and are willing to do so.

That's true. But at some point, you begin thinking about what area of law you may want to specialize or practice in — or which you don't like, aren't passionate about, or aren't good at.

Many law students end taking on internships in multiple areas of law because they find that they really enjoy or are good at more than one. This approach isn't a bad idea because it leaves you open to many different opportunities. It allows you to take advantage of a clinic or two on your campus while also interning off-campus with a firm, or government entity, or private nonprofit.

You may start law school thinking that you absolutely want to practice tax law and then realize after a couple of courses that it's not your area of strength or that you just hate it. You may go in thinking you want to be a litigator only to change your mind and turn to family law when you realize how much research and writing is involved in litigation.

Whatever your path, the beauty of this degree is that you don't have to choose one area of law. Your degree is a foundational degree that sets you up for success in many different areas of law. You're going to gain skills and learn how to work in a way that you never have before. But you also will be privy to a professional degree that has the ability to impact so many aspects of the world.

REMEMBER

Not every ABA law school even has a certificate program, specializations, areas of concentration, and so on. It isn't like undergrad, where you need to declare a major. Many law students graduate law school after having completed a stint in a small business law clinic, an externship with a judge that oversees civil matters, and a job as a research assistant for a professor who's writing a new chapter in constitutional law. Then they end up working for a medium-sized law firm that focuses on employment defense work. In short, law school prepares you to practice law in general, and most grads are open to the job opportunity that's available to them.

Landing a summer job

You have two summers in law school — your 1L summer and 2L summer — as a full-time student. Of these two, the job you find for your 2L summer is by far more important because it's the job that sometimes leads to a permanent offer of employment (particularly at firms). Chapter 20 has detailed information about the summer job search.

During the fall of your first year of law school, your career services/career development officers begin making contact with all their new students. Usually, the officers invite you to programming that helps you learn more about the legal market, which helps you start to narrow in on a summer job. They speak to you about a variety of topics, such as the following:

>> What writing samples from your legal writing program to use

>> How to set up or update your LinkedIn profile

>> What your email signature should look like and what your business cards should contain

>> The do's and don'ts of interviewing

>> How to be prudent about your social media and privacy settings

>> What's negotiable and what isn't negotiable

This process is a time to be open-minded. Explore. Take advantage of the opportunities that come your way. Follow up with attorneys and judges you meet. *Remember:* To remain competitive, you want to ensure you have three to four legal experiences before you graduate. If you're a part-time or evening student, never fear; most law schools have created special opportunities for you to obtain legal experiences that don't conflict with your full-time job, such as work at firms and organizations who have opportunities on the weekends, clinics that operate on the weekends, virtual opportunities, and so on.

You want to take advantage of any networking events your law school hosts; any in-person or virtual panel presentations by firms, organizations, and government entities; and networking with your school's alumni to learn more about what they do and what their firms or organizations offer.

You also want to join any bar associations as a student. These are excellent chances for you to network, identify additional mentors, and so on.

TIP

If you have a full-time job, save your vacation and sick time for midterms, finals, and potential experiential learning opportunities.

Searching for a postgraduation job

Finding any type of job that fits your personality and goals takes time, particularly in a tight legal job market. Graduating 3Ls or 4Ls without a job offer in hand may feel a lot of stress, but with the right attitude, experience, and a good dose of patience, job leads should soon start heading your way. In Chapter 21, I point you in the right direction toward job-searching success and let you in on a variety of job-search tips. In short, persistence and a willingness to tell everyone you meet that you're looking for work are key to landing a great job, whether that's legal or nontraditional, JD preferred, or whatever. (Chapter 23 has more info on nontraditional jobs.)

Passing the bar with flying colors

Becoming a practicing attorney means that you must take and pass the bar exam in the state where you want to practice law. The exam, which is offered in February and July, is typically a two-day affair and varies in difficulty from state to state.

Taking advantage of all the bar-required courses and bar-recommended courses, your program puts on is critical. You want to attend any workshops that your school offers related to preparing for the bar, financing bar-related expenses, deadlines, and so on. Bar prep companies often come to campus and share their bar prep philosophies, tools, strategies, and schedules.

REMEMBER

Many law schools incorporate bar-related costs into the cost of attendance over your three or four years in law school. Doing so helps to defray the cost toward the end when you're already stressed and stretched.

TIP

Plan through law school to ensure that you've saved up money so you don't have to work during your bar prep. Maximize your in-school student loans to avoid the high-interest bar loans where possible because so few bar loan companies exist.

Another consideration is where you take the bar exam. Where's your job offer? Where do you want to live? Every U.S. jurisdiction requires passing a bar exam, with the following nuances:

>> **Wisconsin (diploma privilege):** Graduates of the two ABA law schools can be admitted to the bar without taking the bar exam.

>> **California, Virginia, Vermont, and Washington (apprentice route):** These states allow people to become licensed without attending law school. The individuals must complete a legal apprenticeship under the supervision of a licensed attorney. But they still have to pass the bar exam.

Some jurisdictions allow for *reciprocity* or other pathways for experienced attorneys to practice in other jurisdictions without taking another bar exam. The National Conference of Bar Examiners (NCBE) has the most recent information. Reciprocity gives attorneys the ability to be admitted to the bar and practice law in another jurisdiction without having to take the bar exam again. Of course, there are other factors and rules, including distinctions by the type of law being practiced, the level of court involved, and so on. Additionally, there are a number of parameters and distinctions made state to state. For more info, check out www.ncbex.org.

REMEMBER

Plan ahead. Different jurisdictions have different requirements, deadlines, and fees. The rules, timing, costs, and so on are subject to change. As an example, some jurisdictions require that you register during your first year of law school.

The bar exam isn't something to stress out about extensively (I know, that's easier said than done). But the truth is that most students pass the first time. Taking a bar review course (see Chapter 24) and diligently studying its material can make a huge difference in your confidence levels come test time.

The following sections introduce some of the major bar versions. See Chapter 24 for more details.

Uniform Bar Exam (UBE)

Many jurisdictions have adopted the UBE, which is the standardized bar exam developed by the NCBE. It was designed to test the skills and knowledge that every lawyer should have before becoming a licensed attorney. It consists of three parts:

>> Multistate Essay Examination (MEE)

>> Two Multistate Performance Test (MPT tasks)

>> Multistate Bar Examination (MBE)

Note: The MBE will be phased out with the introduction of the NextGen Bar Exam I cover in the following section. The final administration in jurisdictions fully transitioning to the NextGen Bar Exam is expected by February 2028.

As of February 2025, 41 jurisdictions have adopted the UBE, including 39 states, the District of Columbia, and the U.S. Virgin Islands.

NextGen Bar Exam

The NCBE is developing the NextGen Bar Exam to test a broad range of foundational lawyering skills, using a focused set of fundamental legal concepts and principles relevant to modern legal practice. By July 2028, 29 out of the 56 U.S. jurisdictions are expected to implement the NextGen Bar Exam.

Multistate Professional Responsibility Examination (MPRE)

The MPRE remains a separate requirement in most jurisdictions. The purpose of the MPRE is to assess the knowledge and understanding of established standards related to a lawyer's professional conduct.

The importance of attending an ABA law school usually comes up at this stage. To be able to take the bar exam in other jurisdictions, you must be a graduate of an ABA law school.

Graduating and preparing for your life as a lawyer

The moment you've been waiting for: You're a lawyer! Esq loading.

I know you want to celebrate, but you may need to keep it short for now. If you graduate in May or June and are taking the July bar exam, you need to turn your attention to bar prep.

You want to start thinking about your postgraduation life. Have you saved or borrowed enough money to ensure you don't have to work while preparing for the bar exam? Where will you live during bar prep? If you must move, you want to do so right away because prep begins right after graduation. You want to make sure you don't have too many distractions. If you have a job offer, when do you start? Do you have anything you need to handle before the bar exam? If you don't have a job offer, what's your plan for seeking employment that doesn't interfere with your bar prep?

What are your plans as you await bar results? Did you budget for a vacation (you deserve it!)? Or are you getting started on your career pending bar results? Either way, have a plan.

REMEMBER

Even after you pass the bar, your work is far from over. In your job, you need to spend your first few years extensively learning the trade, putting in long hours, and attending continuing legal education seminars. Your life as a lawyer may not always be easy, but it usually is intellectually stimulating and very fulfilling!

Chapter **2**

Inclusivity and Belonging in Your Law School Class

The idea that law school is different from any other type of education you've undertaken isn't hard to comprehend. But your fellow students may also be a far more diverse and interesting crowd than any other student body you've encountered. Some new first-year law school students (1Ls) walk into orientation amazed to discover just how varied the backgrounds of their classmates are.

REMEMBER

If you're coming straight out of college, facing this kind of diversity can be a major reality check (particularly when you're in a part-time or evening program). When you're used to being in an undergraduate environment where everyone is 18 to 23 years old, the idea of sitting in classrooms with older students who have families or high-powered careers can take some getting used to. The same is true if you're used to being in meetings where you know everything and everyone and being done with your work life by 5 p.m. Law school will change all of that.

Exactly what types of students make up today's law school classes? You find 55-year-old grandmothers taking a civil procedure class with joint *JD/MBA* students (dual degree students in the Juris Doctor and Master of Business Administration programs). You discover people embarking on second careers sitting next to fresh-faced, straight-from-college 1Ls (also known as *K-JD* students) and everyone in between. This hodgepodge of people with diverse backgrounds makes for a challenging and stimulating classroom environment. Just ask anyone who's ever had a former police officer in their criminal procedure class.

Law schools work hard to ensure that the educational experience is as strong as it can be for everyone. In this chapter, I discuss the many different peers you can expect to encounter during your years as a law student. Then I explore in detail how you can make the most of your experiences interacting with such a diverse student body.

Everyone Goes to Law School for Different Reasons

Classroom diversity is much more than racial and ethnic differences. A big part of the diversity you encounter in law school is the variety of motivations your peers have for pursuing a law degree in the first place.

For example, think about your own reasons and motivations for going to law school. Maybe you

>> Just didn't know what else to do with yourself (that was me)

>> Have parents who coerced you into it, or you came from a family of lawyers and law school was the next logical step

>> Want to use your law degree to help people whose voices can't be heard

>> Are passionate about a particular cause, such as civil rights or the environment, and want to make a difference in the world

Whatever your reasons for choosing a career in the law, I bet they differ from those of the student in the seat next to you.

TIP

During your first few weeks of law school, take a few moments to meet the people sitting near you in class (before the realities of law school cliques set in). Talk to them about why they came to law school; you'll likely gain a whole new appreciation for the differences — and similarities — among people's motivations for pursuing a JD.

Changing Times, Changing Demographics

Recent data from the Law School Survey of Student Engagement suggests that "that most law students rate their school experience positively and that increases (or decreases) in campus diversity materially affect student perceptions, belonging, and satisfaction, with students of color often reporting different experiences and needs."

In fact, gender and age diversity of the student body is an area where law schools often outshine other types of graduate education. Unlike top business schools, which sometimes have a female participation rate of only 30 percent, law school has become a 50-50 endeavor. And unlike medical school, where usually only a small percentage of students are older than 30, in law school you're almost as likely to find study groups of 35-year-olds as you are ones of 23-year-olds. Additionally, many law schools have LLM (Master of Laws) programs for international students; these students often audit courses with the JD students, adding another unique viewpoint.

Providing perspective: Older students

Law school is a little like a traditional workplace in the sense that you interact with people of all ages. For the first time in your academic life, some of your peers are old enough to be your kids, your parents, or even your grandparents. Your best school friend may end up being the same age as your youngest child.

The time that the older students have spent away from the classroom can clarify their focus for attending law school because they often have family or career commitments that make the decision weightier than it is for some younger students. When you have to leave an established career or do without the income to which you've been accustomed to pay for law school, you're making more sacrifices than a student straight out of college. Older students also tend to know what they want to accomplish because they've had the opportunity to sample the working world and discover their likes and dislikes about it.

On the other hand, this time away also presents unique drawbacks for the older student, such as getting back into the swing of studying (which I cover later in the chapter) and finding the right balance between schoolwork and social life.

TIP

Check out the helpful article at www.usnews.com/education/blogs/law-admissions-lowdown/articles/advice-for-older-law-school-applicants-to-consider, which is especially helpful for seasoned prelaw students.

Please note that this will require you to set up a free account.

Students who are capitalizing on previous job experience

If you've ever had a job with real deadlines, bosses, and two weeks of vacation a year, you know that you learn pretty fast what you need to do to get by. That means figuring out how you can best accomplish what you need to do, when you're most and least productive, and how much you can do without burning out. These same traits (especially the time management and multitasking) bode well with the law school experience, and older students exhibiting many of these traits are worth emulating.

In general, older law students (and particularly part-time and evening students) handle the tight deadlines and stressful situations that law school presents because they've already been there and done that in their lives. Because they bring more maturity and experience to their studies, they're better equipped to take law school in stride. They're often not as shocked by the required workload; as such, they perhaps don't encounter as many setbacks and disappointments as 22-year-old 1Ls. So when you hear them saying things like "It's just a first semester exam; what's the big deal?" while you're biting your nails down to the quick, you appreciate their "don't sweat the small stuff" perspective (even if you can't quite imitate it yet).

Self-awareness also comes in handy when you're selecting your area of practice. From their on-the-job experiences, older students may realize valuable personal preferences such as their disdain for working in teams, their penchant for research and writing, or their passion for public speaking. Likewise, an older student's previous occupation, whether teacher or accountant, can help them choose an appropriate specialty, such as education law or a corporate/business practice. Younger students who haven't had the opportunity to see what they're suited for in the real world may find these choices harder to make. Harder, but certainly not impossible. And that's the beauty of the first year: exploring all the things you can do with a law degree.

Students who are getting back into the academic groove

Of course, being away from a school environment for many years can have its disadvantages. Getting back into the habit of studying and burning the midnight oil can be jarring and difficult — something that older students may have forgotten about, especially when they're used to going home at 5 p.m. and not worrying about the obligations of their jobs until the next morning.

TIP

Listen to all the advice, tips, and suggestions and then figure out what works best for you. Don't lose sight of what has worked in the past, but be open to new ideas that may make your life easier.

Many schools have student organizations that are tailor-made for older law students. For example, the Older and Wiser Law Students (OWLS) at my law school (and many others) is a group that meets regularly to talk about study skills, deal with life as an older student, and discuss how to parlay your former career into a legal one. To find out more about joining (or starting) your school's OWLS club, attend the student organizations fair (see Chapter 13) that usually takes place each fall semester or contact your dean of students.

Students balancing law school and family

Because law school plus extracurriculars is almost like having a full-time job at times, balancing it with an actual full-time job (for part-time and evening law students) and/or the demands of a family can be difficult. That's true in any type of professional program. For most single, straight-from-college students, this problem doesn't register. They come home after class, feed their goldfish, and head out for a night of studying or partying without giving a second thought to the needs of a spouse or child. For older students with a family life, however, maintaining this delicate balance between work and family responsibilities can be hard.

Students with infants or small children often find law school particularly rough. If an exam is coming up, explaining to your 4-year-old why you can't play or why you need to study so much isn't easy. Having a partner or friend who helps you out during particularly stressful times is ideal. Otherwise, you can seek out other law students with children with whom you can form a playgroup and share responsibilities so that each of you has a chance to study undistracted for a few hours every day or on the weekends.

Taking advantage of opportunities, the law school provides to include your spouse, partner, parents, kids, and friends can help you maintain those relationships. Include them when you can so they understand what you're going through.

TIP

Share the academic calendar for your first year of law school with your spouse/ partner, parent(s), and close friends. You want to make sure they understand that surprise trips or visits during midterms, reading period, or finals will not be the happy surprise they expect it to be.

First-generation students

The definition of *first-generation students* seems to change frequently. If you're in the first in your family to attend and graduate from college and also the first to pursue a graduate/professional degree, you're what many would call *first-gen.*

Law school can bring up issues of imposter syndrome and isolation for first-gen students who aren't familiar with legal lingo, don't have suits for their first law school interviews, and so on. Law schools now have first-gen programming that includes everything from ready-to-work closets to targeted mentoring programs to specific networking opportunities. If you're a first-generation student, make the most of the resources offered to ensure you're successful.

TIP

Many law schools offer prelaw programming to their first-gen incoming students the summer before law school. Take advantage of this type of opportunity! Some programs are free, while others have a nominal cost. Either way, these programs can calm your nerves and get you in the right headspace to build your confidence and start law school on the right foot.

LGBTQIA+ students

If you're an LGBTQIA+ prelaw student, you may have questions about whether your prospective law school has a welcoming environment. At most law schools, LGBTQIA+ students will likely find the majority of their peers, administrators, and faculty members welcoming and supportive. (As with any educational institution, workplace, or religious organization, some people at your school may not know or be close with members of the LGBTQIA+ community. That's just the way life is.)

Still, you may wonder whether the law schools you're considering fit that supportive bill. As you investigate schools, therefore, you may want to consider the following issues:

>> **Deciding whether to be out in your application:** Of course, this decision is a highly personal one. You may want to just be yourself on your application, especially when your sexual orientation and/or identity has a direct link with your desire to attend law school or practice law. Or you may decide that although your orientation is part of who you are, it isn't an important aspect of the law school admissions process. Whichever you decide is up to you.

>> **Checking out the breadth of the school's LGBTQIA+ culture:** One way to judge the atmosphere of a law school is to inquire whether an LGBTQIA+ student organization is active at the school, how many people are members, and what sort of activities or speakers the group presents. If it appears to be a thriving organization, it can be your best resource for discovering the culture of a particular school and identifying openly LGBTQIA+ or ally faculty

members who can answer your additional questions. Don't stop with the law school, however; check to see what if any organizations are available at the general university (if your law school has one).

Also find out whether other thriving organizations at the school seem to be supportive of diversity, inclusion, and belonging in general. If so, that gives you an idea as to the nature of the welcoming — or not — environment you'll encounter.

You can find an excellent resource for prelaw LGBTQIA+ students on the Law School Admission Council's website at www.lsac.org/discover-law/access-and-community-law-school/lgbtq-law-school. It has the results of a survey of law schools regarding questions of importance to LGBTQIA+ students, including whether the school has openly LGBTQIA+ faculty and an LGBTQIA+ student organization, among others.

LGBTQIA+ law students can also go to The LGBTQ+ Bar Association website at https://lgbtqbar.org/ to take advantage of many resources for LGBTQIA+ students (including the Lavender Law resources at https://lgbtqbar.org/annual/) and lawyers.

TIP

Engaging with the law school community early on in the process helps you determine where you feel safe, supported, and seen. Attending virtual and/or in-person events and paying attention to the speakers invited to campus are just some of the ways that you can get a feel for the environment.

Students with disabilities

If you're a student with one or more disabilities, you're far from alone. Law students with disabilities have conditions ranging from anxiety and chronic health problems to blindness, deafness, and paralysis, and plenty of students with disabilities thrive in law school.

The 1990 federal Americans with Disabilities Act requires law schools to make *reasonable accommodations* (determined on a case-by-case basis by your school) for students who have disabilities. The disabilities covered under that law include any physical or mental impairment that substantially limits one or more major life activities.

REMEMBER

Providing reasonable legal accommodations is your law school's responsibility to ensure that you're on equal footing with the rest of your peers. Accommodations may include a special room for taking exams, a smaller testing environment, dictation equipment, special lighting in exam rooms, and extra time on exams, among others. Besides the initial testing, a student who needs accommodations doesn't pay anything for reasonable accommodations.

If you're a disabled law student, you may have many questions about whether your law school can accommodate your disability, including the following:

>> **When should I discuss my need for accommodations with the law schools I'm considering?** Many law students with accommodation requests wait until they've been accepted (after submitting their seat deposits or enrollment fees) to speak with the dean of students, though some mention their circumstances in their applications. In many instances, applicants share details about their disabilities when explaining their grades and/or test scores prior to receiving their accommodations.

>> **What kind of medical documentation do I need to secure the appropriate accommodations?** Again, talk with your dean of students or office of student accessibility to get specific guidelines, but generally speaking, detailed information is required. The documentation you use for the LSAT may or may not be sufficient for your law school and, ultimately, the bar examiners.

>> **How does the law school handle my accommodation requests?** Talking to the office of student accessibility or the dean of students is the best way to find out whether the law school is able to accommodate you. Discuss these matters as soon as you're accepted (at the latest) to ensure everything is in place for your start date.

TIP

Disabled students may want to look into the American Bar Association (ABA) Commission on Disability Rights (www.americanbar.org/groups/diversity/disabilityrights/), where you can find the latest disability law news, research scholarship opportunities for law students with disabilities, and internships with the commission and engage in a mentorship program for disabled law students that pairs you with disabled lawyers.

Neurodiverse students

Neurodiverse law students may experience ADHD, autism, OCD, sensory differences, learning differences, challenges in certain social situations, and so on. These students often self-identity to ensure the law school can provide the appropriate accommodations. Proactively sharing the information can also help the law school identify additional resources like student mentors, classrooms with more suitable lighting and/or acoustics, and specific counselors on campus.

In many instances, neurodiverse students don't share their background and status with anyone beyond admissions and the dean of students. Who you do or don't tell is your call, of course. The goal is to ensure that you communicate your circumstances to get what you need to be successful.

Students juggling full-time work and part-time/hybrid/evening law school

Law school is time-consuming enough for a full-time day student. Students who go to school full time are in class only 12 to 16 hours per week but may complain that they don't have enough time for the recommended standard of studying two hours for every one hour of class time. For those who choose the commendable task of going part time or in the evening, the academic challenges are ten times harder. Imagine working at your job 40 or more hours per week and then going to class afterward four (or five) nights a week for two to three hours per night. When would you study — let alone cook, clean house, mow the grass, run errands, do the laundry, or walk the dog? A social life? Not on your life. Add a partner or kids to the mix, and what you have is Super Law Student!

Hybrid programs are a mix of in-person and online classes. There are at least 35 ABA-approved hybrid JD programs. The format, requirements, and length differ, but graduates from these programs all earn JD. These programs are designed to meet the in-person ABA instruction requirements while also allowing students to meet a significant portion of their legal education requirements remotely.

The variations can include a few weekend in-person courses, along with online/virtual courses throughout the week to an intensive weekend course with primarily virtual coursework.

Going to school part-time or in the evening is undeniably more stressful than going full-time during the day. The biggest questions you need to ask yourself when considering being a part-time, hybrid, or evening student are

>> Will I have enough time to study?

>> Do I have a support system to help me with family responsibilities (such as a babysitter if you have young children or caregiving support for your parents)?

>> Can I get the crucial on-the-job legal experience that I need for when I apply for jobs?

TIP

If you're going to keep working, save your sick and vacation time for midterms, the deadline for that first big research paper, or final exams. You should also have a conversation with your supervisor/manager to get on the same page about how limited your time may and reiterate that you're prepared to handle your job responsibilities along with your law school obligations.

Active-duty and veteran students

Many law schools actively recruit active-duty military members and veterans. The ability to demonstrate your commitment to service, your ability to lead and be led, and your various experiences during your time in the military make for competitive law school applications.

The questions you may ask include the following:

>> Is the school a Yellow Ribbon institution? (This type of school has agreed to partner with the Department of Veterans Affairs (VA) to help eligible veteran students and their dependents cover the cost of higher education expenses not covered by the Post-9/11 GI Bill)?

>> Are other sources of funding or financial aid available for veterans and active-duty students?

>> Does the school have specific department and/or student organization that serves the military population?

>> Is the school connected to Judge Advocate General Corps (JAG) if that's an area of law you may be interested in pursuing? JAG is a great way to combine your military experience and your law degree.

All in all, you want to ensure you find a law school that's a good fit for you and that the support you need is available to you.

Multicultural students

When you combine people of different racial and ethnic perspectives and backgrounds, your classroom environment is a much more stimulating, inclusive, and interesting place than it would be if it were homogeneous. That said, racially and ethnically diverse students may face a harder time adjusting to law school life than their white peers. What can you do to ease your transition to law school as much as possible?

>> **Choose law schools with supportive atmospheres.** You can judge the environment by the breadth and vibrancy of student organizations — not just race/ethnicity-based groups but also military law societies, Jewish law student associations, women law students' associations, and so on. In addition, chat with current students, alumni, and faculty members to get the inside scoop on the atmosphere at their law school.

>> **Find mentors.** Your law school's student organizations may help you set these relationships up prior to law school, during orientation, or during the

first few weeks of the first semester. Some law schools offer faculty mentors along with alumni mentors through the career services office (CSO) or alumni relations. Finding people with similar backgrounds, goals, and experiences may be a source of relief to you as a new law student.

>> **Work to develop as many relationships with people at the law school as you can.** I'm not just talking about other students here but also faculty and staff members from all backgrounds. Getting as much information and knowledge about what law school entails as you can is the best way to succeed.

TIP

Here are a few online resources to bookmark:

>> Check out the ABA's Commission on Racial and Ethnic Diversity in the Profession at www.americanbar.org/groups/diversity/DiversityCommission/ and the Diversity, Equity, and Inclusion Center at www.americanbar.org/groups/diversity/ for comprehensive information on programs, resources, scholarships, and related information for students from diverse backgrounds.

>> For groups specific to a race or ethnicity, head to the National Bar Association, an association for black lawyers and judges (nationalbar.org); the Hispanic National Bar Association (hnba.com); and the National Asian Pacific American Bar Association (www.napaba.org).

Chapter **3**

Choosing the Best Law School for You

What makes a law school good is a question that's both complicated and simple at the same time. A good law school isn't necessarily ranked among the most prestigious in the country, located in a bustling metropolitan city, or endowed with a library bursting at the seams. Instead, it's one that fits *your* individualized needs and is a place where you feel most comfortable and enthusiastic about studying the law.

So how do you find out about what schools are the best match for your personality, budget, professional goals, and geographical preferences? In this chapter, I cover the important law school qualities you need to consider before making your decision. By using the information here, you can evaluate the law schools you visit with an informed and inquisitive eye.

Being a Big or Small Fish in the Law School Pond

One question that's important to ask yourself in choosing a law school is whether you'd rather be a big fish in a small pond or a small fish in a big pond. Many people who prefer the latter like the resources and opportunities available at a prestigious law school, but they don't mind that they don't really shine there. Others prefer to be the big fish at a school that may not be as popular but has the right program, scholarship, and mentor opportunities — somewhere they can make the law review or top-10 percent of the class with relative ease.

Making Sense of Reach, Target, and Safety Schools

As you evaluate law schools, you may find that how you feel about your acceptance chances at each falls into one of three categories. Here's a breakdown:

TIP

>> **Reach:** A *reach school* is a school you'd love to go to (even if they offered you no funding), but you aren't sure whether you'd get in. Maybe your LSAT score and GPA are lower than those in its median range, for example.

Dreams are always worth pursuing. You should shoot your shot, so to speak. No matter how much of a long shot your dream school may be (Stanford, here you come!), apply anyway. You never know when that school may need another philosophy major/debating champion/resident of South Dakota type. They may be looking for someone just like you!

>> **Target:** A *target school* is a school where your admittance can go either way based on your stats. You may get in, or you may be waitlisted or put on hold. These tend to be schools where the data shows various applicants with your profile have been admitted and denied.

>> **Safety:** A *safety school* is a school where your credentials are much higher than the medians. You know you're a shoo-in, unless your clone has also just been accepted. Even if you're not too keen on ever going to your safeties, apply anyway; after all, who knows when your reach or target school will fall through? You don't want to be left without a law school home.

CREATE AN EMAIL ACCOUNT FOR LAW SCHOOL

Be sure to create a new email account for your law school application process. Pick a username that's professional and something that you can use throughout law school. On the off chance that a dean or law school faculty member emails you, you don't want to have an email address that's juvenile or embarrassing and gives them pause about having admitted you!

Don't forget to add the law schools to your safe sender lists. You may want to create folders for each law school to keep yourself organized.

REMEMBER

The competition for law school always is stiff, but in lean economic years and election years, it often becomes even stiffer thanks to the poor economy or simply the growing interest in law when questions about the Constitution crop up. Whatever the reason for the increase in applicants, having more reach and safety schools is even more important now than it was in the past.

Many students wonder how many schools in each of the three categories they need apply to. Some reports show that most applicants apply to an average of five to eight schools total. Another study says that number is five to fifteen. Your strategy may be to apply to

>> Two or three reach schools

>> Three to five target schools

>> Four or five safety schools

This approach gives you a great selection. However, whenever your GPA or LSAT are out of sync with each other — such as having a 3.8 GPA and a 150 LSAT, you may want to apply to more schools because this low/high disparity may puzzle admissions officers. See Chapter 4 for more on the admissions process and how your LSAT scores and GPA figure in to the equation.

Weighing the Key Qualities of Law Schools

Law school is generally three long years (four for part-time and/or evening students). But it goes so fast, and you want to make a good choice. You don't want to randomly pick a school because of the sports team, the popularity of the undergraduate program, or a state on the map, because you may be miserable there. So your best bet is doing a thorough job researching the schools. The following criteria give you a head start.

Using the ABA 509 reports

In 2011, the American Bar Association (ABA) began turning the annual data each ABA law school reports into what's now called a *509 report*. The information includes everything from the admissions statistics to attrition data to employment data to the breakdown of grants and scholarships, plus so much more.

Each ABA law school posts this useful information on its website. The 509 report is also available on the ABA website at www.abarequireddisclosures.org/requiredDisclosure. You can search by law school, and you can choose which year you're interested in.

TIP

This report can be very helpful in putting together your *law school spreadsheet*. This is your working list that contains all of the law schools you are applying to. In this file, you should include the requirements, deadlines, fees, and any other information that you will use to make a final decision about which law school to attend. You may want to include details like the student-to-faculty ratio, the number of scholarships offered, and what the renewal rate is for any conditional scholarships.

State school versus private

State schools are often great deal all-around. There was a time when tuition for in-state students could be half (if not less than half) of what out-of-state students pay. In general, you pay less at a state school than at a private school, even if you're an out-of-state student. Over the years, the gap between the cost of state law schools and private law schools has narrowed. Nevertheless, the cheaper in-state tuition for many state law schools may be a determining factor for many law students.

Some states make becoming a resident for tuition purposes easier than other states, which may impact your school choice. For instance, in some states you must reside in the state for non-school purposes for one full year before you start school to qualify as a resident; other states consider all professional students residents.

REMEMBER

Before you turn your nose up at the idea of a state school, consider that every ABA law school is full of successful alumni, brilliant faculty, and happy law students. Most state schools have solid reputations, and if you're hankering for a large campus with many departmental, joint-degree, and extracurricular offerings, you've found your pot of gold!

Student-to-faculty ratio and faculty makeup

A school's *student-to-faculty ratio* tells you how much face time you'll get with your law school faculty as well as what to expect in terms of class size, faculty mentorships, and faculty availability. This number is something many students that attended large universities for undergrad pay close attention to.

Some students are also interested in how many faculty members are full-time professors versus adjunct professors who are still practicing law. A number of local practitioners may also be part-time faculty members. Lastly, some students want to know which professors are *tenured,* which matters in terms of knowing which professors have long-term commitments to the law school. These faculty members tend to teach most of the foundational first-year curriculum.

Money matters

Tuition at many schools is $50,000 per year. Add living expenses, books, transportation, and housing into the mix, and you're looking at a grand total approaching $150,000 in debt after graduation. (The average is $126,000.)

Cost of living

Make sure you pay particular attention to the cost of living because it impacts your budget significantly in either direction. You may be able to live more frugally in a smaller city. In a small town in Maryland, for example, you may be able to find a great apartment for half the price you'd pay in Chicago or San Francisco.

REMEMBER

Each law school makes adjustments to the cost of attendance based on the expenses of the city the law school sits in. That makes it affordable as long as you attempt to live like a student and not like a lawyer!

Employment opportunities and city size

One key aspect to consider in terms of money has to do with the type of city you're in. Larger cities may have more opportunities for part-time jobs during the school year, which many students hold and which can be a significant source of income. Ask students what types of employment are available nearby and on campus, both for now and for after graduation. For instance, in a small, rural town you're not likely to find an environmental or intellectual property law firm, but in a city, you'll find many.

Scholarship opportunities

Many law schools offer scholarships beyond the incoming merit scholarships. Some of these are based on leadership; areas of law that you're interested in; and your participation in certain student organizations, competition teams, and so on. Additionally, be sure to do your own scholarship research during the application process but also during law school. Check out local, regional, and national bar associations; law firms; major corporations; and the like.

Work-study

Some law schools offer financial aid in the form of *work-study* funds. This option may allow you to earn funding toward your cost of attendance by working as a teaching assistant or research assistant, in the law library, or in the admissions office.

Fellowships

Fellowships are another wonderful opportunity a law school may offer that allows you to further develop legal expertise in tax, environmental justice, or intellectual property law. During a *fellowship*, most candidates earn a scholarship that supports their research for a specific area of law and/or a specific project.

Renewal terms

If you receive a *conditional scholarship*, you need to understand the renewal terms you have to meet to maintain it. Is it GPA or class-rank based? If you fail to meet the conditions and you lose the scholarship, do you have an opportunity to earn it back?

The ABA 509 report I introduce earlier in the chapter has detailed information showing how many scholarships are awarded, retained, and lost at a school each year. However, only ABA law schools that award conditional scholarships are required to report this information.

Reputation

Schools are known to the legal profession (especially employers) in three general ways: as a national school, a regional school, or a local school.

>> **National:** *National* law schools enjoy a reputation across the country, and their graduates often seek jobs nationwide, too. Whenever you mention the name of a national law school, like Harvard, Yale, or NYU, employers instantly recognize the name, whether they're in Boston or Boise, Idaho.

>> **Regional:** *Regional* law schools, on the other hand, may not be well known across the country, but they usually do have that level of recognition in the states, cities, or regions where they're located. They tend to have the best success placing their graduates locally and regionally. If you're at a regional school in Maine, you may have a harder time looking for work in Florida or other distant locales than you would if you were at a national school. It means you have to work more closely with the career development team to seek out those opportunities.

>> **Local:** *Local* law schools are well situated in the community. The community engagement folks, the legal contingent, and local undergraduates are very familiar with these law schools. Local firms and nonprofit agencies are often full of graduates from these law schools. Another positive of a local school is that the level of support it gets from the community can benefit you greatly as you look for a local gym, eatery, or church; affordable housing; good schools for your kids; and so on.

When you have geographical flexibility and get a spot, a national school maybe your best bet. All ABA law schools offer career development opportunities, but some law schools have a proven record of placing their students in certain clerkships, firms, and what have you.

REMEMBER

Some firms, courts, and organizations have preferences for graduates from certain law schools. Some employers may close their doors to you based on the reputation of your law school, especially when you aren't near the top of your class. But this practice is as much a fact of life for law schools as it is for undergraduate institutions.

Safety

Thanks to consumer protection law, every university has to publish a report regarding crimes on and around campus. The report includes information about the safety and security procedures and provides transparency about the campus, the environment, and the incidents that have occurred on that campus.

Geographic location and weather

When you think about spending the next few years of your life somewhere, the location of the law school must be one of your prime considerations. Obviously, knowing where you want to practice *before* you apply to law school can make your search much easier. But you don't actually need this decision right away. Many law students figure it out along the journey by taking internships in other locations, visiting other places for competitions, and so on. And to be honest, most go where the best job opportunity is at graduation.

Another logistical factor to consider is whether you'll be happier in an urban or rural location. For students who attended an urban college, a rural or suburban law school may be a welcome change of pace, or vice versa. If school spirit is what you're after, keep in mind that an urban campus may not have as much of a collegiate atmosphere when compared with a college town. So if a swinging nightlife is what you value, you're likely to quickly tire of the same old bars in the same small city. But pay attention to what the student organizations offer in terms of social activities. That may be enough to make up for a small city if the law school meets your other criteria.

Likewise, be sure to take note of what surrounds the school. I visited some schools that had little in terms of restaurants, shops, gyms, and college hangouts around the law school. Others had a rich variety of cute sandwich and coffee spots and local shops. If the setting is important to you, visiting the schools gives you the most accurate reading. (See the "Visiting Law Schools" section later in the chapter for more information.)

Weather is another factor for many. Do you love the change of seasons? Are you freezing if the temperature dips below 70 degrees Fahrenheit? Do you need to touch the water every so often? If weather impacts your mental health, choosing whatever climate makes you feel like you're in a good space weather-wise is key.

Duration of law school

If you want to get done in a hurry, some schools (but not all) offer full-time students the opportunity to graduate in two-and-a-half years rather than three. You can do so in one of several ways:

>> Starting in the summer before the traditional first year of study begins (if allowed)

>> Taking summer school to gain credits quickly

>> Taking a heavier credit load each semester

Some people choose a combination of all three so they can take advantage of an earlier graduation date.

For most part-time programs, law schools last four years. In some part-time programs, the students must attend summer school to finish the program in four years.

Note: Some law schools offer accelerated programs that are different from you simply choosing to complete your degree more quickly as I outline here. Often, these students complete their JD program in two-and-a-half years in programs that usually involve intense summer sessions. These are formal programs (approved by the ABA) with specific requirements, and students make commitments to participate in them.

ABA-approved versus non-ABA–approved

The majority of American law schools (198 of them, to be precise) are approved by the American Bar Association, which is the accrediting body for law schools. The ABA accreditation requires that law schools meet specific standards, and these law schools are evaluated every ten years.

If you're in an ABA-approved school, you have an easier path because you can take the bar exam in any state. If you're in a non-ABA–approved school, generally you can take the bar exam only in the state where the school is located.

WARNING

Keep in mind that some employers may regard a diploma from a non-ABA school with a bit of suspicion. Firms often take the quality of your law school into account when making hiring decisions.

Some law schools are accredited by their states rather than the ABA, but the standards aren't the same. Do your research. A state-accredited school may work for you if you have no plans of leaving the state or practicing outside your home state. But the risk is there: What if you change your mind? What if your dream job opens up in another jurisdiction and you can't take the bar there because you attended a non-ABA law school?

You can sometimes find workarounds to this rule, but they vary from state to state. Some states allow a non-ABA–accredited law school graduate to sit for their bar exams after the graduate has been practicing law in another jurisdiction for a certain number of years. Other states have other options, such as making non-ABA–approved graduates eligible to sit for their bar exams after they've earned a master of laws degree (LLM) from an ABA-accredited law school. For the most up-to-date requirements for your state, consult the National Conference of Bar Examiners at www.ncbex.org/, where you can link to every state's bar admission office.

Dual degree/joint degree opportunities

Many *dual* and *joint degree* opportunities are available, combining a juris doctor (JD) with other disciplines. The JD/master of business administration (MBA) is the most popular. But some people work toward joint degrees like JD/doctor of medicine (MD), JD/master of arts (MA), JD/doctor of philosophy (PhD), JD/master of library science (MLS), JD/master of social work (MSW), and the list goes on.

If you're interested in earning a joint degree, you need to consider law schools that are attached to a university or standalone law schools that have established arrangements with other institutions. When enrolling in a joint-degree program, you usually apply to both degree programs simultaneously or apply to the other program during your first year of law school. For ABA law schools, you must start the dual/joint degree program in the law school.

TIP

Be sure to double-check the scholarship opportunities as well as terms and conditions for dual-degree programs.

Pursuing a dual degree has a big impact on your career options. Do plenty of research to decide whether a dual-degree program is right for you.

REMEMBER

Specialization in one or more areas

Some people know as prelaw students that they want to specialize in a particular area, such as environmental, family, tax, or intellectual property law, so they choose a school that specializes in that area of interest. A law school that *specializes* offers a certificate program in the field, has a larger number of professors and course offerings than usual, or provides clinics focusing on the particular area of practice. Some schools are known for certain specialties. For instance, Vermont Law School and Lewis & Clark are known for environmental law and Santa Clara and Chicago Kent are well known for intellectual property law.

TIP

I encourage you to be open-minded. You're exposed to so many areas of law in law school, including things you've never heard of. At the end of the day, the area of law that offers you a job will be your favorite for the time being. Get the experience, test the waters, and try something else.

However, going to a school that specializes in a particular area of the law can potentially pigeonhole a student, which can be good or bad. On one hand, it helps you because your résumé and transcript lean heavily toward one subject area; all things being equal, you'll be better suited for getting a job in a niche market than someone else. On the other hand, having a specialty can make exploring other areas of the law later on more difficult.

Teaching quality

The quality of your professors is a major factor in determining the overall quality of your education. An outstanding professor makes the material come alive in ways you never imagined. I've taken several courses that, judging from their descriptions, looked utterly boring — only to come away with an amazing educational experience because the professor's enthusiasm and competence in an area made all the difference. Conversely, some interesting-looking classes with great potential have been botched by professors with poor teaching and interpersonal skills.

You need to find out ahead of time how good the professors are at the schools you're interested in. The first step in evaluating a school's teaching quality is browsing its website. Check out the faculty biographies. What are their levels of experience? Have they written many publications, like textbooks or scholarly papers? How often is their work cited and quoted? Are they fresh out of law school themselves, or have they been practicing, clerking, or teaching for a while? What's the ratio of full-time to part-time professors? Men to women? Diversity among professors?

TIP

The best way to get the dirt on profs is by visiting the schools and sitting in on a class or two. Do the professors seem bored or lively? Do the students seem interested? Do the professors use many examples, overheads, or gestures, or do they read from lecture notes in a monotone voice? When you're visiting, make sure to ask students for details about the professors. Who are the good ones? Are there more good than bad? Before you know it, you have an excellent idea about the faculty's strengths and weaknesses.

You can also use the ABA 509 report (which I cover earlier in the chapter), current students, alumni, and the Law School Survey of Student Engagement (LSSSE) for law schools that use this resource to get additional info on a school's faculty.

Course selection and breadth

One big question you may have is when you can start taking electives. Many first-year (1L) curricula are set in stone: You take certain required courses, and no electives are offered. A few law schools do allow 1Ls to take one or two electives during the spring semester. The majority of schools allow all 2Ls and 3Ls to take entirely electives while meeting the required course minimums. There may be bar-required courses, upper-division writing requirements, and/or experiential learning requirements. This just takes planning and a thorough review of the academic course schedule to plan things out.

The ABA now requires that law schools have an experiential learning requirement. Other schools may require clinical experience or a public-interest externship to graduate. Besides the typical courses, you may be interested in clinics, externships, and courses that prepare you for the business of law. (I discuss clinics and externships in Chapter 18.) You also want to look in the brochure and on the website and talk to students about the availability of these types of classes.

Commitment to the public interest

From the outside looking in, you may think many law schools seem to focus on corporate law. Consciously or unconsciously, they send a corporate message to their students through course selection, guest speakers, and graduate placement. If you're instead interested in the public interest, you may want to find out about the school's commitment to it by doing the following:

» Looking at the number of clinics, institutes, or centers that are public-interest-focused

» Seeing whether the law school has its own public-interest scholarships for new students

» Checking out whether the law school offers loan repayment assistance programs

» Seeing whether the school's career services office (CSO) or career development office (CDO) has a staff member whose sole focus is public-interest placement, public-interest job fairs, and so on

» Getting a handle on how many public-interest organizations, firms, and entities recruit at that law school

» Looking at the number of graduates who choose public-interest careers

» Asking about the indebtedness of the public-interest graduates

Global study opportunities

You've probably heard again and again that law is becoming a global profession, meaning that it involves business, intellectual property, and legal systems in countries beyond the United States. That may mean you may want to supplement your legal education with opportunities to study abroad, participate in exchange programs, and/or take an international internship. Or you may just want to go abroad for fun. Either way, check out the study-abroad opportunities, exchange programs, and placements in countries of interest at the schools you're considering.

Some schools offer a plethora of their own programs in addition to the opportunity to earn credit for programs sponsored by other schools. Others have strict rules about allowing their students to go only on their programs or on programs at a select few other schools. Some don't let you do any studying abroad/exchange programs during the year — only during the summers. The best strategy is to review the student handbook and website to learn about what opportunities are available, or meet with your academic affairs team or an upper-division student. See Chapter 18 for more about studying abroad.

TIP

Study-abroad programs can be a year, a semester, or a summer long. If your dream school doesn't offer a study-abroad program you're interested in (or any at all), you may be able to attend as a student at another ABA law school. Touch base with the academic dean and/or registrar to determine your eligibility and what courses may be approved to transfer.

Well-endowed library

A stuffed library may be at the top of your list of school attributes. After all, you'll be spending a bunch of your time there. But the idea of a well-endowed library can mean more than the number of volumes in it. Sure, that's important, but how many of those tens of thousands of volumes are you actually going to use?

TIP

More important, in my opinion, is the number of computers, group and individual study spaces, research stations, and law librarians a library has. Other questions you may want to ask are these:

>> Is the library bright and airy or like a dank dungeon?

>> Is food allowed? The answer may be important to you, especially when you're the type who stays at the law school all night. My school's library permitted food, and I've seen pizzas ordered to study rooms in the library — it's a pretty great privilege!

>> Is it conducive to your being able to study? Is it quiet? Do students respect no-talking areas? Are people using cellphones?

>> How many librarians are lawyers?

>> What technology will you be trained on?

>> What tools and resources do you get for being a student, and what do you have to pay for?

>> Are the chairs comfy? This point is crucial because studying can take its toll, and sometimes you just *need* a nap.

Employment data

Everyone is concerned about jobs these days, given the depressing state of the economy. When you go into hock for $110,000 -180,000 of total debt as an average law student, you want to make sure that you're going to be gainfully employed so you can pay it all off, preferably sooner than later.

You should do some research to find out what percentage of a school's graduates have jobs at graduation and then at nine months after graduation. The best way to do that is to inquire directly with the CSO or CDO at a particular law school, keeping in mind that employment statistics sometimes are vague. To find out the entire picture, visit the CSO/CDO data. Learn about the percentage of graduates employed in legal jobs and in nonlegal jobs and how many are unemployed or still looking for work. Review the average starting salary.

If the percentages of gainful employment are low, you may want to investigate a little deeper to find out why. Some of the categories you want to pay close attention to are the employment rate at graduation, at nine months, and JD Advantage jobs (jobs that do not require bar passage, but there is a distinct advantage to candidates with a law degree). Use the ABA 509 report I cover earlier in the chapter, the law school's website, and the National Association for Law Placement site (www.nalp.org).

Visiting Law Schools

Visiting law schools — either before applying or (more realistically) after being accepted — is essential to making an informed decision. When you visit law schools, the most important thing to do is ask questions. Talk to students, faculty, administrators, and admissions people. Have lunch in the cafeteria or student lounge and hang out in the library. Corral a few students and ask them in-depth, probing questions about their school. After all, wouldn't you love to speak your mind about the good, the bad, and the ugly regarding your undergraduate school? I'm sure you wouldn't have hesitated to describe in excruciating detail how bad the cafeteria food was or why prospective students absolutely must take particular classes. Law students are exactly the same way. So don't overlook this valuable resource!

WARNING

The worst time to visit schools is during midterms and final exams. Schools try to avoid scheduling visits then, but sometimes that's the only time a student can make it. Whether exams were being held never even crossed my mind (even though it was prime exam season — the end of April). As a result, my visit wasn't that useful. I didn't get to talk to any students because everyone was scurrying back and forth from the library like voles running for cover. I wasn't able to sit in on classes because none were in session. All I was able to do was take a tour and walk through the silent halls, trying to make eye contact with stressed-out students. Try not to make this mistake — you'll get a much better picture!

TIP

You need at least half a day to visit each school. If you have time to do more besides just take the law school tour, consider sitting in on a class, vising the bookstore, and/or speaking with a faculty member. If you have a little more time than that, be sure to check on the housing and parking/transportation opportunities.

Soaking up the atmosphere of the school

Doing a few specific things can greatly enhance the quality of your visit. Although these activities aren't mandatory, they help you get a better feel for the school, the student body, and the quality of life there.

>> **Interviews:** Many law schools offer interviews as part of their admissions process; in fact, some require them as part of the traditional admissions review process or the waitlist process. These meetings are informational sessions with an admissions representative, just to gain information about the school. Although rarely do such interviews change your status, playing up your selling points and presenting your sparkling personality sure can't hurt.

>> **Sitting in on a class:** Checking out the classroom interaction can help you learn a lot about the school's culture and environment. Observe the formality of the class: Are people being called "Mr." or "Ms."? Are they being asked to stand when answering questions? Does everyone have a seat available? If you have a few hours, try sitting in on classes other than the typical first-year courses, which the admissions department usually arranges for you. Try to request one or two first-year classes and a few electives. Doing so helps you see the different class sizes, atmospheres, and teaching styles that the school offers.

>> **Scoping out the city:** If you have a free afternoon, you may want to drive around the city, especially if you've never been there before. Does it seem like your kind of town? Does it offer activities you enjoy doing, whether that's skiing, doing art gallery hops, or eating out at a new restaurant every week? Is it a place you'd feel comfortable in?

>> **Scheduling appointments with key people:** One efficient use of your time during your visit is scheduling appointments with the financial aid staff, career services staff, any admissions staff you may want to chat with, and deans. These appointments can be particularly helpful for gauging the law school

atmosphere and vibe. Note that you need to call ahead to schedule these meetings. Use your time in them to ask important questions and get a feel for the staffers' attitudes toward the school and prospective and current students.

Making the most of tours

If you're on campus and no tour guides are available (for example, during the summer), use the self-guided tour information or check the website to get a lay of the land so you know what to look for. And don't hesitate to ask whether a staff member is available to assist you even if the students aren't available.

You may be on a tour with other prospective students, and your guide could be a student or an admissions staff member. Taking the law school tour (hopefully one run by a current student) may be your prime opportunity to put in some one-on-one time with a current member of the student body. Develop a solid list of questions for your tour guide. What do you want to know? As you're meandering through the hallways, ask all your most detailed questions, but keep in mind that this person is representing the school, so their answers may be edited.

TIP

If you're a bit introverted, bringing a friend or a sibling with you when you visit campus may help you relax and focus on what you need to learn about the law school you're visiting.

SET UP YOUR VOICEMAIL

Be sure to set up the voicemail on your phone. If a law school calls you, it wants to ensure it has reached the right person. Additionally, confirm any music you've selected is tasteful and appropriate. Better yet, just record yourself and state your name clearly and plainly. This approach avoids all potential controversy if the dean or a current student calls you.

Chapter **4**

Using Battle-Tested Application Strategies to Succeed

For some people, the decision to go to law school is a step toward a lifelong dream. For others, this professional degree is simply a better alternative than medical school or business school. No matter when or why you make this decision, be prepared for the competitive application process. It can seem tedious and overwhelming, but if you stay organized and stick to the deadlines, you can do it.

REMEMBER

In spite of the continued interest in law, the number of law schools and the number of seats they offer hasn't changed drastically. That means you have to put your best foot forward.

In this chapter, I help you do just that. I cover the details on your personal statement, letters of recommendation, and writing sample and how to stand out in a positive way. I also talk more about the role the Law School Admission Council (LSAC) plays and how to navigate the decision-making process.

Demystifying the Application Process

In this section, I dive into some basic information regarding the law school application process. Some of it may seem pretty obvious, like "Don't spell your own name wrong or mention a different law school in your personal statement." (Yes, these mistakes happen regularly.) But other aspects are more nuanced — submitting a thoughtful and competitive application, deciding how early to start the application process, and so on.

Setting a realistic timetable

You want to plan to apply about a year out from the time you intend to start law school. So for a fall start, you should begin the application process the summer of the year before.

REMEMBER

A few elements of the application impact your timeline, such as the LSAT/GRE test dates and preparation time and how soon you need to take the test to meet the law schools' admissions cycles. You also need to plan time for ordering transcripts and submitting them to LSAC, which I cover in Chapter 1, and gathering and submitting letters of recommendation.

Early decision programs

The big decision facing most applicants is "if I'm admitted early decision (ED), I'm willing to follow the parameters of the program."

REMEMBER

Early decision is a specific program that allows you to apply to a law school via a binding process earlier in the admissions cycle. You agree to commit to the law school if offered a seat.

Most early decision programs have binding requirements like the following:

>> Withdrawing all your applications to other schools, even if you haven't received a decision

>> Accepting the offer without financial aid information (for some schools, that includes merit scholarships)

>> Accepting the offer prior to visiting any law schools or participating in admitted student conversion or yield events (admissions activities designed to showcase the student experience, programs, faculty, and so on to help you convince you to attend that specific law school)

>> Accepting the offer before tuition is set for the law school

But ED programs do have positives:

>> You find out early where you're attending law school, eliminating the stress of waiting on a decision.

>> You may be able to lock in your dream school.

>> You may be eligible for specific scholarships.

REMEMBER

ED programs are designed to give you and the law school some peace of mind by figuring out very early in the admissions cycle where you're going. Then you can turn your attention to preparing to move, applying for scholarships, paying down your debt, and getting excited about your first (1L) year!

This decision comes down to how much you want to attend a specific law school and your willingness to accept the offer within a limited time frame and without the full financial aid picture or decision-making help from the activities that schools host.

Scheduling the LSAT and/or GRE

I discuss taking the LSAT in the later section "Improving Your LSAT Savvy," but here are a few points to consider as you get ready to register for it:

>> **Look at the LSAT registration deadlines and test dates.** This point is particularly important for international students because their test dates are much more limited.

>> **Back into the law schools' deadlines.** What's the last LSAT and/or GRE date a school will accept for that admission cycle? Additionally, you also want to make sure that you give yourself time to retake the test if you don't love your first score.

>> **Make sure that you account for any necessary accommodations (such as a distraction-free space or additional time).** Pay attention to the LSAC deadlines for submitting your paperwork based on the LSAT administration you're signing up for.

Obtaining letters of recommendation

Review the law schools' application instructions. Do they have their own recommendation services or require that you use the LSAC letter of recommendation service? Do they require or recommend that you waive the right to see the letter of recommendation? How many letters do they require, and how many will they accept?

I'll be honest: Most letters of recommendation are just blah. That is, they aren't persuasive; they don't help the admissions committee members understand more about who you are, what your skills are, and why they should admit you. This blahness happens because students don't give the people they're asking enough time and information to craft a great letter of recommendation.

To obtain the best letters of recommendation possible, you have to put in the time and work. You want to ensure that you give your recommender enough information to write a strong letter, not just plug your name into their form letter.

TIP

Ideally, give them the following pieces of information:

>> A list of law schools you're applying to

>> A draft copy of your personal statement

>> A copy of your transcript

>> A copy of a paper, exam, or project you submitted

>> Three or four points you want them to focus on, such as

  ● Your ability to work with groups and independently

  ● Your willingness to seek assistance or guidance when struggling with a course or project

  ● Your ability to learn new things quickly

  ● Your ability to overcome obstacles

You get the picture here. The more effort you put in, the better chance you have of getting a great letter of recommendation as opposed to one that doesn't enhance your application.

REMEMBER

Investing in the right recommenders can have a significant impact on the decision a law school makes. Choose wisely!

Getting your transcripts in order

I know you know that you need to submit all your transcripts to LSAC. "All" includes all coursework that goes toward your bachelor's degree and study abroad program transcripts (these may already be incorporated into your *degree-granting* transcript from the college or university awarding your undergraduate degree). The transcript process is where we often see delays. Some schools have automated systems that you use to order transcripts, while others are a bit more old-school.

Clearing the hurdle of transcript holds

If LSAC conducts its transcript review and contacts you because you have a hold on your transcript — usually a financial hold or one related to a book or library issue — clearing it up as soon as possible is in your best interest.

WARNING

A transcript hold may delay the processing of your application. Many law schools won't mark your application complete if you have a missing transcript. Additionally, such an issue may give some schools concerns about your ability to pay your fees at their institution. It becomes a character issue.

Addressing academic issues

Unreported academic action and academic probation notations on your transcript can raise a major red flag. The mistake is usually innocent enough. Most students simply forget how homesick they were the first semester of freshman year and how bad their grades were. The problem is that the law school application asks about academic action, probation, and so on; if you've checked "no" but schools see this notation on your transcript, eek!

WARNING

Though some law schools may give you a chance to amend your application and note that you were actually on an academic supervision plan because of your grades, that isn't always the case. Some law schools make a note of it and bring it up during the review process/hold it against you without your knowledge. Others simply report you to LSAC for misconduct. That means that every American Bar Association (ABA) law school you've applied to receives a notification from LSAC that another ABA law school has raised an issue and investigation is underway. You want to avoid this scenario at all costs!

Fixing incorrect or outdated information

TIP

Obtain copies of all your transcripts now and review them thoroughly. If you see anything that doesn't seem accurate, contact your undergraduate institution right way. Human beings staff these offices, and everyone is capable of making a mistake. Double-checking is the right way to go.

If you're in undergrad and applying, check out the instructions from each law school about submitting updated transcripts. If you submit your application in October and your fall semester grades boost your GPA, you probably want the law school admissions committee to use this new GPA in its review process.

Preparing if you're an international applicant

LSAC evaluates your international transcripts, academic records, mark sheets, and degree certifications.

LSAC creates the Credential Assembly Service Authentication and Evaluation (CAS A&E). The documents must come directly from the institution; LSAC doesn't accept documents sent from the applicant, even if they're sealed. Please plan ahead because this process can take a long time.

The American Association of Collegiate Registrars and Admissions Officers (AACRAO) is the organization that will evaluate your international credentials and verify the documents submitted by your institution(s). When this evaluation is completed, it becomes part of your CAS report.

Be sure to check the law school requirements to ensure you're providing what the law school needs.

Take some time to review the LSAC website to ensure you're (promptly) submitting the correct documents based on the transcript requirements for each country.

TIP

The process of obtaining, submitting and having your international transcripts evaluated can take some time. As soon as you decide to start the application process and create an LSAC account, order your transcripts and begin the process with LSAC and ACACRAO. LSAC doesn't accept submissions from the World Education Service (WES).

Lastly, be sure you contact the office that processes visas and I-20s (the form that identifies your nonimmigrant student status). Getting those documents in order can take a while, and you don't want to miss out an opportunity to attend law school because the institutions don't have enough time to get your visa and I-20 processed.

Taking care of character and fitness issues

As I explain earlier in the chapter, now is the time to review those transcripts for any freshman probation notices or academic action information. You also want to obtain a copy of your credit report in case an old roommate never paid that cable bill that was in your name. I bring up these issues because getting your hands on records, especially old records, can take some time. You don't want to create delays because you can't completely answer a question.

REMEMBER

You have an ongoing duty to disclose information related to your character, both during the application process and throughout your time in law school. Any questions listed on the application are issues that you must disclose. That means that if you get a DUI after your "almost graduated" happy hour, you have to tell your law school about it as soon as possible.

TIMETABLE CHECKLIST

Here's a quick checklist to help you keep tabs on your application timetable. Ask yourself these questions:

- When do I want to start law school?

- What are the application due dates?

- Will I apply for early decision/early action?

- When do I want to have all my applications submitted?

- Do I anticipate an improvement in my cumulative GPA during the application process?

- Do the law schools I'm interested in accept the LSAT and/or GRE?

- When do I have time to prepare for the test?

- How will I prepare for the test?

- What test dates are available to me?

- Do I have the paperwork to get accommodations if I need them?

- Have I identified the people I want to write my letters of recommendation?

- Have I given them the information they need?

- Have I given them a due date?

- Have I ensured I have no holds or barriers that may prevent me from ordering my transcripts?

Delving into the Minds of Admissions Committees

Usually, a law school admissions committee is made up of admissions professionals and faculty. Some law schools also have alumni and/or current students who serve on the admissions committee.

People often ask what the admissions committee wants — what it's looking for. The answer is that it varies. What jumps out at a school's admissions committee depends on your academic profile, your major, your writing ability, and what your recommenders say about you.

I get into this idea more in the following section, but remember that law schools spend a lot of time putting together their applications and their instructions. The law school admissions committee wants to see someone who

>> Answers all the questions posed

>> Understands the importance of being detail-oriented

>> Recognizes the importance of actually following rules, details, and instructions — like a good lawyer does

Details matter. Your ability to follow directions is a key factor in admissions.

Admissions committees want applicants who are ready for the rigors of law school. And you demonstrate that readiness by highlighting your experience; educational background; skills, strengths, and talents; and adaptability throughout your application materials.

Each person on a committee is different; they all have different preferences, experiences, biases, and so on. What matters most is really identifying candidates that they believe can be successful in the program, in the law school community, and in the legal profession.

Standing out by falling in line

One of your primary goals as an applicant is to literally follow the directions on the application and share your story within the confines of those instructions.

A huge misconception about the law school application process is the allure of "standing out." The students who stand out in this process typically do so for the wrong reasons — they generally aren't well prepared, don't follow all the rules, and/or fail to adhere to deadlines, page limits, and so on.

The law school application is a space where you want to demonstrate your ability to fall in line. You want to show the admissions committee that you understand who you are and what your goals are but also that you also understand the importance of following the guidelines. Schools spend a lot of time crafting their application instructions. They're asking for the things the committee wants to know about you.

TIP

Show the law school that you're mature, focused, and detail-oriented by doing exactly what it asks. As one of my colleagues often says, "Don't answer the question you wish we'd asked. Just answer the question we asked."

REMEMBER

The way you demonstrate that you're a good candidate for a school is by ensuring that you've done your homework and are able to articulate why this particular law school is a good fit for you and vice versa.

It's simple advice, but committees often find themselves reading documents that have nothing to do with the prompt. The quickest way to have your file moved into the "no" pile is to discuss a program, clinic, or professor affiliated with another law school. It happens so frequently, and it's incredibly disappointing and frustrating. It shows your inability to pay attention to detail, and it makes you stand out in a negative way.

Analyzing the ideal applicant

Following the application directions as I explain in the preceding section is an important part of painting yourself as a strong applicant. But other factors also shape an ideal candidate.

These things include, but aren't limited to, strong writing ability, diversity of major and/or minor, strong and competitive letters of recommendation, and leadership experience.

Here are a few ways to strongly position yourself as an ideal applicant:

>> **Ensure your documents follow the parameters outlined in the instructions.** Doing so tells a law school that it doesn't have to worry about when you join its class.

>> **Highlight your leadership, community service/engagement, and extracurricular activities.** Show the law school that you're likely to participate in its community organizations, committees, journals, and competition teams.

>> **Have recommendations that highlight your academic skills, receptiveness to feedback, perception by classmates, your level of participation, and so on.**

Charting challenging coursework and playing up your work history

Admissions committees also consider factors such as your major and minor, the courses you took (and when), and how many hours per week you were working. Working on hard projects and accepting different and difficult challenges are all part of being a law student (and ultimately being a good attorney).

REMEMBER

Play up the good stuff! Don't be afraid to brag about the difficulty of your courses or the challenging job that you've taken on or project that you completed. You want to make sure you're showcasing your academic and work history in your application process.

You may want to highlight a difficult major or competitive minor, specific courses you took, or a particular project you worked on that was particularly competitive. You definitely want to list the hours you worked while you were in college. If you don't recall the exact numbers, that's fine; provide approximate hours per week per job, internship, or whatever.

Adding your work hours is really important because it gives the reviewers some context for your cumulative GPA. For example, if you work 25 hours per week from your sophomore year through your senior year, this information may give the committee something to think about while reviewing your transcript — particularly when they're looking at another candidate who has a similar GPA but didn't work at all and wasn't involved in any extracurricular activities or any leadership roles.

REMEMBER

Your goal is to fill in any gaps and answer any questions the committee may have when reviewing your file. Tell them anything you want them to know about circumstances that impacted your GPA.

Solving the "major" problem

Not all majors are created equal. I know that's not what you want to hear, but the reality is that some majors — such as the hard sciences (like physics and chemistry) and engineering — are deemed more challenging than others.

That's why you want to take the time to explain why your major is competitive. It's an opportunity to highlight your willingness to take on hard things and show the committee that you don't take the easy route!

GETTING THE MOST OUT OF YOUR PRELAW ADVISOR

If you're fortunate enough to have a prelaw advisor on your campus, please take advantage of their time and expertise.

When your prelaw advisor hosts a prelaw event, attend. They put a lot of time and energy in getting the law school representatives to your campus or virtual event. When they're offering you workshops to work on your personal statements, letters of recommendation or your résumé, take advantage of those opportunities. The larger prelaw community on your campus can also be an outstanding and free resource.

Additionally, the letters of recommendation from prelaw advisors often go very far with admissions officers. That's because they trust these advisors' judgment. They know you well, how hard you work, and how committed you are to obtaining a law degree.

Tip: Sometimes a letter of recommendation from a prelaw advisor can make the difference if the advisor has especially good connections with a particular law school's admissions committee or if many past alums of your college were successful in gaining admission to that law school.

You can also use this discussion to explain how your major will impact your perspective in the classroom and in the profession. Show the committee what others can learn from you because of the diversity and/or difficulty of your major.

If you've chosen a major that's more competitive at your particular university, ask one of your recommenders or your prelaw advisor whether any written documentation is available that highlights that fact. For example, some majors at some institutions that are considered difficult to get into or are more challenging than other majors. Pointing this out can help you stand out positively!

Making Your Application Stand Out for the Right Reasons

Earlier in the chapter, I point out that applicants who try to get clever in distinguishing themselves often just end up proving they can't follow directions. But you still want your application to stick in the minds of the committee. The following sections offer six steps for successfully standing out for the right reasons.

They can help you put forth the best application possible and present yourself in the most positive light.

I suggest you focus on one application as a time. This approach ensures you don't accidentally submit the wrong materials to the wrong law school. Unfortunately, this silly but costly mistake happens too frequently.

No. 1: Getting great letters of recommendation

Letters of recommendation can really make a difference in an application. If your academic statistics are so-so, a recommendation can significantly impact a reviewer, particularly if it's focused on the skills and assets that actually matter in terms of being a successful law student or lawyer.

Start by asking your professors, TAs, internship coordinator, organization advisor, or whoever whether they can write you a competitive letter of recommendation. If they agree, ensure they have all the information they need, including the following:

>> A draft of your personal statement and résumé

>> A list of schools you're applying to

>> A reminder of things that you've worked on together

>> A list of three or four that you want them to address, such as your work, your research skills, your ability to work independently and/or in small groups, and your ability to take directions

Getting your recommenders this info proactively is your responsibility. They're doing you a favor, so make their job easy.

No. 2: Writing an authentic personal statement and/or essay

The *personal statement* portion of a law school application is essentially a 2–3 page, document that serves as an interview, a writing sample, and shows reviewers who you are beyond your stats.

Start your personal statement with your why. Why are you doing this? Why do you want to pursue a law degree? Why do you want to work this hard? You want the committee members to get a good sense of why you want to go to their specific law school and are a good fit for their mission and why they'd be excited to have you and all you bring to the table in their classroom, campus, and community.

Strong writing is as important as being authentic. Remember that this statement is your primary writing sample. Use a style guide and grammar tools, and work on multiple versions of your statement. Be sure to let your mentors, supervisor, and best friend read it. If they have no idea what you're talking about by the end of it, you can be pretty sure the reviewers won't, either.

Be genuine

Law schools want to get to know you. Your story is your story, so focus on yourself — your genuine and authentic self — and not on other people. Be sure you're giving the committee a picture of who you are beyond your stats and what's on your résumé.

Avoid the temptation of using artificial intelligence (AI)

A few law schools have policies that allow you to use AI in your application, but they're the exception and not the rule.

You're joining a profession where your word and your integrity are everything. Be sure you know the exact rules for each law school you are applying to, as it relates to the rules on ChatGPT and usage.

To be safe, just write your own personal statement (as well as any other items like an adversity statement and LSAT and/or GPA addendum). You don't want to ruin your career before you get started because you used AI to apply to a school that checks up on that. It's just not worth it.

No. 3: Proofing your application

What's the saying — the devil is in the details? That's definitely the case in the law school application process. You want to ensure you've answered every question thoughtfully and thoroughly. Being a lawyer involves attention to detail, so you want to ensure you check everything before you submit.

Adjust your timeline so you build in enough time for a thorough review. Although most applicants submit everything electronically, printing everything and reviewing the hard copy is worthwhile. Read every document out loud for tone, messaging, and clarity. Are you saying what you meant to say? If not, edit and revise.

TIP

Slow down. You don't want to submit your application only to find out it has minor errors you could've fixed had you given yourself more time to proofread every single document.

If you can, allow a trusted advisor, family member, supervisor, and/or mentor to review everything. Having a fresh set of eyes can make all the difference. When you look at your own documents over and over again, missing minor typos and grammar errors is easy.

No. 4: Deciding whether to include attachments

Most law schools allow you to provide additional attachments and documentation to explain anything that aligns with specific character fitness questions. This stage is when following instructions is really important. Being transparent and providing as much information as possible about a dip in your undergraduate performance or character and fitness issues can assist you in answering any questions an admissions committee may have about these issues. Your goal is to ensure that you disclose any pertinent information about yourself. The decision you make can be instrumental in allowing the admissions committee to resolve any concerns they may have and can lead to favorable decisions. You can read more on this topic in Chapter 6.

How many attachments are too many attachments? Use your best judgment here. If you have too many things to explain, that becomes the focus of your application rather than the positive aspects.

No. 5: Filling out all financial aid applications

REMEMBER

Make sure you complete whatever documents each specific law school requires. If a school wants the FAFSA and a need-based form, complete both.

Here are a few other financial aid considerations:

>> **Make sure you know who else's information you may need to submit.**
Not all law schools require parental financial/asset information, but some do. Income information for your spouse or partner may also be necessary.

- » If you've created a new email address for law school, use it for the application process and all these documents.

- » **Keep all your documents together.** Make copies of everything you submit and all formal emails.

- » **Meet all the deadlines.** Specifically, pay attention to the priority deadlines for the FAFSA and any need-based documents the law school requires. If a school has supplemental scholarships you can apply for, be sure you do so on time.

- » **Have your own process for identifying outside scholarships.** No joke: A ton of money goes unclaimed every year. Thousands and thousands of dollars don't get awarded because candidates don't apply.

REMEMBER

If your decision about law school is tied to the amount of financial aid you receive, do your part. Turn in those forms as soon as possible, and submit the FAFSA even if you're waitlisted.

No. 6: Making sure your application is complete

One way to ensure you are organized throughout the application process and ensure you don't miss anything is to create a spreadsheet! List all of the law schools you are interested in, deadlines, and requirements for each one. Revisit this document frequently. Check items off as you complete each one. This will help you stay on top of things. Depending on when you created the document, visit each law school's website to ensure nothing has changed since you initially created your list.

TIP

Stay organized. Label your documents and date them so you know which version you're working on. Nothing is worse than accidentally submitting version 1 when you meant to submit version 15.

Improving Your LSAT Savvy

The *Law School Admission Test* (LSAT) is the main standardized test U.S. law schools use as an admission requirement. Some students find preparing for it overwhelming, while others find it fun. Either way, you need to be prepared. That's where this section comes in.

REMEMBER Though lots of conversations about the LSAT continue to swirl, keep in mind that the majority of ABA law schools still require it, and many merit-based scholarships are tied to it.

Discovering what's tested on the LSAT

Things have changed over the years, but the basic idea behind the LSAT is that it's testing your skill set — the skills you'll use throughout law school and your legal career. It's an aptitude test, not an intelligence test. The LSAT consists of the following elements:

>> Three multiple-choice sections:
  - Reading Comprehension
  - Logical Reasoning
  - Analytical Reasoning
>> LSAT Argumentative Writing, which replaces the Writing Sample.

The LSAT was designed to predict how law students would perform in their first year of law school.

Though many law schools have years and years' worth of data showing how students will perform in their first year of law school, the two factors that most applicants have in common are an LSAT score and a cumulative GPA.

Figuring out the best way to prepare

Do you know your current learning style (because it may have changed over the years)? How do you generally perform on standardized tests? What resources do you have available to you? These are some of the things that you want to consider as you prepare for the LSAT.

The only way you get better at a skill is by practicing, whether that takes you two to three months or a year. Some applicants can study on their own, while others need the structure of a test prep company and the study schedule. Some may even find they need a private a tutor.

REMEMBER LSAT studying is a big prospect. You may need to save more money for test-prep resources (though you can find free ones as well), cut back on your hours at work for a period of time, and so on.

Here are a couple of potential places you can find help:

>> LSAC, which administers the test, offers resources (some of which are free).

>> Many LSAT prep companies offer opportunities to take the test before you study so you can see where you stand and figure out what you need to work on.

Deciding when to register for and take the LSAT

When you take the LSAT is directly related to when you plan on applying and to which school(s). Each law school identifies the last LSAT date it wants to accept for that specific admissions cycle. Most applicants work backward from that date. For example, to start in the fall at a law school where January is the last acceptable LSAT, most people sign up for the LSAT administrations in June and early fall of the year before. This approach ensures they have a few additional test dates available if they feel the need to retake the test. (And can afford to do so; finances can factor into the number of times you can take the LSAT.)

Of course, your school and work commitments and obligations are other factors that affect when you can schedule your test date.

Glimpsing what LSAT scores can get you into law school

The LSAT is a key part of the application process. Your goal is to do the best you can on the LSAT. But you also can be strategic here about what a school may be looking for based on your LSAT score.

Looking at how past students' scores fared

This task can be a little tricky, but here are a few tips.

>> **Pay close attention to the information provided on the ABA 509 report and on the law school website.** The *509 report,* which I cover in Chapter 3, is comprised of data ABA schools report to the ABA. The class profile from each academic year or admissions cycle can give you some insight into past success.

>> **Attend law school events to learn more about a school's focus on the LSAT.** Is that the primary factor this cycle? Is it as important as the GPA?

>> **Check out the LSAC Official Guide** (www.lsac.org/choosing-law-school /find-law-school/jd-programs). This resource can help you understand what LSAT scores schools deemed admissible in the last admissions cycle. That information may impact your decision to retake the test, to obtain two academic letters of recommendation as opposed to one, and/or to provide a more thoughtful *LSAT addendum*.

An LSAT addendum is a brief explanation of your LSAT performance. When your LSAT score(s) is not where you want it to be, and you fall closer to the LSAT 25th percentile or below the median, you may want to provide aa statement of facts about why. Using facts and evidence, you will want to explain why this score is not the best reflection of your capabilities.

For example, if the LSAC guide indicates your LSAT score is closer to the 25th percentile (meaning that 25 percent of the class had that score or lower), you want to point out that your skills and abilities aren't actually similar to those of that group of applicants. One way to do that is to ensure your letters of recommendation focus on skills related to being successful in law school (specifically, the things that are tested on the LSAT, such as reading comprehension skills, analytical skills, and logic).

Using online tools to determine your odds of admission

You can find so many tools that let you put in your highest LSAT score and your cumulative GPA and get a sense of what your odds of admission are. They also may help you determine your recommendation strategy (where and who your letters come from and what they focus on). You may even identify more law schools that seem like a good fit for you!

Here's a list of tools and resources. Remember that most of these sites use public data (the ABA 509 reports). They don't take into account the fact that law schools are conducting holistic reviews of your application materials, have data that show them candidates who have been very successful in their programs despite their numbers, and so on.

>> **LSAC Official Guide** (see the preceding section)

>> **Law School Predictor Sage:** https://7sage.com/predictor

>> **Law School Transparency** (behind the paywall via LSAC.org): https://app. lawhub.org/law-school-transparency

>> **LSD.Law:** https://lsd.law

Taking the GRE for Law School

Some applicants feel more comfortable with the *GRE* (short for Graduate Record Examinations), a standardized test many graduate schools use. For some, it's because they've taken it before. Others have just heard horror stories about the LSAT. The following is a quick Q and A about using the GRE for law school.

» **How many ABA law schools accept the GRE?** As I write this, approximately 115 out of 200 ABA law schools allow a GRE score. The most important piece of information involves how many applicants who take the GRE are admitted and how many actually enroll. Check out the ABA Standard 509 report, which has this information broken for you, at www.abarequireddisclosures.org/requiredDisclosure.

» **How do law schools award merit scholarships for GRE applicants?** I can't answer this one specifically for you because it varies by school. For this critical piece of information, you definitely want to ask each law school. I suggest taking it a step farther and asking whether the policy has changed over the years and/or whether the school anticipates further changes.

REMEMBER

At the end of the day, you have to do what works best for you, and you have to take the test required by the law schools, whether that's the GRE or the LSAT.

Navigating the Nuts and Bolts of the Law School Admission Council (LSAC)

TIP

You should have the Law School Admission Council site saved on your tablet, computer, phone, and any other bookmarkable device. In addition to registering for the LSAT on this site, you can find many tools and resources you'll use throughout the application process.

Looking at LSAC's credential assembly service (CAS)

Credential assembly service (CAS) is a compilation of your LSAT score, the score bands or range your LSAT score falls in, the average score, your writing sample(s), your letters of recommendation, information about whether you attended law school previously, and a thorough evaluation of your transcripts. The law school you are applying to will request a CAS report from LSAC, and you pay for each CAS report.

Law schools rely heavily on the CAS report for a couple of reasons:

>> **LSAC does a lot of the work for them.** It takes your transcripts and provides grade trends for each year. The report shows the mean information for applicants from your specific undergraduate program, if there are enough law school applicants within the last three or five years. The report also shows your *cumulative GPA* (if you took courses at more than one institution for your bachelor's degree) along with your *degree GPA* (created from the classes you took at the university that awarded your bachelor's degree). Law schools see all your transcripts, so they'll know what your degree GPA is.

>> **LSAC manages to level the playing field among the thousands of universities that have a variety of grading scales.**

The LSAC site has a solid explanation for this leveling, but here's a quick example: Say applicant Y goes to school F, which has a grading scale of 0- to 4.33 and no + grades, while applicant Q goes to School T, which has a grading scale of 0 to 4.0 and uses – and + grades. LSAC ensures that applicant Y and applicant Q are on the same scale.

REMEMBER

If you fail a course your freshman year and then repeat that course in your sophomore year and earn an A, most schools count only the A. For grade normalization purposes, though, the A and the F both count in the calculation of your cumulative LSAC GPA.

To help decrease the cost of applying to law schools, applicants can ask the law schools for a CAS report waiver. A waiver can helpful because most ABA law schools require a CAS report, and the fees can add up. CAS waivers aren't as common, but some law schools do award them.

Note: The CAS report is for students whose got their degrees from schools in the United States. LSAC works with another company to provide law schools with credential evaluations for candidates whose degrees came from international institutions.

Requesting transcripts

You want to make sure you get your transcripts in hand early. Most candidates' biggest issue is that they obtain their transcripts and find a discrepancy, or some other issue they weren't aware of, too late in the process. The last thing you want to do is find yourself in this situation *after* you've submitted your transcripts to LSAC for your CAS report and to the school. For more on reviewing your transcripts and dealing with any issues or incorrect information, head to the earlier section "Getting your transcripts in order."

From there, make sure you keep a copy for yourself and then send one or more directly to the law school admissions council following whatever directions the school has laid out.

REMEMBER

You may need multiple copies of your transcript for the same school. An ABA standard requires that your final degree-granting transcript must be on file with the law school. That means an ABA law school must have a copy of that transcript after the degree is conferred. Some law schools accept the degree-granting transcript that's in your CAS report to satisfy this condition, but others require you to submit a second copy after you're admitted to their programs.

Processing recommendation letters

Each law school will tell you how many letters of recommendation it requires and how many letters it will accept. But just as important is how it wants to receive these letters. Follow the instructions for each law school on the individual site and/or the LSAC website.

Using the LSAC's submission service works for most law schools because LSAC vets the authenticity of the letter, confirming that the recommender actually wrote it. Other law schools may have their own processes.

Ask the law school how it wants to receive letters from alumni, especially if an alumnus is writing the letter on your behalf because you've been waitlisted. In that case, also confirm whether the law school makes any exceptions to the maximum number of accepted letters.

Providing the LSAC writing sample

The LSAT writing sample has always been part of the CAS report, but it may not be the only one you submit. If you take the LSAT more than once, your CAS report will contain all of your writing samples.

REMEMBER

These writing samples are supposed to be an example of your true, raw writing skills. They're unpolished, unvetted versions of your analysis and grammar skills and your writing ability. They can be persuasive, particularly if your academic profile may be considered a little less competitive.

Not every law school views these writing samples the same way. Some of my colleagues will tell you that they don't even read them. Some law schools read them for every single applicant, and others just for candidates that they've waitlisted.

Regardless of which school you end up applying to, you should take the writing sample seriously. My colleagues often refer to samples where an applicant chose to write a poem or include a statement within their sample that says, "No one is going to read this, so I'm not going to bother." These types of submissions, which are actual examples we've seen, are immediate red flags that make a law school admissions committee not view your application seriously.

Understanding notes regarding test center disruptions

LSAC automatically includes a notification with your CAS report if any disruptions at your test center during your LSAT administration. This notification can be helpful if the incident impacted your ability to focus and do well on the LSAT.

Feel free to also provide an explanation about how the disruption impacted your ability to focus on the test in your LSAT addendum.

Requesting application fee waivers from LSAC and/or law schools

You can apply for a fee waiver through LSAC's fee waiver program. Many ABA law schools will honor the LSAC fee waiver which makes things easier for you because you only have to submit your information once.

Many schools offer free waivers for attending their events. Some law schools actually waive their application fees for a certain time frame to get you to apply earlier in the cycle. Other law schools will waive the application fee if you've been awarded an LSAC application waiver. Some law schools will send out fee waivers to prospective students based on their undergraduate GPAs, LSAT scores, the year they're applying to law school, which state they're interested in attending law school in, and so on. So don't opt out of receiving emails when you set up that LSAC account. You can miss out on these fee waivers!

Recognizing the impact of extracurriculars

You should highlight your experiences. Consider the following:

>> What clubs, student organizations, or extracurricular sports were you part of?

>> What leadership roles did you hold? What fundraisers did you participate in?

>> Were you active in your place of worship or local/regional/national political campaigns?

>> Were you committed to working with a particular community, such as seniors or animals?

Whatever your activities are, this is your opportunity to showcase other aspects of who you are. Remember that schools are building a class. They want to know what you do for fun, what your hobbies are, and what instruments you play and languages you speak. They want to know what your favorite movies are. All these things give the reviewers information to focus on other than just your stats and help them learn more about you.

TIP

Don't limit yourself to activities or clubs and organizations that are law related. Showing reviewers the political engagement, the work with the local school district, the youth sports team you coached, and so on allows them to see a bit more about who you are and how you contribute to your community. It tells them how you'll contribute to their community.

REMEMBER

Your extracurriculars are important, but how they relate to your courseload is also important. Be sure to list the organization, the dates, and then the hours per week you participated in meetings, events, fundraisers, or whatever for each activity on your résumé.

Advice for undergrads

Extracurricular commitments can gets a little tricky for undergrads. You to want to be thoughtful about how extracurricular activity may impact (or seem to impact) your cumulative GPA. Maybe you don't want to pick three or four different extracurricular activities if balancing that many on top of your classes means your grades will suffer.

Advice for those out of college

If you are already out of college and are thinking about how to explain extracurriculars on the application itself, you may want to include information about why you chose the activities or causes, particularly if those activities aren't tied to why you want to go to law school and why you're pursuing a law degree.

Handling the Outcome of the Application Process

The moment you've been waiting for — you have an answer! Whether you've been accepted, waitlisted, or denied at one or more schools, the following sections help you through the next steps.

Receiving law school decisions at different times throughout the cycle

You may start to hear from schools at different times — as early as November or December or not until April or May. This lag can be maddening, but it's part of the process. Be sure you

>> Are keeping track of your deadlines for deposit or confirmation.

>> Are aware of any financial aid dates, deadlines, and opportunities.

>> Think through your wish list as you begin to weigh acceptance offers. What do you hope you get from your law school experience? What do you need to be successful?

Celebrating your acceptance

You're in! Take a moment to appreciate the fact that you have an offer on the table. No matter what happens, you have a seat in a law class.

After you come down from that high, go back to your checklist. What additional questions do you have now? What else do you need to know about the offer? Do you have what you need to make a decision? Can you visit in person or virtually? Are the deposit or deposits refundable? Partially refundable by a certain date? Be sure to get your questions answered in time to meet the deposit deadline if the acceptance is from a law school you're serious about.

REMEMBER

You need to stay organized. Keep an eye on deadlines, to-do lists, and your list of non-negotiables.

This moment may be a time to check in with a mentor or prelaw advisor. Another great resource may be a colleague or friend who is going through the application process at the same time. It will be important to maintain your sanity, decrease your anxiety while you wait to hear from the law schools, and stay excited about the next step in your journey to becoming an attorney!

Deciding between two or more schools

If you've been accepted at more than one school, bust out your list of what you're looking for and break down the pros and cons of your options. Here's a short list of things you can consider while deciding between multiple offers.

>> What do you like about each law school?

>> What programs, clinics, concentrations, and/or emphasis programs interest you?

>> Are any perks associated with the university or campus the law school sits on?

>> What do the students say is the best quality about their law school?

>> What/who do the alumni believe is the most impactful course, professor, or clinic has impacted their career the most?

>> What's their favorite place to study?

>> How is the weather? Does that jibe with your preferences?

TIP

Don't be afraid to ask to speak to more students, faculty, and alumni if you want more information about why they chose their specific law school. What you're looking for and what you need may be different, but hearing other people share what tipped the scales for them can be helpful.

Committing to multiple law schools

You applied to multiple schools and have multiple offers. But now you find yourself in a situation where you just don't want to make the final decision (or any decision) just yet.

Many candidates submit more than one deposit in this scenario, meaning they're holding more than one seat at one time. Law schools call this *commitment* to more than one school. During this time frame, some candidates visit the law schools and the respective campuses, compare their financial aid offers, and/or ask to speak to current students and alumni.

REMEMBER

When you're committed to more than one law school at a time, some of those schools reach out to say, "We see you're deposited at more than one school. We have other candidates on the waitlist, so if you'd let us know one way or the other whether you're enrolling at our law school, it would be helpful for us." It's an important decision for you. It's a business decision for the school. Trust me, you won't hurt a school's feelings if you believe another law school is a better fit for you.

Handling the waitlist

Landing on the waitlist can be pretty awkward for everyone involved. It's not a yes, and it's not a no. It's a maybe.

TIP

Don't make assumptions about why you were waitlisted. Some applicants can figure out pretty early on why they were waitlisted, but asking the law school for information doesn't hurt. Was it your GPA or LSAT/GRE score? Did you not have enough academic letters of recommendation? Was it the timing of your application? These are all reasons that some candidates may end up being waitlisted.

REMEMBER

Sometimes the law school and the admissions committee are just trying to figure out how their class is going to come together. They may be waiting to see how competitive the rest of their applicant pool will be.

Here are some tips for navigating being waitlisted:

>> **Be sure you follow any instructions or rules the law school outlines for waitlisted candidates.**

>> **If a school asks you to confirm your intent to stay on the waitlist, do so.** Within the specified time frame, of course. However, don't accept a spot on the waitlist if you aren't seriously considering attending the law school.

>> **Submit any recommended additional letters of recommendation or other materials.**

>> **Take advantage of any opportunities to participate in an interview.** Most prospective students can easily speak about why they want to go to law school, why they've applied to a specific law school, and so on.

>> **Ask whether the waitlist is ranked.** This information may help you figure out what your chances are.

>> **Be prepared with questions about the waitlist process.**

- How will the school contact you?

- How much time will you have to decide?

- What's the likelihood that you'll be awarded a scholarship if you're on the waitlist?

- Can you submit updated transcripts or test scores? Also, ask what type of document a school wants if it hasn't given you suggestions to allow you to share a promotion or a new job title.

>> If the law school accepts one continued letter of interest and another allows for multiple letters of continued interest.

>> **Find out whether you need to make an appointment for tours and/or visits and schedule ahead of time if necessary.**

>> **Submit your FAFSA with the appropriate law school code.** You can read more about FAFSA and school codes in Chapter 5.

Dealing with a rejection

Many law school applicants find themselves receiving a rejection notification. This result isn't ideal, but it does happen. If you find yourself in this situation, take time to reflect on what happened, but ultimately, you have to move on and focus on the other opportunities that you're waiting to hear about.

Deciding to defer

Deferments are a good option when you realize that you need a little more time to get yourself ready for law school. Students defer for a variety of good reasons, such as the following:

>> A great job opportunity or promotion comes along.

>> You get the chance to join an organization like the Peace Corps or Teach for America.

>> Your military deployment plans change.

>> You or a family member becomes ill.

>> You hit a rough patch financially.

These are reasonable reasons to ask the law school whether it'll hold your seat until the next admission cycle. If you're offered the opportunity to defer, be prepared for

>> Additional fees

>> A request to submit an updated application

>> A request to agree to not enroll in another law school

TIP

If you've been awarded a scholarship of any kind, ask whether the scholarship is part of the deferment offer and whether you're eligible for additional scholarships if the parameters change. (Many law schools change the awarding criteria for scholarships each year. You want to ensure that you lock in the amount of your current scholarship if the law school will move to more restrictive criteria.) I also suggest asking whether you can expect an increase in your scholarship if you obtain a higher GPA, higher LSAT score, or GRE score. For those of you applying during your last year of college, your final GPA may be higher than the GPA on the transcript you submitted when you applied. This could be an opportunity to obtain additional funding!

Chapter **5**

Financing Your Legal Education

This is the main question most prospective law school applicants have: How do I pay for this? Everyone knows that law school is expensive, but another perspective is that it's an investment in your future that can pay for itself in terms of opportunities and legacy building. And remember, law schools want you to start and complete the program.

As far as financing goes, there are more options than you may realize, and we will explore some of them in this chapter.

Submitting Your FAFSA

If you used financial aid to pay for college, you filled out the Free Application for Federal Student Aid (FAFSA). You use the same form (available at studentaid. gov/h/apply-for-aid/fafsa) to apply for law school financial aid.

WARNING

The most important issue is ensuring you use the correct school code. Some law schools use the code for their associated university, but some have their own code. Getting this information right is important because errors may delay your ability to obtain financial aid information upon being admitted to the law school.

TIP

You should submit your FAFSA with the appropriate school codes for every school you're applying to. Doing so prior to being admitted or waitlisted speeds up the process after (fingers crossed) your status changes. But at a minimum, be sure to submit it for the schools that you've been waitlisted at in addition to the schools you've been admitted to.

Reviewing Your Financial Aid Award Letter

You've probably heard all the jokes about people going to law school because they hate math or don't "do numbers," but know that your math skills come into play here. You need to pay close attention to your financial aid award letters to make sure you

>> Compare apples to apples when reviewing your offers.

>> Understand the terms of your scholarships and how to renew them (or get them back if you lose them).

>> Know how much tuition increases every year as you're comparing offers and making three-to-four-year decisions about your law school program and budget.

REMEMBER

Be sure you pay close attention to the renewal terms for the scholarship. You also need to be aware of any other stipulations associated with accepting the scholarship. For example, does it convert to a loan if you transfer out after your first year? Do you have an opportunity to renew the scholarship in your third year if you lose it after your first year?

TIP

The ABA 509 report can be useful here (see Chapter 3). All law schools that have conditional scholarships are required to post five years' worth of scholarship renewal data.

Exploring Other Financing Options

Beyond traditional financial aid, you may be eligible for additional opportunities to pay for your law school education. The following sections cover some possible options.

Tuition remission

One perk of working at a university is often *tuition remission*, which is an incentive or a benefit that provides some type of discount toward tuition for the school's employees. For many universities, the discounts are less for the graduate and professional programs, if they're available at all, than the benefit for traditional undergraduate programs, but they're definitely worth looking into.

REMEMBER

Be sure to check any eligibility requirements. Does the remission apply to spouses and partners, children, or grandchildren? Do you need to be aware of any terms or conditions?

Military educational benefits

If you've served or are currently serving, thank you for your service. You've earned a benefit known as the *Yellow Ribbon Program* that can drastically reduce the cost of law school. You may also be eligible to use your parent(s') or spouse's benefit if they served.

Start by looking your law school up on the Yellow Ribbon Program website at www.va.gov/education/about-gi-bill-benefits/post-9-11/yellow-ribbon-program/ to see whether it's part of the program.

TIP

Get in touch with your school's veterans' affairs office or department that supports military-aligned students (if one exists). It can be a great place to start getting a broader understanding of how that specific school's services and programs work.

If your law school is part of the Yellow Ribbon Program, the next question is figuring out what percentage of funds the law school will match. Some law schools are 100 percent matching schools, while others match at 25 percent. Some have a limited number of yellow ribbon scholarships they award each year, in which case you want to set things in motion sooner rather than later.

REMEMBER

Some law schools ask you to use your military benefits first and then take advantage of the institutional scholarships (that is, scholarships the school offers). In these instances, you want to make sure you have in writing what happens when your military benefits are exhausted.

Vocational rehabilitation benefits

If you've been approved for vocational rehabilitation benefits, the Veterans Affairs Office may cover your tuition. Check out rsa.ed.gov for more information.

Vocational rehabilitation services include job development, placement, and coaching; bar exam resources; disability, rights, information, and so on. These resources are often referred to as *Chapter 31 benefits*.

International student considerations and opportunities

TIP

Pay close attention to the information each law school provides regarding international financial support. This info may include merit scholarships, specific school-related scholarships, loans from private entities, and so forth.

Obviously, to obtain an I-20, you need to study in the United States and to have provided documentation that shows you can pay your tuition and living expenses for the year. (That doesn't mean that you don't want to obtain as much free money as possible; rather, you can get by without the free money if you don't receive any.)

An I-20 is the government document that is issued to international students that have been accepted into a student and exchange visitor program by an approved US institution. The student also must meet the eligibility requirements for an F-1 student visa.

Here are a few questions you may want to ask:

>> Does the school have specific programs for international students to pursue?

>> Are there designated scholarships for international students? DACA students (also known as *Dreamers*)?

>> Are merit scholarships open to all applicants?

>> Are institutional funds available that international students can take advantage of in case of an emergency?

>> Does the university have a program that hires international students to work on campus to help keep their costs down?

TIP

Some law schools maintain lists on their websites for all international and DACA funding resources.

Several lenders loan educational funds to international and DACA students. Many of them require a U.S. cosigner or sponsor of some sort. Ask each law school whether it has a list of preferred lenders the law school and its students have had success with in the past.

TIP

NerdWallet (www.nerdwallet.com) has a list of international student loans. It also compares the interest rates, makes recommendations based on the rates with a cosigner and without, and so on.

Continually Searching for Scholarships

TIP

Throughout your entire law admissions process, you should have a scholarship search on your calendar. Every weekend, spend 30 to 45 minutes searching for free money. It's out there — everything from Rotary clubs to houses of worship to local, regional, national, and *affinity* bar associations (such as those for women, first-generation law students, or specific ethnic groups).

REMEMBER

These scholarships can range anywhere from $100 to more than $25,000. The reality is that most people won't make $1,000 or even $100 an hour at a job, but you can do just that by taking the time to apply for a scholarship here or there!

Many of these outside scholarships require some type of essay or application, along with a copy of your résumé and a law school acceptance letter or email.

TIP

Here are some important tips to keep in mind when searching for and applying for scholarships:

>> **Pay attention to the law school website; it may show opportunities available to you.** Additionally, many law schools send out opportunities that come to the attention of the admissions team.

>> **Make sure you complete the FAFSA with the appropriate school code (as I discuss earlier in the chapter).** If the scholarship you're applying for has a need component, you'll have the info ready to go and won't have to wait to apply.

>> **Keep copies of every single document you submit.** Your tax returns, the FAFSA, the student aid report that you received that comes from the FAFSA submission, any scholarship documents that you submit, scholarship contracts, email communications with the financial aid office and business office, etc.

>> **Order a few copies of your transcripts.** Some organizations may want a hard copy rather than an electronic copy.

>> **Save the essays you create for scholarship submissions.** After you've done a few, you can generally use them repeatedly by tweaking them for a particular group's requirements.

Chapter **6**

Preparing for Pre-Orientation and Orientation

The summer leading up to the start of your law school career can't be all fun and games. You need to attend pre-orientation activities as well as your official law school orientation.

Orientation is an opportunity to welcome you into the law school community, the campus, and the city. You learn more about the administrative processes, where the bookstore is, what office you go to if you have an emergency, where the lockers are, and how to brief cases.

Orientation itself can vary drastically from law school to law school. Some law schools have virtual portions of the program in addition to in-person activities and sessions. Some of these programs last two to three days, while others may last two weeks.

REMEMBER

One of the most important things to figure out is when you actually need to be on campus. Take a look at the academic calendar and get a sense of when you need to move or get settled. You may want to think about when you should stop working or plan to get in that last vacation or outing with family and friends.

TIP

Don't be surprised if you constantly hear from the law school that it doesn't want you to do anything but relax and have fun the summer prior to law school. It's because the orientation programs are set to give you everything you need to get through those first couple of weeks of the fall term. So go to the movies, read for fun, go on that trip, spend time with your loved ones. Just make sure you take care of the pre-orientation tasks I cover in this chapter.

Getting Yourself Ready during Pre-Orientation

Some law schools offer a reading list for the summer prior to law school or run prelaw programming. These *pre-orientation* programs can include academic sessions, social activities, housing info sessions, financial aid primers, and more. They're designed to ensure you have what you need to get situated in your new city, prepare physically and financially for the start of your law school journey, and help you reduce your stress and anxiety as you anticipate what your new life will look like and transition to your new city or campus.

For example, pre-orientation may cover what to do if you don't have financial aid yet. You still need to ensure you have enough funds for rent, moving expenses, your books, and so on.

TIP

Your law school may have a checklist you can use to handle pre-orientation and orientation tasks, so don't hesitate to ask if you can't find one on the website. Getting organized brings a sense of relief.

Checking your email regularly for communications from the law school

Various law school departments will communicate with you leading up to the start of classes about things like student health insurance, setting up your school email account, making sure you have your class schedule, and ensuring that your bank account is associated with your student account. Make sure that you're checking that email daily.

TIP

Put the law school's addresses on your safe senders list so you have no issues receiving their emails. Some items may be time-sensitive, such as deadlines you need to meet, and you don't want them relegated to the spam folder.

Hitting all the deadlines for accommodations

If you need accommodations (such as extra time, a private space, etc.), keep an eye out for any request for information to set those up. The documentation you used for your undergraduate program or graduate school may or may not be sufficient for the law school experience, so you want to ensure you have everything you need prior to starting law school.

Adhering to the school's deadlines is crucial because the accommodations process may involve various departments within or outside the school. You want to make sure you're all set prior to the start of law school so you can focus on your studies. If you have any questions, be sure to reach out to the student services or student affairs office.

Testing for a learning disability

Many students have undiagnosed learning disabilities that are more apparent when they start law school. If you suspect you have an unidentified learning disability, you may want to set some funds aside to get tested as soon as possible. Law school tests different ways of learning and communicating, and for many students, it's the first time where just memorizing and regurgitating the facts isn't enough.

REMEMBER

Sorting out any learning accommodations now is also critical for the bar exam (see Chapter 24). That may seem far away, but these three or four years will go fast. To ensure you have what you need for the bar, get that accommodation testing done and hold on to the paperwork.

Meeting your ongoing duty to disclose

Throughout the admission cycle (and law school itself), you have an ongoing duty to disclose any issues or incidents that you're involved in that may be related to the character and fitness questions on the law school application (such as a DUI). So if anything comes up between the time you submit your application and the time you start law school, you have to report that situation to the law school.

REMEMBER

Many law schools send reminders throughout the admissions cycle, prior to the start of school, and again (perhaps multiple times) during orientation. But proactively updating your school is ultimately your responsibility. Don't put yourself in a situation where you risk your entire law school career because you fail to disclose something that you could've easily communicated to the law school and had that be the end of it.

TIP

Always reach out to the law school if you have any questions or concerns about what you should or shouldn't report. Their job is to support you. You can also look at the reporting criteria for the state bar examiners information in the state you think you want to be licensed for guidance.

Submitting your final degree-granting transcripts

As I note in Chapter 4, the American Bar Association (ABA) requires that law schools have a *degree-granting* (official) transcript on file for all students. Though you typically submit this transcript with your application, be sure to send through any updates that your final semester grades may create for potential scholarship enhancements. But the ABA requirement must be met. Some law schools send reminders throughout the pre-orientation process and during the first few weeks of the term, but making sure you get it done falls to you. Some law schools will utilize the transcript you submit to LSAC while others will require a formal, final degree-granting version to be sent directly to the law school. If you do not meet this deadline, a law school may revoke your offer of admission even if you are several weeks into the term.

Say cheese: Submitting photos for your ID card

Many law schools ask you to submit a photo prior to orientation; others take your photo when you arrive. These photos are often used in photo books for the faculty's rosters and seating charts, so the photo will be around for the entire year. Make it good!

Updating your contact information

Before school gets underway, you want to make sure your contact information (mailing address, phone number, and so on) is up-to-date so you don't miss out on important info about, say, your financial aid *refund* (living expenses). If you're unsure about where to update your information, ask the admissions team.

Attending Orientation

What should you expect at orientation? Anything and everything! Prepared to be overwhelmed and excited and to have some bouts of self-doubt. You may start questioning whether you made the right decision. All these reactions are natural.

You're going into something completely new, and being nervous is okay. Use that nervousness to get focused for the task ahead.

Ask questions. Take advantage of all the opportunities. But also take care of yourself. If you feel overwhelmed, find someone to chat with about it, whether that's an upper-division student, administration, orientation leader, or someone else.

Getting started: You've got homework

You may have literal homework for orientation. That's an opportunity for you to get a feel for what preparing for class, getting called on, and taking notes are like. Most professors give you ample time to prepare.

Getting ready for classes

Check your new law school email for any information from your new professors. Some may already have your first assignments ready for you during orientation. That means you need to review the syllabi for your classes, get your books, and schedule some study time in the midst of enjoying that last weekend of freedom. You want to start law school off on the right foot, and showing up prepared, even if you get it wrong, makes a good impression on your faculty.

Dressing properly: Orientation attire

Depending on the activity or session, the law school may provide specific guidance about what you should wear. Obviously, you want to be casual and comfortable, but you also have to remember that you're starting your professional career and want to make a good impression on your faculty and staff members, administrators, and fellow students. Generally, business casual is a safe way to start.

Attending oath or pinning ceremonies

Many law schools have introduced some type of professionalism oath or swearing-in ceremony for brand-new law students. These rituals help you understand

>> The importance of the journey you're about to begin

>> The level of responsibility you have in becoming an attorney, a judge, an advocate, and so on

Some law schools have you pin yourself, while others have alumni, faculty, and current students pin you.

This event is a huge introduction and welcome into the new profession, so business attire is generally required. Students are often encouraged to bring their family members and close friends. Some law schools actually stream the event so people who can't attend in person can still see you take the oath of professionalism as you join your new profession. All in all, a pinning/oath ceremony is a serious but joyous occasion. It marks the importance of your embarking on a brand-new path.

CONSIDERATIONS FOR TRANSFER STUDENTS

Many law schools have specific programming for transfer students, though some incorporate transfer students into regular first-year orientation.

Another important consideration: fall recruitment/on-campus interview deadlines. If you are a transfer student, be sure you contact the law school to understand how the process will work. The submission of résumés and transcripts may be critical to obtaining interviews with the firms and organizations you are interested in.

2

Getting What You Came for: The Law School Experience

Get the tech and school supplies you'll need.

Make a smooth transition to law school.

Understand the 1L course load.

Have the right mindset while staying on top of your classes.

Manage your time.

Chapter 7

Shopping for What You Need to Start Law School

Whether you love to shop or hate it, you can't get around the fact that starting law school means you're going to need some gear. This chapter covers several items you may want to put on your shopping list before classes begin. Buy what's best for you and what you can afford.

Making Sure You Have the Tech You Need

As you may expect, you're going to need a computer and other tech-related tools if you're going to attend law school.

Laptop and monitor

A laptop is where you take most of your notes (even for professors who don't allow them in the classroom), create your outlines, work on your papers/memos, and do research.

You want to ensure that your laptop is compatible with whatever example software your law school uses. Most law schools actually tell admitted students which type of laptop is most compatible with their software, but you may also be able to find that info on the school's website. If not, don't hesitate to ask the admissions office.

Many law students find that having an additional monitor or an additional screen helps them stay organized, read, and add information to their outlines.

TIP

I suggest buying a new laptop so you can keep the same device throughout law school. The last thing you need is for your ancient computer to crash the night before a major assignment is due — taking all your outlines with it — or right before (or during!) final exams. That level of stress and chaos isn't worth it.

REMEMBER

Most law schools allow you to adjust your financial aid at least once to buy a new laptop. You may have to buy the laptop out-of-pocket, submit the receipt, and be reimbursed, but just know this is an option.

Tablet

You may be interested in working on a tablet throughout law school in addition to having a laptop. Tablets are lighter and easier to carry around. Most are compatible with laptops and PCs and allow you to take handwritten notes in class that you can then transcribe into typed documents.

Printer, paper, and ink cartridges

I know. I know. Saving trees and all that. But the reality is that many law students want to print their papers, outlines, old exams, and so on. Your law school may give you a certain number of copies for free, but when you need to proof your paper one final time at 11 p.m., you'll want to print it yourself, make those edits, and then update the information on your laptop.

Headphones or earplugs

If you're someone that needs a bit of quiet but also likes to be in a space around other people, some sort of noise reducer is helpful. Depending on your tolerance for noise and where you plan on studying, investing in noise-canceling headphones may help you out quite a bit. Otherwise, good old-fashioned earplugs also work. Remember that some libraries have a zero-tolerance policy for noise, while others are a little more lax about students talking and giggling.

REMEMBER

Some law schools allow you to use earplugs, but not noise-canceling headphones, during exams. So you may actually want both options available; be sure to check the rules.

Portable chargers

Because of how long your days may be, I recommend having a portable charger for your laptop or tablet and for your phone. You may even need one for a recording device, if your law school allows recorders or they're a part of your accommodations.

The Books Every Law Student Needs

You encounter tons of opinions about what you should read before law school. What follows are my suggestions for fun and informative reads. I could easily list 25 or more books, but here are just a few:

>> *Black's Law Dictionary* (Thomas Reuters)

>> *To Kill a Mockingbird* by Harper Lee (Harper Perennial Modern Classics)

>> *Law School 101: Everything You Need to Know About American Law* by Jay M. Feinman (Oxford University Press)

>> *The Elements of Style* by William Strunk, Jr, and E.B. White (Pearson)

>> *Mindset: The New Psychology of Success* by Carol S. Dweck, PhD (Ballantine Books)

>> *Letters to a Young Lawyer* by Alan Dershowitz (Basic Books)

>> *Getting to Maybe: How to Excel on Law Exams* by Richard Michael Fischl and Jeremy Paul (Carolina Academic Press)

>> *Law School Confidential* by Robert H. Miller (St. Martin's Griffin)

>> *One L* by Scott Turow (Penguin Books)

>> *Thinking Like a Lawyer: A New Introduction to Legal Reasoning* by Frederick Schauer (Harvard University Press)

Stocking Up on Office Supplies

I'm calling these items "office supplies," but I realize your office space may just be a corner of your studio or campus housing. Get what works for you.

Desk and desk chair

You'll be spending a lot of time studying, reading, taking notes, working on papers, and doing research. The last thing you need is a strained neck, lower back problems, and cramping in your hands.

That's why you need a comfortable space to work. Even if you primarily study in the library, you'll have to do some of your work at home; most libraries close at some point. A good desk means you can have your laptop, notebook, handouts, supplements, and whatever else out for hours at a time.

That includes a sturdy desk chair. You don't want to get back and neck problems from spending that much time in a flimsy chair.

Desk lamp

Stop me if you've heard this one: You read a lot in law school. A good desk lamp can make a huge difference in helping prevent excess eye strain. Some students actually purchase a book lamp in addition to a desk lamp.

REMEMBER

The goal is to get items that make your eyes less tired and ensure you can stay awake when it's late at night and you have another 20 pages to read or another set of edits to go through for the next day.

Highlighters

This suggestion may seem old school, but as much as the world has moved to electronics for most things, many law students still find comfort in using a highlighter to emphasize rules, policy, arguments, other cases, and so on. So line up your favorite colors and stash some extras at home, in your locker, and in your backpack just in case.

TIP

Be judicious with your highlighters; don't fall into the trap of highlighting everything. Then you can't distinguish what's actually important. Your law books shouldn't look like a rainbow.

Notecards

Some law students find creating their own notecards for rules, policy arguments, and important cases for each class helpful. If this technique interests you, or has worked for you in the past, consider picking up some index or other blank notecards to try it out.

Notebooks and folders

Your notebook needs depend on how you plan to take notes. For many students, typing their notes and outlines and using those typewritten notes to create note-cards is sufficient. For others, writing their notes in class and then retyping them is a solid way to start to memorize rules, case law, and so forth.

REMEMBER

The laptop policy for each class is an important consideration. If a professor doesn't allow laptops, you need a notebook. Check the syllabus or ask your upper-division mentors on the policies for each professor so you can plan ahead.

Commercial flashcards

Each course in law school has flashcards for law school study and exam prep.

TIP

Don't rush out to buy premade flashcards right away. If you get lucky, your men-tor may have flashcards you can borrow, or a recent graduate may offer their cards or sell them at a discounted rate.

If you're pretty certain you can benefit from this learning style and you don't have access to used cards, check in with your new classmates and the academic support/success team about their recommendations for the best companies to buy from.

Dry-erase board

For many law students, mapping out schedules, difficult concepts, rules, and case law in the book or on a computer can be a dreadful experience. Some people just need to visualize what they're processing.

For example, many students find creating flow charts that show when a court has jurisdiction helpful for civil procedure. Dry-erase boards are also good for study groups.

REMEMBER

Be sure to get some markers and an eraser as well!

Shopping for Personal Items

The following items may not be at the top of your shopping list as you prepare for law school, but they're certainly useful.

Reusable food containers

This suggestion may seem silly, but be sure you have some reusable containers in your backpack or locker. Let me explain: Law school campuses offer a lot of events and activities, and schools often over-order a bit on food (to make sure they have enough for guests). That means leftovers, which are often available to law students. (In many places, you can't donate food from events to local shelters.)

TIP

Some law schools have a website where they post where the food is and what time you can show up and fill up your containers. Others send out some sort of group message. Figure out what your school's system is so you can stock up and save money.

Water bottle

You need to stay hydrated. One way to do that is to ensure you bring a water bottle with you everywhere. Even if your law school doesn't allow drinking in the classroom (and some don't), it's nice to have a bottle in your backpack when class is over.

Backpack or book bag

Just like when you first started pre-K, getting a new bag for school always generates a little buzz of excitement. Unlike preschool, the main factor you're looking for in a law school bag is the ability to withstand the weight of the books associated with your classes. The books are very heavy, and if you're at a law school that doesn't have lockers, that means you may be carrying all your books for the day with you after you leave home. Depending on how active you are, that may or may not be painful. But it's most definitely uncomfortable if you're lugging around two or three classes' worth all day.

TIP

Some new students opt for backpacks with wheels. This option is particularly helpful if you have a bad back.

Spare eyeglasses or contact lenses

TIP

Get your eyes checked before law school begins so you can be sure your glasses or contacts are good to go.

Take the time to ensure you have an extra set of glasses along with an extra side of contact lenses. Life happens, and if you break a pair, you don't want to suffer. I also suggest getting an extra prescription just in case something goes awry and you need to get new items after you get to your new city. For contacts, have extra solution in your bag or backpack as well as in your locker (if you have one).

REMEMBER

Be prepared for the fact that your eyesight may change during law school thanks to the volume of reading! Many of my classmates who didn't need glasses when we started school definitely wore them by the time we graduated.

Creating a Wish List for Family and Friends

Many law students have family, friends, mentors, and other folks that want to support them. One way to facilitate that is to create some type of electronic wish list that you can share with family, friends, and mentors. You can add items as they come up, and people can purchase at their leisure. This approach also helps people who may not be able to afford to buy you a laptop but who can afford 5 bucks here or 50 bucks there.

TIP

Add the things you need along with the things you wish you could have! Don't be shy. Ask for what you need/want.

The following list isn't exhaustive, but it offers some general ideas you may want to start with:

>> Your laptop, a tablet, and/or notetaking devices

>> A second screen or dual monitor

>> Your favorite pens and highlighters

>> An additional stylus in case you lose one or need to leave one on campus in your locker

>> Eyeglass cleaner or contact lens solution

>> Personal items like your favorite snacks, a nice pillow, comfy fuzzy socks, an extra sweatshirt, or a light jacket

>> Gift cards for food delivery services such as DoorDash, Grubhub, or Uber Eats

You can also share your preferences for receiving funds, which may include your handles for services like Cash App, Zelle, Venmo, Apple Pay, and so on.

Chapter **8**

Getting into the 1L Groove

Congratulations! You've made it to law school after a grueling application season. You conquered the LSAT and/or GRE, and now's the time for you to get everything ready so you can hit the ground running during your first year of law school (1L)! Before you officially begin the school year, getting your life, living situation, and law school lingo up to speed is a wise idea so you don't have so much to worry about as the semester gets underway.

REMEMBER

Moving to a new city, starting a new school, and opening a new chapter of your life is often scary and uncomfortable — at first. However, this chapter helps arm you with all the tricks of the trade to make your transition as painless as possible. Here, I discuss some of the best ways for new 1Ls to acclimate themselves to the law school mindset and start the year leaps and bounds ahead of their peers. Think of how much fun it will be to look back on your first year after graduation!

Performing Crucial Tasks before School Starts

Think of the one or two months before the school year starts as being the prime time for you to get all your affairs (everything) in order. Yep, you need to start packing up your old place, confirming your new place, and reading about your new city. This section describes several key actions you must take *before* your classes start because that's when you have plenty of time and energy to deal with them. The last thing you need as a 1L is to be worrying about things that you can easily handle beforehand.

Take control of your personal life

First-year law students don't have much time for socializing, including dating. The reason: Almost all their free time is devoted to staying on top of reading, freaking out about exams, and trying to figure out exactly what this thing called law school is all about. But the problem is especially difficult when the angst of a relationship back home already causes you mental anguish. Everyone goes through tough times with their partner, but you need to iron out any significant relationship issues before starting law school. You're starting a new phase of your life, so you need to make sure that your relationships are prepared to withstand the time commitment and stress of law school.

Doing so, however, may mean deciding that you need to break up or separate before you start law school. Some of my peers who had a love interest back home at the beginning of law school broke up during the first semester. Many of them cited the same reason: The other person just couldn't relate to what the 1L was going through. The ones that made it work were on the same page; their partners were supportive of the 1L's goals and understood their "why." They were willing to make short-term sacrifices for a long-term career opportunity.

On a happier note, however, many new 1Ls decide that heading to law school is the perfect time to solidify a relationship. You're starting a new chapter of your life, and getting engaged, getting married, or starting a family or adding a new addition to the family may be a wonderful way for you to begin your new path as a soon-to-be law student. (As long as you have a budget, a plan, and clear communication about roles and expectations.)

TIP

Even when your relationship is in great shape, I recommend explaining to your significant other that you're not going to have as much time to spend with them for at least the first year of school. You need to explain that law school may mean putting a cap on nightly four-hour marathon conversations or twice-weekly dinner and movie dates. If you have children, you and your significant other need to plan ahead on sharing responsibilities. Involving them from the beginning can help manage expectations.

But also reassure your partner that this 24/7 time commitment to law school is only temporary; after the first year is over and you're better able to gauge how much time you need to put into your studies to get the grades you want, you can probably devote more time to all the areas in your life, including your partner. Of course, part-time and evening law students, who will likely work full-time during their entire law school careers, may need to explain to their partners that their free time probably won't increase appreciably from the first year to the rest.

Put your finances in order

No one likes worrying about money, especially when you have a million other things to think about. You don't want to be halfway into your first month of law school only to find out that your *refund* (living expenses check) won't be arriving on time because you forgot to fill out the required paperwork, failed to complete entrance counseling, used the incorrect student ID, or whatever. As soon as you arrive on campus, check in with the financial aid office and go through the following steps:

>> **Read all the materials that you get from the financial aid office closely and double-check that your information is correct on every document you receive.** Keep copies of everything. When possible, carbon copy yourself on correspondence.

>> **Resolve any snafus right away, and don't hesitate to contact the financial aid office with any questions.** If you don't understand a charge or a fee, the timing of disbursements, what your next steps are, and so on, speak up right away to avoid any delays.

>> **Determine how you want to receive your refund (if you decide to take out loans for living expenses) before school starts and make the appropriate arrangements.** Whether you want the funds to be deposited directly into your account or the check to be mailed to you, get that set up now. For physical checks, make sure you have your mailing address updated in the system.

Create a law school budget

Review the cost of attendance. What do they think you spend monthly on rent, transportation, food, and so on? It may be a bit of shock but remember, the goal is to live like a student, not like a lawyer. Yet!

TIP

Calculate what you need for your new life and ensure you have that much saved up and/or available through credit. Don't forget you need funds to secure your new place, transportation, moving to the area, new supplies, and so on.

Make sure you have enough funding to support yourself the entire first month of law school in case the school doesn't disburse financial aid until after the add/drop period. Some law schools may start processing refunds during orientation, especially if you're technically starting law school during your orientation program, but don't count on that. Better to be safe than sorry . . . or broke.

Secure comfortable housing

In the same way that a comfortable bed helps you sleep much better, which in turn enables you to work more productively (when you're not falling asleep at your desk every five minutes), a comfortable home is another key to success in law school.

When your neighbors are a bunch of loud fraternity or sorority members, unruly friends, or other forms of around-the-clock party animals, you're unlikely to arrive at law school adequately rested each day. This also holds true if you have an inconsiderate roommate who insists on keeping odd hours. The presence of annoying neighbors and roommates or loud bass thumping through your walls at 4 a.m. may also negatively affect your ability to study undistracted at home.

WARNING

To avoid these unfortunate circumstances, securing your housing well in advance of your arrival in town is a good idea. (I went on one trip looking for housing four months before school started.) Doing so enables you to aim for the best housing selection, which is particularly important when you're in a college town where move-ins and move-outs are often timed to the start and end of the school year. Otherwise, when you show up without housing or any clue as to where you're going to live, you may be forced to move into whatever housing is left over or get stuck with a roommate you may not be compatible with. Some hapless 1Ls end up with apartments that have rodent problems, broken appliances, and inattentive and uncaring slumlords. Doing some advance research into which housing complexes are quieter and better maintained greatly adds to your peace of mind when school starts.

Coordinate your move

A few weeks before moving into your new place, you need to develop a plan for getting out of your old home that includes

>> Setting a packing timeline

>> Scheduling movers

>> Turning off the phone, Internet, cable, water, electricity, and other utilities

>> Changing your mailing address with the post office and the law school

In preparation for moving into your new spot, be sure to inquire whether they'll be ready by the time you arrive in town. Having to stay in a hotel with all your belongings while waiting for former occupants to move out is a huge hassle. For some buildings, you must schedule your move-in time and reserve the elevator designated for moving.

How long before school starts should you plan on moving into your new place? A good guideline is at least two weeks; otherwise, you'll be in a rush to get everything done. Many of my students moved in three to four weeks before school started and found this time frame to be ideal. They had plenty of time to furnish their apartments, get household supplies, and learn their way around town. When you arrive at your new place, make sure your Internet, electricity, and other utilities are turned on, that your mail is being delivered, and that your cable can be hooked up.

Establish a routine

A couple of weeks before law school begins, figure out what sort of routine you need to establish so that everything gets done. Some people may equate the notion of a *routine* with a boring, predictable life. But when you're faced with so many new experiences and the time-consuming study requirements of law school, you'll be hard-pressed to do everything that needs to be done on a daily basis without a routine.

After figuring out what I need to plan for during the day, I've always found that making a rough weekly schedule is helpful — penciling in class and study times, workouts, meals, and fun/rest/relaxation. Developing a rough plan now of when you'll do things helps you feel more at ease later on when law school is in full swing.

Take care of a few more important considerations

With so much going on in the lead-up to law school, some things can slip through the cracks. To avoid face-palming a day or two after you arrive at law school, ensure the following:

>> **You have all your medications, equipment, and so on ordered.** You want to confirm you have everything you may need in case finding a new doctor, therapist, allergist, or whatever takes some time. Being prepared reduces your stress and makes sure you have what you need.

>> **You keep copies of all your accommodations paperwork.** If you've received accommodations in undergrad or your graduate program, be sure you know where your copies of that documentation are. For testing you've sought prior to law school, ensure you have electronic *and* paper copies of everything.

TIP

If you're seeking out testing prior to law school, ensure you know exactly what your law school accommodations office requires. These tests can be very expensive and time consuming. (The admissions office, student affairs office, and/or office of student accessibility will be able to provide this information.)

>> **You ask for referrals for therapists or counselors if you're currently in therapy.** Law school can be stressful. See whether your current therapist has recommendations for a new therapist in the town you're moving to. If possible, ask your therapist to make the introduction for you prior to your last session. Anything you can do to reduce your stress and anxiety prior to your move and prior to starting law school will help you tremendously.

TIP

As soon as you can, identify a place of worship, gym/workout facility, favorite grocery store, and so on! Finding the places that will keep you grounded and make your new home feel like home is key to having a smooth transition. Spend some time exploring your new location. Figure out the best days and times to shop and go to the gym and where to park for free. Or figure out public transportation (and whether it offers student discounts).

Taming Your Transition

Almost every transition is stressful, regardless of whether it's starting a new school, moving to a new town, or starting a new job. It's a life change, and getting used to life changes takes time.

Getting your bearings

I have a pretty good sense of direction after a few times around the block, campus, or city. But if you always take a while to figure out where you're going, be sure to factor in enough time to get acclimated before or during orientation. That way, you can find the fastest routes to bookstores, grocery stores, pharmacies, and other places that are important to your routine. Here are a few tips:

>> **Arm yourself with maps of the campus so you become acquainted with where the nearest study spots, faculty offices, law library, lecture halls, and campus gym are located.** Update any map apps to ensure they can help you navigate your new campus and city.

>> **Head out on foot, by car, or by other means to figure out how to get to where you need to go.**

>> **Check with the city's chamber of commerce or tourism office to stock up on any activities brochures, coupons, or other benefits it may offer.** The law school may have some of this information for you as well, so be sure to review what's online, in the new-student portal, or on the newly admitted student page.

TIP

Knowing where you'll park is also important given the scarcity of parking spaces at most large universities and big cities. You'll want to figure out your parking options well in advance, including university-owned parking and private parking nearby. If you don't want to deal with university parking, ask around at the admissions office to find out about any out-of-the-way private lots near the law school and about public transportation.

Perusing your book-buying options

If you've never seen a *law school casebook* (a thick hardcover book filled primarily with appellate court cases), you may find that taking an advance trip to the bookstore to check one out is educational. Sure, you're risking a heart attack finding out just how much these babies cost (and weigh), but you can at least flip through one, contemplating the vast amounts of knowledge it holds.

TIP

Ask current students for their advice about which courses may be best for using electronic books or used books, which are often less expensive. If you're lucky, a mentor may have saved a book or two that you can borrow (but that also likely means you can't write or highlight information in the book). Similarly, some of your new law school classmates may offer their used books for free or at a discounted rate. Keep an eye out for message groups or social media posts. These books can go quickly because the prices are usually much less than the ones at the regular law school bookstore. The selection, however, is necessarily hit or miss. You can also find great deals on a variety of study aids this way (see Chapter 14).

TIP

Some books you can rent, but the issue is figuring out whether your financial aid will arrive in time to get the books that way. Some law schools allow you to purchase your books with a voucher at the university/law school book store if you have pending financial aid. As always, double-check with your law school to know your options.

Finding out what the university offers

One advantage of attending a law school that's attached to a university: You have access to all the resources the university offers. You're also surrounded by a multitude of departments — graduate and undergraduate, research institutes, resource offices, and specialized libraries. Take a look at the university catalog on the website and review the department listings. This information may come in handy if you want to audit a course for personal interest.

Meander through the student union/center and check out the information or activities desk, where you can often find brochures and schedules of fun activities. Many unions offer inexpensive classes like massage, drawing, photography, or foreign languages, all for students who want to try something different in a no-stress atmosphere without grades. While you're at the student union, you may want to find out what restaurants or food courts are available (and when), where any movie theaters are, and what recreational activities are offered, such as racquetball, bowling, or billiards.

You may also want to find out what kind of student organizations the university/law school offers. Even if you aren't at a big university that offers loads of amenities, most schools have a student organizations fair at the beginning of the year or as part of orientation. However, signs and posters advertising the times and locations may not be posted in the law school on bulletin boards or electronic boards. Check the e-newsletter, weekly updates from student affairs, and/or the Student Bar Association (SBA) to familiarize yourself with various organizations and what they do.

Attaining the Law School Mindset

As a newly minted 1L, you may need some time to get used to doing things the law school way. When you're a 1L, everything is new to you. You may find practices unfamiliar (like the widespread use of seating charts) or disconcerting (speaking in front of 100 other people). Relax.

Getting used to seating charts

I can't remember a single college class where I had assigned seats, but most of my law school classes had them.

The way the seating charts work is that on the first or sometimes second day of classes, professors pass around large paper maps or charts of their room's seats, and you're expected to sign your name on the space that corresponds with where you're sitting. A day or two later, professors are likely to have taped photos from the class viewbook to the charts next to each corresponding signature, making identifying everyone in the class easier for them.

REMEMBER

Because seats are assigned on the first or second day of classes, you need to choose where you sit carefully. Strategize by getting to classes early on the first and second days, because if you choose a poor seat — or seatmate — you're stuck there all semester.

TIP

Here are a few approaches to maximizing your seating chart position. None of them are foolproof, though; be prepared no matter what!

>> If you don't want to be called on too often, choosing a seat that's out of the professor's direct line of sight sometimes helps. I had a little success with this technique, especially by sitting on extreme sides of the first row. The professor almost never looks directly at the first row or the extreme sides of the room in any location, so you may well be safer in those areas.

>> When you actually want to get called on, however, be sure to sit right in the middle — rows three through six — and in the center.

>> Beware of sitting in the very last row. Many professors become annoyed by students who do so when plenty of other seats are available in the room.

Getting used to the same classmates

Unlike college, where each class you take is made up of a different set of people, as a 1L you attend classes with the same set of people for virtually the entire year. At most schools, each 1L class is divided into *sections* or *tracks*. At some schools, a class of around 200 to 220 people is divided into six to ten sections for legal research and writing courses, each with about 18-22 or so people. For the other standard 1L classes, each individual group is usually melded with between two and four other groups; that means about 50 to 70 students per track/section. *Note:* In spite of what you read, at most law schools, the process is completely random.

Before I started law school, I'd heard of this practice and worried that being with the same people day in and day out would become highly annoying. To my surprise, I never once felt that way. Instead, seeing the same faces every day was somewhat comforting during those times when law school was such a maelstrom of uncertainty. As 2Ls, 3Ls, and 4Ls, the sections or tracks don't apply, and you're with different people for each class again. I rarely had the same people in any of my 2L and 3L classes, and some classmates from my first year I rarely saw again because we must have had completely different schedules.

Surviving Orientation with Your Sanity Intact

Orientation can be a two- to three-day event or even two weeks of activities preceding the start of classes. Most orientations are set up the same way: with introductory comments from people in all the major facets of law school life. For example, you may hear a representative of the career services office (CSO) and the various deans speak, followed by meetings with various faculty members and lunch with your peers. A few law schools incorporate the start of your classes into the orientation program.

Many schools assign small groups of new students to 2Ls, 3Ls, and 4Ls who serve as *peer mentors*. Your peer mentor group meets for meals, goes to social events together, and serves as a support group through the early weeks of the semester. Members of these groups often become long-term friends.

If you want to get the most out of your orientation, follow these tips:

>> **Attend every meeting and activity.** Most law schools email you orientation materials along with the schedule a few weeks before the program is slated to begin. The information generally includes attire for the various activities, things you need to bring with you, and so on. Remember that going to everything during orientation is always best, no matter how tired you are or how lame you think it may be. You never know when you'll miss out on an important piece of law school trivia or find out something interesting about your classmates and faculty.

>> **Tag along on tours, even if you've visited previously.** When you're new to law school and don't know where anything is, be sure to go on as many tours as you can, including tours of the law school, main university, career development office, and law library. Library tours give you a general overview of where everything is, although many of the books the librarians point out

have such complicated-sounding names that you may not remember them. Still, when you have a general idea of where things are located, you're a step ahead of the game when classes start.

>> **Go to all the social events (or as many as you can).** The first few weeks in law school are critical for meeting new people and forming friendships. Social events during orientation — whether organized by the school and/or put on by student organizations — are great ways to mix and mingle. I recommend going to everything: the welcome barbeque/picnic, lunch with your peer group, and the late-night party hosted by your new neighbor. Cliques tend to form fast in law school, so you want to meet as many people as you can initially and try to keep an open mind. Often, the people you meet during orientation will still be your friends when you're 3Ls or 4Ls and beyond.

REMEMBER

When you're an older student or a student with obligations beyond law school, getting out there during the first few weeks is especially important for meeting new people before the frenzy of law school life kicks in. It ensures you make connections with your classmates, upper-division mentors, staff, and faculty.

>> **Involve your family in orientation as much as possible.** Orientation is great for you because you get a solid snapshot of the school that reveals its mission and its offerings. However, your spouse or family usually isn't so lucky. Although some schools formally involve families in orientation, many more don't. In that case, letting your loved ones know what you've discovered in orientation and what services or aspects of the school may be beneficial to them is up to you. Keeping them involved helps them understand how hectic your schedule will be and why you're working so hard to keep up.

Preparing to Create Your LinkedIn Profile

LinkedIn can be a useful tool in finding your first law school internships and connecting with classmates, alumni, and organizations like firms and nonprofits.

When you're setting up your LinkedIn page, take some time to check out the profiles of upper-division students for guidance on setting the right tone, using the right action words, and so on. Remember, this site is your professional networking tool and resource.

TIP

Take advantage of your 1L headshots for your new LinkedIn profile. They're free! Spending money on professional shots when your law school is offering them to you is pointless. You also probably have an orientation photo (and a classbook photo too if your law school creates one).

IN THIS CHAPTER

» Making sense of your 1L courses

» Getting a feel for class organization

» Maximizing classroom time

» Developing good relationships
with your professors

» Knowing what to do if you're
unprepared for class

Chapter **9**

Surviving First-Year Classes: A Crash Course

Why do people say that law school is the most rigorous and intellectual education of all the professions? Because you're *constantly* being challenged. Law school isn't like memorizing the anatomy of the body by rote; you're finding subtle weak points in an argument. In class, you're not passively taking notes in a huge lecture hall; you're bombarded at every turn with your professor's relentless Socratic questioning (see Chapter 12). Dozing off when an overhead projector switches on isn't an option; lively debates among your peers keep you on your toes, and the pace of the class forces your brain to be in constant overdrive.

If that isn't enough to stimulate you, well, perhaps 50 to 100 pages of reading per night or that shot of adrenaline you feel when you're caught unprepared will do the trick. The good news: If you follow the advice in this chapter, you'll be ready to hit any kind of pitch that law school or your professors throw at you out of the park. This chapter describes what courses you'll take, how they're organized, and how to avoid falling behind. Want to know when to perk up your ears in class and how to know what your professor considers important? It's all here, so grab your syllabus, start flipping through your casebook, and prepare to discover what your first-year classes are all about!

Understanding the 1L Curriculum

Most law schools offer the similar required courses (including legal research and writing) that comprise the standard 1L curriculum. How many credit hours and how many semesters/quarters the respective law schools allot to each course varies, however. For instance, some schools require two semesters of contracts or property, whereas yours may require only one (or vice versa). At some schools, you may take one or two of these 1L courses in the second year rather than the first.

REMEMBER

Although all law professors have their own perceptions of what material within a single course deserves more or less coverage, the basic substance of 1L classes is similar from one law school to another. Regardless of course length or instructor focus, rest assured that all 1Ls are pretty much learning the same material.

Note: For part-time and evening students, the concept of a first year falls apart to a certain degree because they don't take all the following courses during their first year. At many part-time and evening programs, students take the traditional 1L courses during their first *and* second years, taking fewer credits each semester than full-time students. The third and fourth years of part-time and evening programs are when students take upper-class electives.

Torts

If the only tort you've ever heard of is the kind that goes well with coffee and a scoop of ice cream, you're far from alone. (I hate to break it to you, but that one's actually a torte.) Basically, *tort* is the French word for "a wrong." More specifically, *torts* are civil wrongs where some sort of remedy (usually damages in the form of monetary compensation) can be obtained. Torts class covers many of the same things you'd imagine personal injury lawyers handle — car accidents, erroneous amputations, battery, and heavy objects falling out of windows and injuring people, just to name a few.

I liked torts class, but it wasn't my favorite subject! Reading the details of horrific surgical mishaps, train wrecks, defective products, wild animal attacks, and slips and falls was a refreshing change of pace from drier courses like contracts. One thing's for sure: After a stimulating semester of torts, you never look at a banana peel lying on the sidewalk in the same way again! And I was reminded about why some people pursue law versus medicine.

Civil procedure

Civil procedure (or *civ pro*) is all about how to sue someone for noncriminal penalties. The course shows you the steps you need to go through to begin proceedings against a defendant in state or (more frequently) federal court, the structure of the court system, how to determine which law (state or federal) controls, and under what circumstances a case can be brought in state or federal court. Many law schools use the most recent edition of the *Federal Rules of Civil Procedure* as one of the main teaching tools for the course. You also find out how to file a *complaint* (which signals the start of a lawsuit), how to handle responses to complaints, and how lawyers use a host of motions and counterclaims to stymie the proceedings.

One of the most surprising tidbits I got out of civ pro is the tiny percentage of lawsuits that ever make it to court (most are either settled or otherwise terminated). Some sources say something like 20 percent of cases actually make it to court, though others have it as low as 5 percent. Think about it for a moment: In the litigious society you're familiar with, many times more lawsuits are initiated than are actually ever tried!

Criminal law

If you're fascinated with the criminal mind or have an image of the criminal lawyer as the prototypical attorney (you know, like the ones you see on TV shows), this course is sure to captivate you. Here, you discover the notion of *mens rea* (the guilty mind), endlessly discuss the concept of punishment, and focus on the notion of intent. You find out about the significance of the due process clause in the Constitution and examine the insanity defense in depth.

TIP

I think criminal law is the most practical and useful of the 1L courses because the concepts are easier to relate to everyday life. Criminal law seems to be the one law school course that's useful for everyone to take because, for the most part, everyone knows at least a little about it. After all, crimes are an unfortunate part of everyday life in today's world, and knowing how they're classified and how the prosecutorial system works is valuable knowledge for anyone.

Contracts

In *contracts* class, you work on the nuts and bolts of your garden-variety contract. You learn

>> What makes up an *offer* (an attempt to initiate a contract), an *acceptance* (agreeing to the terms of the offer), and *consideration* (something of value required for an enforceable contract)

>> What constitutes a transaction

>> When you can revoke a contract without penalty

You also find out about *breach of contract* and how to interpret contracts.

After taking this class, you're much more informed and capable of dealing with routine things such as your apartment lease, health insurance contract, or employment agreement. One result of this class: You'll never again sign your name to anything without going over it with a fine-toothed comb!

Property

Property is the course that's all about the relationship of rights and duties to land or objects. In this class, you talk about issues such as rights in personal-property and landlord-tenant issues and how people's estates are divided up after death.

REMEMBER

Property, however, involves more *abstract thinking* (heavy on the theory) than other law school courses and is harder to relate to on an everyday basis. That's why some consider it to be by far the most difficult first-year subject. For example, you learn about complicated concepts such as *future interests* (where possession of property occurs in the future) and *adverse possession* (getting title to property through possession under certain circumstances). You also draw plenty of diagrams, which may help you conceptualize some of the more theoretical ideas (particularly future interests).

You'll certainly learn some interesting new vocabulary, like my all-time favorites: the rule against *perpetuities* (common law definition regarding property held in a trust and what happens after 21 years) and the *fee tail* (a particular type of estate).

Constitutional law

Constitutional law (or *con law*) is all about the law that comes from the Constitution. In this course, you talk about governmental powers (the three branches), due process, and the Bill of Rights. You also delve into topics such as separation of church and state, equal protection, and the commerce clause. One of the great things about con law class is that you touch on many important issues facing American society today, including racism, civil rights, abortion, school prayer, and the death penalty, just to name a few. You read landmark cases like *Roe v. Wade*, the *Bakke* case, *Bush v. Gore*, *Citizens United v. Federal Election Commission*, *Miranda v. Arizona*, and *Marbury v. Madison*.

REMEMBER

Con law is unique in its emphasis on a *balancing approach*. Many con law cases have no clear-cut answers, so the courts attempt to weigh the competing interests to arrive at reasoned (or *balanced*) solutions. When you finish the course, you'll have a greater appreciation of the difficult jobs judges have.

Legal research and writing

Ah, the joys of legal research and writing (LRW), sometimes known as Legal, Analysis, Writing, and Research (LAWR). It is one of your required 1L courses, but it's very different from the others in the preceding sections.

At my school, legal research classes accounted for fewer units, yet it often took up more time than all my other graded classes combined. How can a (usually) two-credit, pass/fail course take up so much time, you ask? For one thing, legal research is the only law school class that actually has regular homework (other than reading) assignments. (I know, the mere mention of the word *homework* may summon bad memories of high school.)

Almost every class features *citation exercises* (where you find out the correct legal citation style for sample cases and other works cited in legal memos and briefs) to hand in, research exercises to perform with library reference materials, and many long reading assignments to work on how you perform various legal research tasks. You also must complete several large writing assignments, ranging from writing analytical memos to researching and writing a *brief* (a persuasive document in which a lawyer advocates for why the client should prevail in a lawsuit) and then arguing that brief in the spring before a mock judge panel.

WARNING

Beware of blowing off legal research class! Many students are tempted to do just that because the class is often only one or two credits per semester. However, it's one of the all-time most important classes you ever take in law school. The concepts you discover are crucial to your success as a lawyer — and they come into play heavily during your summer legal jobs (see Chapter 14). So do yourself a favor and treat legal research class like the graded, five-credit class it deserves to be.

TIP

Don't sell your legal research and writing books. They'll come in handy during your summer legal jobs. Using them as a reference or guide can be crucial to your success. Rereading them, or at least skimming them, prior to starting your summer jobs (as a review) is also a good move.

Reviewing How a 1L Course Is Organized

A 1L class is fundamentally different in terms of pace, structure, homework, and expectations than many of your college courses. Probably the biggest difference between law school and college is the lack of traditional homework (except for legal research and writing class; see the previous section). You almost never have a single nonreading homework assignment: no papers, quizzes, or any other sort of non–final exam evaluations. In my entire law school career, the only pieces of homework I ever had to do were a short writing assignment based on trips to court for civil procedure (a class I cover in the earlier section "Civil procedure") and several short papers (two to three pages) for two upper-level electives. In general, the only homework you have is reading. And staying on top of your outlines, briefs, and so on, of course.

WARNING

The problem with the lack of traditional homework is that many people become lazy about keeping up with the reading. They take a few days off, and suddenly they're 100 pages behind. It's so easy to do; I remember the desire to slack off on a subject I found relatively easy creeping up even on me. You may be tempted to think of reading as not real work, but after you fall into that dangerous mindset, everything goes downhill. You fall so far behind that you can't keep up in class, and you become really nervous when you're inevitably called on and haven't glanced at the material in days. Keeping up with the reading always makes your law school coursework go easier for you.

Just the facts, folks: Surveying the syllabus

The only real handout — okay, it may be an electronic file — you're likely to receive during an entire semester (except in legal research and writing) is the almighty syllabus. In your college classes, you probably got a several-page, detailed, descriptive syllabus that featured an explanation of the course and its goals. In law school, however, brevity is the name of the game. Many syllabuses are plain one-page jobs with a brief intro sentence or two and the schedule of reading topics and corresponding page numbers. That's it.

As you skim your bare-bones syllabus, you may notice that you're supposed to cover 30 to 50+ pages of reading *per class session*. This amount of work may come as a shock to students who are used to covering that many pages *per week* in college. Just keep in mind that you get used to the reading load pretty quickly and soon find out how to keep up with the rapid-fire pace.

More like rabbit than hare: Checking out class pace

You may find that law school classes move at a quicker pace than what you're used to from college. Each day in class you cover several topics or concepts, and you may find that the professor spends less time on each one than you're comfortable with. That's why your typing/note-taking skills become super-important. You have to keep up with the conversation, be prepared to be called on, and take notes that are coherent enough that you know what you meant when you're looking at them later.

REMEMBER

The only way to keep up with class pace is reading your assigned pages on time and trying to keep up with class discussions. Make your own notes about cases, policy issues, and so forth that you still have questions about. You may find that joining study groups (see Chapter 13) comes in handy, especially when you notice that you're missing points made in class or you're not grasping topics.

One exam, one chance: Freaking out about the final

What seems to make new 1Ls the most nervous is the concept of taking only one exam. (See Chapter 15 for more on exams.) When you have only one factor determining your grade, trying not to flip out at the end of the semester when the stress really piles on is difficult. (If it makes you feel any better, class participation may count in some circumstances.)

I think the one-exam concept is challenging and can be counterproductive to real learning because you don't receive any feedback all semester on how you're doing. It doesn't bode well for students who suffer from test anxiety or have more success with intermediate grading opportunities throughout the semester. Additionally, no matter how diligent you've been with your reading or with showing up for class every day, when you blow the exam or you're sick that day, your entire grade for that class is shot.

Thankfully, many law schools have introduced midterms for some 1L courses. Many academic support professors and law students find midterms to be helpful because they provide a good check-in point to see how you're doing. Are you grasping the material? Are you able to analyze the cases and provide a thorough analysis in response to your professor's questions? If yes, great! If not, you have time to course correct before final exams.

So although the one-exam concept may be a big-time pain in the peach, just prepare as well as you can if that's how your school does it. Address your test anxiety, identify coping mechanisms for exam day, rest, and hydrate. If you need help, Chapter 12 gives you a head start with some great tips for studying for exams.

Making the Most of Your 450 Classroom Hours Per Year

The American Bar Association (ABA) Standard 310 specifies that law students must attend a certain number of class hours per semester, amounting to a total of 450–500 hours per year. For the most part, that means if you skip too many classes, your grade may be lowered automatically, or you may even be excluded from taking the exam.

Because you need to attend the majority of your classes, you may as well find out how to get as much out of them as possible. In-class time is most crucial for finding out what your professor thinks is important, what you need to study for the exam and what you can skip, and what your professor's own special take is on a given subject.

TIP

The best way to prepare for class: Read the assignment beforehand, highlight the important areas, and jot down any notes or questions you may have in the margins. Have your brief ready to go (I discuss case briefs in Chapter 12), and look up unfamiliar terms in your Black's Law Dictionary (see Chapter 14).

Arguing with your classmates (in a good way, of course)

A great benefit of going to class is the opportunity it provides for you to challenge your classmates' assertions. Saying, "I disagree with Mr. Brown," and then stating your take on an issue is a rush. In fact, classmates often say things that you may find outrageous or just plain wrong. Your time in the classroom is your chance to volunteer and to refute their comments. Formally arguing back-and-forth in class is great practice for becoming a trial lawyer because those lawyers not only need to state their cases out loud and succinctly but also must listen closely to every word their opponents say and every issue they raise.

Doing extra reading

Some topics you just may not understand, no matter how thoroughly you read about them before class. Sorry, but skipping over these troublesome topics in the casebook isn't a way you can increase your classroom comprehension. Instead, make notes. What are you missing? What doesn't make sense to you? Then go see the professor during office hours and/or talk to your TA. (Flip to the later section "Seeking help during office hours" for more on making the most of this opportunity.)

TIP

Whenever you're having trouble with a course topic, ask your professor to recommend a good hornbook. *Hornbooks* differ from study aids in that they cover individual topics in a more scholarly, in-depth way. Hornbooks include good definitions, background material, and examples. However, because they're usually very expensive, you'll want to check them out from the law library. See Chapter 14 for more information about hornbooks.

Knowing when you absolutely can't miss class

The end of the semester is when you definitely don't want to miss class. Starting about four to five weeks before the exam, your professors often go into super-speed mode, trying to get through as much material as possible in preparation for crunch time. They may decide at the last minute to cut items from the syllabus, and you definitely don't want to miss out on knowing what you no longer need to study.

Toward the end of the semester also is when professors start dropping hints about what's going to be on the exams. If you hear one say, "Equitable servitudes may show up on the exam," that's a good clue that something is crucial. You don't want to miss any other discussions about exams, either. Professors sometimes explain — sometimes unannounced — how they want their particular exams written, much to the dismay of students who skip those classes.

Handling Your Professors

Professors, like students, come in all types. For example, even in first-year classes, some may rely more heavily on the Socratic method (see Chapter 12) than others. Some may be more easy-going and conduct their classes in a discussion-type format, where they heavily rely on volunteers, while others may favor a pure lecturing style. Because you'll experience a handful of different professors and teaching styles during your first year, knowing how to deal with them in advance is the best strategy for success.

Staying on your professor's good side

Generally, professors have likes and dislikes that mirror those of the general population. They like it when students come to class, seem interested, are prepared, and participate. They don't like it when students frequently skip class or come late, are unprepared on a regular basis, or are noticeably checking social media when they should be taking notes.

REMEMBER

On the other hand, professors typically make a definite distinction between talking for the sake of hearing your own voice and contributing something meaningful to the discussion. In other words, raising your hand ten times during an hour-long class and offering some mundane or self-serving comment isn't the best course of action. Professors prefer that you think before you speak and try to make your insights thoughtful and relevant.

Figuring out what your professor thinks is important

Professors often have subtle ways of telling you that something is important and thus is likely to appear on the exam. For example, they

>> **Write important concepts on the board or screen:** The general rule is that anything written on the board needs to go into your notes (and be highlighted).

>> **Cross-reference or repeat major concepts:** Professors may refer to something you learned in the beginning of the course or constantly make analogies to a particular discipline. When they do, take note; it'll probably be on the exam. And check their old exams because you may begin to pick up on a theme or their favorite rules, cases, and concepts.

>> **Put their own unique spin on a topic:** Some professors approach a discipline from a particular angle: an economic, policy, or feminist one, for instance. When you figure out that your professor is taking a specific approach to a course, be sure to get a handle on this spin and tailor your exam responses accordingly.

Seeking help during office hours

Professors lament office hours as an underutilized phenomenon. Many law school professors have office hours every week; however, they also report that few people ever show up. Why let your professors just sit there, twiddling their thumbs?

Think of office hours as your prime chance to get a private one-on-one Q and A session. If you're too nervous to go by yourself, go with a classmate or two.

WARNING

Don't go to your professor's office unprepared. Don't say something general like, "So what's this I hear about con law?" Instead, be ready to ask several concrete, specific questions about the reading or class discussion. If you didn't understand a hypothetical (see Chapter 12) in class, now's your chance to rehash it.

REMEMBER

The other benefit of office hours is that they give your professor the chance to get to know you. When you're in a class with 100 other students, your professor is likely to remember you more if you've stopped by a few times. Because many internships, clerkships, scholarships, and summer jobs (and permanent ones, for that matter) require an academic reference or two, asking for one from a professor you've gotten to know through office hours is a great idea. Of course, you also need to do well on the professor's exams to make good use of that endorsement, but going to office hours is a great first step toward getting a stellar letter of recommendation.

Keeping study aids easily accessible

Many wise students bring their study aids to class, leaving them open to the case they're studying at the moment. (These aids may be the commercial outlines I discuss in Chapter 14 or the self-compiled outlines I cover in Chapter 13.) This backup method has helped quite a few 1Ls who needed extra reassurance survive their Socratic questioning (see Chapter 12).

TIP

Try keeping the study aid on your lap, out of sight, or hidden by most of your casebook so your professor doesn't notice you reading out of it during class or when you're called on. Study aids aren't necessarily forbidden in class; professors just want to see you really *thinking* rather than getting the material spoon-fed to you out of a study aid. But some professors *are* downright hostile to the notion of study aids; you really can't tell which ones, so keeping it out of sight is a good idea.

WARNING

Study aids aren't a replacement for getting a handle on reading and briefing cases. If you're using supplements only, you may find yourself in trouble when you're called on in class or tested on a very specific rule of law and the policy issues during an exam. Use the supplement as a backup to solidify what you read, what your notes say, what your brief contains, and so on.

IN THIS CHAPTER

» **Having the right mind-set**

» **Taking steps to avoid letting law school take over your life**

» **Prioritizing your health**

» **Allotting time for family and friends**

» **Figuring out where you fit in the school's social spectrum**

Chapter **10**

Keeping Academics in Perspective

Some people have an uncanny knack for taking everything in stride. They can tell you that your contracts final is "no big deal," dismiss your concerns about your legal writing assignment with an exasperated sigh, and never look the least bit stressed out, even when they're caught unprepared during class. These same people seem to know the importance of keeping everything in perspective. In other words, they don't sweat the small stuff. After all, is the world really going to end when you get a B rather than a B+ on your civ pro exam or you don't get the exact summer job you wanted?

Probably not. Maintaining this kind of healthy outlook about your law school and personal life goes a long way toward keeping you sane (and smiling).

This chapter discusses some simple, painless strategies for better allocating your time between work and play. I explain the importance of maintaining your pre-law school interests and ways that you can develop new hobbies while in law school. By making time each day for the most important person in the law school equation — you — you'll have a much more well-rounded and enjoyable law school experience.

Law School Isn't a 24/7 Affair

Just because you're a law student doesn't mean that law school needs to overwhelm your life. Although being in law school makes you feel like you're caught in a whirlwind of never-ending responsibilities, you do get *some* free time in your day. Everyone needs a break!

TIP

Use your time between classes to catch up on your property reading and multitask during lunch so you can read *and* eat tort(e)s. Some law students, especially those with families, like to treat law school like a 9-to-5 job. They come in early in the morning to get their work done and stay a few hours after their last class to avoid taking too many books home.

Of course, if you're a part-time or evening student, time is at a premium, so finishing off even a few pages of reading whenever you get the chance can make your life much easier on weekends, when you'll likely be doing the majority of your studying. Whatever your situation, be sure that you take advantage of any priceless downtime whenever you can.

REMEMBER

Often the people who are loudest when claiming to be too busy to do anything besides study purposely make their lives that way because relaxing feels unproductive to them. These same people may feel restless during school breaks, believe that doing nothing is lazy, and use "I don't have time" as their favorite catchphrase. The next time your fellow classmates claim to be too busy to have a cup of coffee with you, don't freak out over all the work they seem to be doing that you're not. Their claim of having no time may simply be their own "never-stopping-for-breath" work ethic, which isn't necessarily healthy.

Law students who never take a breather are prone to being so absorbed in the law school scene that they rarely make time for themselves. However, repeatedly sacrificing your own mental, emotional, spiritual, and physical health so that you can hit the books soon takes its toll. Falling hopelessly behind because you're so rundown that you miss a week of classes or being sick with the flu during finals is the last thing you want.

That's why the most well-adjusted law students routinely make time for fun. If you plan your day right, you won't feel too crunched to take a long walk, browse in your favorite store, or cook your favorite meal. Part-time and evening law students also need to make time for themselves, even though that's easier said than done between working a full-time job and going to school part time. Even the smallest things, like playing with a pet or taking a hot bath before bedtime, can make all the difference between stress and success.

Developing a "marathon versus sprint" mentality

Endurance is key. You have three or four years ahead of you during which you need to:

>> Stay healthy

>> Rest/sleep

>> Attend to your physical, mental, and spiritual health

>> Maintain your relationships with family and friends

TIP

You can't learn everything on the first day. You won't get everything right, right away. So look at your calendar, the academic calendar, and your syllabi assignment and exam dates. Then think through what you need to do *throughout* the next quarter or semester.

Figuring out what works for you, what your favorite subjects are, where you can turn for support and guidance, and how to balance all the things on your to-do list helps ensure you stay in the race for the long haul. That's the person your professors need to show up for final exams, not the stressed out, overwhelmed, and unhealthy you.

Using the law school's counseling services

I'm so happy to discover how many law schools offer free or nominally priced counseling services. Let the school help you. That's what the staff is there for.

Many law students can benefit from this resource. If any of the following sounds like you, consider checking out your law school's counseling options.

>> You need help managing stress and anxiety.

>> You're dealing with being away from home for the first time.

>> You're struggling with becoming a full-time student again.

>> You need a good sounding board to deal with belonging, feeling like an imposter, and questioning whether law school is for you.

Meeting with your mentors

Mentors can be upper-division law students, faculty members, and/or alumni. If nothing else, they're people who have been through what you're going through and can be the voice of reason and a shoulder to lean on.

Mentors can be instrumental to your success in law school. Many students meet their peer mentor during orientation. This is an important time to make a connection, touch base about expectations, and figure out when you two can connect.

REMEMBER

Meeting with your mentor should be more than just chit-chat. Decide what you need from your mentor and have an agenda in mind when you meet. Are you unsure of your work and need validation? Would you like a copy of their contracts outline? Do you want or need them to check in once a week so that you don't isolate yourself? Do you just need practical info like guidance on the cheapest places to park near campus?

Achieving School-Life Balance

In your first year as a law student, balancing work and play may seem difficult. When you're not sure what preparing adequately for class or doing well on exams takes, justifying a daily two-hour nap or a weekly facial is hard, no matter how much those activities may recharge your batteries.

Assessing your situation

After your first few weeks of the fall semester, you're better equipped to know what doing well requires. That's when you can best decide how to allocate your time. The following sections give you some strategies for striking a healthy balance between work and play.

Keeping a checklist or a to-do list

This list is just a homemade record of what you do every hour of the day. Depending on how you roll, you may want to use a planner, an electronic checklist, or an online calendar. Simply jot down when you're in class, when you study, when you participate in law school extracurricular activities, and when you eat meals and how long each activity takes. The point of the log is to figure out exactly how and when you spend your time. After seeing that information in black and white, you discover that you actually have an extra few hours left over for recreational activities.

Part-time and evening law students who try this exercise may find they can squeeze in an hour of reading during the morning public transit commute (seriously, don't read and drive) or wake up a little earlier on the weekends to get extra work done. And students with families to care for may discover they can get more done than they originally thought while watching the kids' Little League game or early in the morning before everyone is awake for the day.

REMEMBER

Whether your free hours are clumped in a large block of time or spread out in 30-minute increments, the important aspect is that you realize when you can fit in your hobbies and interests. But I also want you to pay attention to how much you accomplish each day.

Figuring out how much you procrastinate

When you actually sit down to study, are you able to power through, or do you take a lot of breaks? For example, on a typical school night, you can do one of the following:

>> Spread your studying over a six-hour period, taking many little procrastinatory coffee, sleep, or Internet breaks (but not really enjoying them because you know you have more studying to do)

>> Bite the bullet and work straight through for three hours, finishing everything and using the remaining time to fully relax and enjoy yourself

In other words, you'll study far more successfully as a law student if you work productively for shorter periods of time instead of concentrating half-heartedly and spacing your studying out. Plus, I know from experience that reading and digesting an assignment in its entirety is easier than giving it only piecemeal attention, which results in your retaining far less of the material.

REMEMBER

Relaxing when you feel like you need to be doing something is difficult, so finishing one thing before you start the next is a great way of getting even more out of your personal time. And if you love a list, checking off a completed item makes you feel accomplished!

Making a list of your favorite leisure activities

Think about how many of your interests you ideally want to fit into an average day. Doing so means you need to classify your favorite activities according to which ones:

>> Fit into smaller chunks of time

>> Require an afternoon or entire day

>> Can be multitasking activities (such as reading an article while eating lunch or getting a walk in while checking in with your parents or your partner)

>> Require your full attention

When you can see on paper exactly what you need in your life, you're often better able to accommodate your favorite leisure activities. Part-time and evening students usually have less time than full-time day students to engage in their favorite activities on a daily basis, but fitting in a few pages of novel reading before bed or drawing in a sketchbook at lunch may be manageable ways to fit leisure into jam-packed days.

Maintaining your previous interests

Some law students believe that the moment they enter law school they must abandon their love of working out, playing video games, or having long Sunday brunches. The truth is that law school and your previous interests can peacefully coexist. Treat your previous interests as the precious gems that they are and never think that you have to postpone your weekly softball game or photography hobby for three long years.

REMEMBER

In fact, maintaining your previous interests is a great way of relieving stress. What better way to unwind after a stressful week of studying than a day of hiking, cooking your favorite meal, or simply doing whatever it is that floats your boat?

Taking in city life every month

Making your entire presence on campus revolve around the law school is tempting. You may step outside the law school to eat or shop, but for some law students, that's the extent of their campus exploration.

TIP

Ignoring the multitude of educational and entertaining things to do throughout your university's campus, such as attending a dance performance at the auditorium or watching a sporting event, is definitely a mistake. By the time my third year rolled around, I realized that I hadn't made as much use of the rich resources on my campus as I would've liked. I hadn't explored many of the museums, cultural opportunities, and university events, and graduation was just around the corner.

That's why I decided as a 3L to check out one new restaurant, museum, or activity every month. I found out about these events by perusing the university's website for any special activities or exhibits. I usually opted for the free events and/or the events that served food or offered happy hour prices. These opportunities gave me an appreciation for the city I lived and attended law school in while also serving as a study break.

Keeping Active and Healthy

Between classes, law school activities, and all your other hobbies and interests, you may think you have little time left to exercise. Many law students are grateful just to exercise once a month, let alone every (other) day.

Being physically and mentally healthy is as important in law school as it is in everyday life. If you neglect your body, your brain may soon follow. Eating bags full of fast food, cutting corners on your sleep, and feeling constantly sluggish don't help your intellectual stamina.

TIP

Take the time to devise a good health plan for yourself. Doing so soon pays off because you need plenty of energy and endurance for the long path ahead of you as a law student.

Fitting exercise into your busy day

After making a commitment to stay healthy, you need to take the momentous step of figuring out *when* you can exercise. Now, I'm the first to admit that exercise was definitely last on my priority list. Normally, I was so tired after a full day of commuting, attending class, and studying that I could barely make it up the one flight of stairs to my apartment, let alone actually hop on a treadmill or stationary bike. Sound familiar? But many law school students successfully work out a few times a week.

One way of exercising (that doesn't really seem like exercising) is joining an intramural or university team sport. Many law schools offer informal or sometimes even formal athletic opportunities, from intramural basketball to pick-up football and softball games. Although part-time and evening law students generally don't have the time to participate in these activities during the week, they may be able to take advantage of any sporting activities offered on the weekend.

Eating well

Although many law students are fond of the traditional student fare of cheap eats — wings, pizza, and beer — adding variety to your diet by cooking (or at least eating) "wholesomely" some of the time is a good idea.

Eating well gives your brain and body the nutrients they need to operate at peak performance. (Can't you just hear your parents telling you to drink your milk and eat your Brussels sprouts?) This point is especially true during midterms and finals, when you want your brain fueled by nutritious fare and not greasy fries and empty-calorie sodas. I know fitting trips to the grocery store into your already jam-packed schedule is hard, but if you go just once a week for an hour, you can buy all you need for a week's worth of meals. Or try sharing a grocery delivery membership with a family member so you can order what you need and have it delivered.

Some law students I knew did all their cooking or meal prep on Sunday afternoons. They cooked up some substantial dishes like hearty soups, stews, or lasagnas and froze them in individual portions. That way, their meals were ready to defrost quickly and eat on the run. You can also make up a huge salad, and voilà: You have a week's worth of great meals at minimal work for you. Sure beats the same old chicken wings and beer at the cheap happy hour down the street from the law school five days in a row.

Getting enough shut-eye

No matter how many hours of sleep you require, make sure you establish a routine that works for you. Here are some helpful suggestions:

>> **Vary your bedtime according to your productivity level.** If you're a morning person, going to bed early so you can wake up early to do your work may be easiest for you. On the other hand, if you're a night owl like me, you may want to arrange your class schedule so that your first class doesn't start too early. (If possible, this option usually isn't available during your first year but may be for 2Ls and beyond.) That way you can stay up late working and then sleep in.

>> **Prioritize sleep over work.** Whenever the choice comes down to staying up for an hour reading that last case or getting an extra hour of sleep, choose the sleep. You can always get to class a few minutes early and skim over that case or read it during lunch. But a botched night's sleep may affect your ability to concentrate all day long, and with tuition as expensive as it is, the fewer classes you miss the better.

>> **Nap.** A nap a day keeps dozing off at bay. When you feel tired, take a power nap. A *power nap* usually lasts 10 to 20 minutes; any more than that, and you may feel more tired than before you fell asleep. Many people find that napping before 6 p.m. doesn't affect their ability to fall asleep later on but that napping any later than 6 p.m. inevitably does. And if you suffer from insomnia like I do, you want to be thoughtful about your sleep cycle. Being well-rested before class and exams is important.

Making Time for Loved Ones

Part of achieving the right balance between your studies and your personal life is spending a healthy amount of time with your friends and family. Only you and your partner and family can decide how much time feels right. Spend too much time together, and your schoolwork may suffer; spend too little time together, and your relationships may take a nosedive.

Although being with your significant other ideally falls under your *relaxation time,* many law students feel stressed out because their partners want more of their time than they can afford based on the volume of reading, outlining, and class time.

TIP

As soon as you decide to apply to law school, or when you're accepted, sit down with your friends and loved ones and talk honestly about how they view the amount of time you're able to spend with them. You may also want to have this talk yearly so you can gauge how they've felt the past year and what you can try differently in the coming school year. Ask them to rate the quality and quantity of your time together, and explain that even if you can't meet the *quantity* they want (given the demands of being a law student), you certainly aim to satisfy the *quality* aspect.

Making time for your friends and family doesn't need to feel like a chore, but you do need to be intentional with your time. When you live together, perhaps spending an uninterrupted hour together works best, enabling each of you to unwind from the day before bedtime. When you live apart, setting aside a few days a week for after-school snacks, drinks, or even dinner may work for you. If you're a part-time or evening law student whose free time is at a premium, you can always ask your friends and family to meet you for an early breakfast or dinner on campus. Cuddling in a booth or holding hands across the table can help you communicate to your special someone that every bit of time you spend with them is of the highest importance to you.

Surveying the Law School Social Scene

Although all law students have their own ideas about fun activities, from intimate dinner parties with friends to "bar reviews" at the local pubs, you're bound to find like-minded people at every school, no matter where your socializing interests lie.

Some law schools are more into the social scene than others. All you have to do to get an idea of how yours measures up is to hang out in the student lounge on Monday mornings. You're sure to get an earful on what happy hour gatherings or parties went on and what crazy antics occurred at them.

No matter what your preference, hanging out with fellow students is a great way to relax, find out about your classmates, and perhaps even discover a golden nugget of law school advice from a seasoned upper-level student.

IN THIS CHAPTER

» Looking at popular planners and apps

» Blocking out a schedule

» Reviewing your syllabus as soon as possible

» Staying on top of scheduling with a wall calendar

» Giving yourself some grace as your schedule adjusts

Chapter **11**

Time Management 101

For most students, law school is their first time being a professional student. It's different from any programs you've already participated in or graduated from, and it will challenge you in ways you may not anticipate.

For the first time, you may read something three times and still need help deciphering what it really means. That perfect thing you've written will meet with tons of edits, critiques, questions, and few answers.

REMEMBER

As I note in other chapters, law school is a marathon, not a sprint. Utilizing time management tools helps you stay focused, feel like you're on top of things, and maintain your relationships with the people that matter.

In this chapter, I discuss time management — why getting yourself organized is important and why creating a schedule helps you be successful. I share a few ideas and tools that can help you figure out how to juggle all that law school brings on top of, you know, the life stuff you still have to deal with.

REMEMBER

You may be thinking, "My goodness, all this time-management advice seems excessive." But the reality is that until you've started law school, you have no idea how many things you need to do each day just to get prepared for class.

Choosing a Planner or Planning App

So many tools are available to help you with time management. You must figure out whether you're an app person or whether you need an old school traditional planner.

Some law schools may give you a planner as part of your orientation swag. But if that doesn't happen, you want to be prepared with an app or your own planner to get your schedule straightened out as soon as possible.

TIP

The options can be overwhelming, so be sure to ask your mentors or classmates whether they recommend specific scheduling planners or apps that work well for them. Don't hesitate to ask the admissions office staff whether they have suggestions as well.

Paper planners

The website testprepnerds.com makes these recommendations for paper planners in the article "The 4 Best Planners for Law School Students 2025":

>> Academic Planner|School Agenda – Erin Condren

>> The Luxe Digital School Planner

>> Luxe Papeterie PDF Download Planner

>> Law School Planner PDF Download

TikTok offers tons of videos that share a variety of planners. It really just depends on how much time you want to spend going down that rabbit hole.

TIP

To help you narrow it down, consider whether you want a dated or undated planner, whether you need accessories for the planner, whether you want a spiral binding or regular binding, and so on.

Planner apps

Here are some app-based planner options, which come from Lucy Rome's article "Best time management apps for students":

>> Evernote

>> Focus Booster

- >> Remember The Milk

- >> RescueTime

- >> Google Calendar

- >> Trello

- >> myHomework Student Planner

- >> Todoist

- >> 2Do

You can find the full article at www.educationalappstore.com/blog/best-apps-will-help-students-manage-time/.

TIP

Some of these apps may offer trial versions or limited-feature versions for free, so you can give them a try before committing to buying them.

Creating a Tentative Schedule Using Time Blocks

Getting organized and keeping track of your time may be easier if you schedule all your activities into time blocks. And I mean do mean all of them — everything from sleeping and eating to studying for specific classes, outlining, study breaks, and anything else you spend time on.

For many new law students, using blocks of time really helps them:

- >> See how much time they're spending on each task, project, or class

- >> Rethink their approach to getting things done

- >> Identify when they're procrastinating and when they're most/least productive

So if you know you're not a morning person but you need to get up to get to class on time, your blocking will likely skew toward scheduling most of your activities and studying later in the evening (while also incorporating enough time to get enough sleep so that you're sharp as a tack if you get called on the next day, of course).

TIP

Familiarize yourself with your academic calendar, which will have information about orientation, the add-drop period, midterms, deadlines for accommodation materials, final exam schedules, and so forth. You don't have to memorize it, but as soon as you can, download or print a copy so you can start to think about where you want to block off time as necessary.

Getting Acquainted with Your Syllabi

Depending on the law school you attend, some of your professors may have their syllabi available prior to the start of classes. If that's the case, go through and review them for rules, suggestions, and — most importantly — the attendance policy and assignment or midterm due dates. You want to make sure you're prepared with any questions for the first day of classes.

TIP

If a professor doesn't make the syllabus available until the first day of classes, you can always utilize your upper-division mentors about what if anything you need to be aware of or ask about.

Using a Larger Wall Calendar to Map Out the Term

In addition to reading, making notes, updating your outlines, and rereading some of the materials, you want to schedule as many things out as possible.

That's why I recommend buying a big wall a calendar and using it to plan your entire term. Seeing the big picture gives you a good sense of how much time you have throughout each quarter or semester. It may seem like you have all the time in the world, but then you're going to look up and realize that you're already in November and the reading period is just around the corner. This means final exams will be starting sooner than later. You want to make sure you are not too far behind on your outlines because you weren't paying attention to where you were in the term.

Being Patient with Yourself

Law school is a new experience for you. You won't get it right on the first day. Maybe not even the first week or two. But you'll figure it out. Be patient.

Along those lines, be prepared to make adjustments as you get used to the grind. What you try the first week may not be what you need by week six. Maybe that class you thought would take you hours to read or prepare for turns out to be one that comes easily. In that case, adjust your schedule to spend a little more time on a class that's tripping you up.

REMEMBER

The most important thing is to make sure you're doing what works for you. Thinking through what you learned during orientation, from your mentors, or from your new classmates is fine. But at the end of the day, it's your schedule, your life, your sleep pattern, and your sanity. Do whatever you need to do to make it work for you.

TIP

If you're still struggling after a week (or two or three), please go see your mentors, your dean of students, your academic support professors, or whoever has the resources you need. Don't isolate yourself; the worst thing you can do is try to figure it out on your own. You have access to plenty of people who have been through this who want to help you. Let them.

3

Studying Law: Secret Techniques That Really Work

Solve problems like a lawyer.

Study efficiently and effectively.

Make use of study aids.

Do well on exams.

Plan for your first summer break.

IN THIS CHAPTER

» Understanding how lawyers solve problems

» Beating the Socratic method

» Getting the most out of reading cases

» Breaking down brief-writing

» Gearing up for class participation

Chapter **12**

Thinking, Talking, and Writing Like a Lawyer

Almost everyone has heard the cliché that law school teaches you to think like a lawyer. But what do those thoughts really mean? That after law school you're able to spout off in legalese anytime you get the chance? That you view every new situation as a potential lawsuit? That you completely shed your pre–law school personality and instantly morph into a lawyer-in-training? Not quite.

This chapter demystifies the law school learning process with an eye on facilitating your shift toward legal thinking as soon as you're ready. It also shows you how to beat the Socratic method and dazzle professors with your class participation and discusses the most efficient ways to attack your reading assignments and brief cases.

Does Law School Really Change You?

How long does it take to start "thinking like a lawyer?" Is it definitely guaranteed to happen? These probing questions are at the front of many new law students' minds, but they're hard to answer because learning the law is such an individualized process. In the same way that children learn to walk and talk when they're ready, law students begin thinking like lawyers at their own pace.

You don't suddenly wake up and find you're a lawyer. But you may gradually notice subtle differences in your:

>> Logical reasoning powers

>> Ability to see two sides to every issue

>> Interpretation of news stories

>> Confidence in holding your own in an argument

Additionally, you gain a brand-new legal vocabulary and a much better understanding of the political and judicial processes than before you began law school. That's right: In addition to your newfound legal mind-set, you also become a more informed and concerned citizen.

One professor I spoke with felt that the transition to thinking like a lawyer tends to happen toward the end of the first semester, or at the latest, by the end of the first year of law school (but certainly not in the first month of school). Professors can tell when the proverbial lightbulb goes on for students by comparing the complexity of the arguments they make in class at the beginning and the end of the first year (1L) fall semester. In other words, they can tell that thinking like a lawyer occurs when students start seeing complex *issues* (the conflicts between rules) that they never would've picked up on earlier.

One of the ways *you* can judge whether you're on the right track is how well you understand what's going on in class discussion and in the reading. If you don't feel like you're really getting the material by the end of your first few weeks, talk with your dean of students, academic success/support professor, TAs, and professors to identify any problems with your comprehension, briefs, note-taking, and so on to figure out how to fix things.

Because the shift to "lawyer" is such a subtle change, seeing it in yourself is often difficult, though your family and friends may begin to notice the changes right away. In fact, when I think about my own transition to thinking like a lawyer, I'm still not sure when it happened. At some point, I no longer took forever to get the point of a certain holding or why a professor emphasized a certain set of facts. Reading, working on my briefs, and preparing for class became routine and not overwhelming. I wasn't freaked out that I didn't understand the assignment or terrified to engage in a conversation with the professor when I was called on. Nervous, yes, but not nauseous. Whether this shift is indicative of my thinking like a lawyer is anyone's guess.

REMEMBER

The ability to explain a legal principle or case in a way that your non-law school family and friends understand is one thing. Being able to communicate with your law school classmates, mentors, and TAs may mean you've arrived!

Introducing a new method of thinking

The way lawyers think is supposedly different from the population at large, and that's because lawyers are known as problem solvers:

>> One way lawyers solve problems is through rational, analytical thinking that tends to disregard their own individual opinions or perspectives in favor of what's objectively fair.

>> Another way is by being able to analyze a problem from different angles — in other words, understanding both sides of a problem. A good lawyer should be able to argue either side of an issue, which is what the Socratic method helps teach you. (See the upcoming "Braving the Socratic Method" section for details.)

The best way to demonstrate how lawyers think is to consider the nature of the legal process itself. Society doesn't want judges making decisions about cases based on the way they personally feel about the parties involved. Likewise, lawyers are taught to coldly analyze a situation rather than hastily come to a conclusion about a problem. In other words, they try to keep their own personal prejudices, assumptions, and feelings out of the analysis.

REMEMBER

Some people equate legal analytical thinking with a lack of creativity. In fact, lawyers sometimes are stereotyped as being less creative and artistic than other professional groups. If you're a creative type who's worried about losing your creativity in law school, hone your creative side as much as possible by engaging in your favorite art, writing, or dramatic activities on a regular basis. (See Chapter 10 for ideas about balancing law school with other activities.) Doing so can prevent your newfound analytical side from completely taking over.

Seeing the world through a lawyer's eyes

One significant way lawyers differ from the rest of the world is that they see issues better than anyone else. *Seeing the issue* refers to seeing the conflicts between legal rules. More specifically, lawyers want to find what's debatable — the conflicts — and use those to bolster their arguments. One way they accomplish such a refined insight is by separating the essential from the nonessential. In other words, when you walk into a law office and begin telling your lawyer a saga about your car accident, the first thing they do is determine the real issue of your case by *mental filtering,* which involves segregating every detail you explain into the factors that are irrelevant and the ones that are important.

Your lawyer then takes this information, recalls (or looks up) governing laws, and prepares arguments on your behalf, detailing why you should prevail over the other party. Most people look for tough lawyers — notably those who make the most forceful and gutsy arguments, the ones who refuse to back down or be intimidated by the opposite side.

You know that you're internalizing this type of thinking when you see a banana peel lying on the floor of a grocery store and think to yourself, "tort liability," rather than just, "someone should clean this up." When these kinds of thoughts start passing through your mind on a regular basis, you know that you're starting to see the world through a lawyer's eyes.

Speaking your new mother tongue: Legalese

I felt like I'd been immersed into a foreign language course on my first day of law school. Sitting in those first law classes, positively clueless, felt the same as when the professor speaks only Spanish in your Spanish class. In law school you're basically thrown into this new language, legalese, and expected to sink or swim on your own.

Learning *legalese* — that vocabulary unique to lawyers — takes time and patience. Although you may feel like you and your *Black's Law Dictionary* are joined at the hip, you'll find yourself growing less and less dependent on it as you grow more comfortable with the words and phrases. However, don't even consider tossing your dictionary in a corner where you'll never look at it again. Even as a 2L, 3L, and 4L, you'll be confronted with new bits of legalese that you'll need to look up, so your trusty dictionary should always stay close by.

TIP

One great way to speed up your legal language comprehension is to read opinion pieces, your local legal newspaper, a national legal newspaper, and/or a law journal in your spare time. Seeing these words and phrases in other contexts helps cement them in your mind.

One of the reasons legalese is so hard to learn is that many times the legal words don't suggest their meaning at all. For instance, in property class, you'll hear the word *fee tail* thrown around quite a bit. At first glance, you may think that has something to do with costs — or furry animals — but alas, the *fee tail* is an estate inheritable in a particular way. Who would've guessed? That's one of the reasons catching on to legalese took me awhile. During my first few weeks of law school,

I repeatedly wondered how I was ever going to remember complicated-sounding terms such as *tortfeasor* and *summary judgment*.

Much to my relief, I learned all these words, and probably 200 more, by the end of my first semester. Reviewing your notes, case briefs, and outlines can help. Flashcards (see Chapter 14) may also be helpful, but for the most part, I just repeatedly looked up new words whenever I encountered them in my casebook or in class.

REMEMBER

It gets easier. Little by little you start picking up these unfamiliar words and even begin using them yourself in your class discussions.

Braving the Socratic Method

Perhaps nothing is quite as hyped in law school as the Socratic method, which is sometimes jokingly known as the "sarcastic method." Prelaw and law school students alike generally regard this unique and aggressive teaching style with dread and fear. However, for all the negative publicity surrounding it, the Socratic method has several positive aspects. If it didn't, it wouldn't have lasted this long as an integral part of the legal curriculum.

The *Socratic method* (named after Greek philosopher Socrates) is an ancient teaching strategy that involves carefully questioning and probing students until they discover answers on their own. Christopher Columbus Langdell, then the Dean of Harvard Law School, introduced it to legal education in 1870 based on his opinion that students learn the law best by figuring out legal principles on their own rather than by being passively taught. Law schools around the globe have incorporated this method ever since.

REMEMBER

The key to the Socratic method: Students answer the professor's questions instead of the professor answering questions posed by the students.

Basically, you don't find any lecturing with the Socratic method. Instead, the professor calls on one or more students during the course of a single class and intensely questions them. Some professors call on a student to answer only a few questions; others call on someone to grill for the entire hour (or more). Yikes!

For instance, a typical Socratic dialogue may go something like this: Your professor starts questioning you about a case assigned for class. You're getting the easy questions right, so you're pretty pleased with yourself — that is, until the professor lays a really hard question on you. As soon as your answers become the slightest bit ambiguous, your professor turns into an argumentative wolf pouncing on prey, trying to get you to recognize the error on your own by asking you more and more probing questions. Soon, you feel as if you're genuinely being interrogated, because your anxiety level is mounting as you have less and less time to think between questions.

Understanding why law classes are taught this way

Although you may think the Socratic method sounds a little sadistic, you nonetheless come to appreciate having gone through it by the time you graduate law school. That's because the main difference between the Socratic method and, say, undergraduate lectures, is like the difference between active and passive learning. Many students probably admit to preferring lectures because you don't really have to prepare on a daily basis and can otherwise just sit there, daydream a bit, and relax. After the lights dim and the overhead projector goes on, no one knows that the professor's voice has lulled you off to sleep (unless, of course, you start snoring).

With the Socratic method, you don't have a chance to tune out, let alone doze off. That's because you constantly need to be on your toes, waiting for the moment that strikes fear into every law student's heart: when the professor glances down at the seating chart and then up at you. Even as a 3L, my heart raced when I knew I was about to be called on. You must intensely follow the course that the class discussion takes just in case you're chosen to pick up where someone else leaves off or as co-counsel if a classmate is struggling. You can see why the Socratic method is the epitome of active learning.

REMEMBER

Learning by the Socratic method is good practice because lawyers, particularly trial lawyers, need to be constantly on alert. When you're in a courtroom, the opposing counsel can make a statement that drastically changes the course of your arguments. If you're not paying rapt attention, you'll be ripped to shreds. You need to know how to think on your feet to be able to dramatically refute your opposition's arguments. The Socratic method teaches you how to do that.

If you truly despise the Socratic method, a remedy is in sight. As an upper-division law student, you find that your professors have eased off the Socratic method somewhat. That's because the first year is when most of the work of teaching law students to think like lawyers happens. Many professors in upper-class courses use purely volunteers, call on one person very informally to get the discussion going for the day, or call on three people at once (so one person isn't put on the spot). After your 1L year, you also can choose your classes based on which professors teach Socratically and which don't — after you've consulted with upper-class students on this point, that is. Just find out which classes aren't being taught in the Socratic method and register for them.

Because professors ease off the Socratic method in the second and third years, slacking off is easier than it was as a first year. Many classes are largely lecture (or discussion), so you may be tempted just to let the volunteers raise their hands and contribute. But beware of falling hopelessly behind in your reading. Taking more than a day or two off at a time can put you in a major bind come exam time. And you still want to keep your grades up and maintain a good relationship with your professors.

TIP

If you absolutely dread public speaking, choose classes in small rooms. In my experience, classes in smaller classrooms tend to be more laid-back and discussion-oriented rather than Socratic, and speaking in front of a small group is much easier. After you become familiar with your law school, you can remember the size of the classroom based on its classroom number when you register for classes. You also know more about the courses and professors at that point and can make some decisions based on your comfort level.

Beating Socrates at his own game

REMEMBER

The best way to beat the Socratic method is by being thoroughly prepared. Simply put, read for substance and understanding, make notes, complete your briefs, have your materials organized for quick reference, and think about or anticipate what the professor may ask. Some other helpful ways to prepare in advance include the following:

>> **Be extremely comfortable with the facts of the case, such as the identities of the parties, the reason for the dispute, and who initiated it.** Know these facts really well so that you can at least answer the professor's basic questions. If you stumble over the basics, you may get in your head and be more nervous about answering the more challenging questions, which is likely to annoy the professor.

>> **Try to understand the arguments the judge makes in the opinion.** Then go a step farther and try to anticipate the arguments the judge *didn't* make. In the Socratic questioning, your professor may ask how you would've ruled differently. Thinking about what's *not* in the case helps prepare you for these questions.

When you're a 1L, I suggest bringing your *case briefs* (short, well-organized summaries of cases) with you so that you have something to glance at during those first few tense minutes of questioning. Whenever you encounter any ambiguous or confusing facts in the case, make a special note in your brief, because your professor is sure to zero in on them.

Having a relaxed attitude helps, too. After all, eventually everyone is called on (professors keep track on the seating chart or a class roster), so you're all in the same boat. Don't sweat it too much; just ride it out when you're called on. As I explain in the later section "Recognizing the Importance of Class Participation," your classroom participation usually only influences your grade if it's extremely frequent or infrequent, so just try your best. It gets easier eventually. By my third year, if I wasn't prepared for class, I'd just read the case a few minutes before the discussion and still be as well prepared as I'd been in my first year after putting in an hour or more on each case. (Obviously, the success of that technique depends on the class and the professor, though.)

Hammering hypotheticals

Hypotheticals, or *hypos* for short, are one of the main tools of the Socratic method. Hypos are hypothetical situations based on the facts of the case that you're assigned to read. The professor simply takes certain facts from the case and twists them around, making a slightly different scenario.

Your professor uses hypos to test your understanding of the principles of the case. For example, your professor may ask something like "Suppose the child who drowned was blind. Would that make a difference?" or "Suppose the fence was high enough but had just been broken by a rainstorm the night before; how would that be reasoned by the court?"

At that point, your job is:

>> Remembering the facts of the original case

>> Figuring out whether changing the facts changes the result of the new case scenario

>> Identifying any potential policy issues that may impact the facts

>> Explaining the logical reasoning behind your answer

As you can see, hypos engage you in active learning, and they help you apply what you've discovered to new situations. That's what attorneys must do every time a new client walks in the door to their offices.

TIP

You can best prepare to respond to hypos by asking yourself a few of your own when you read about a case. After you finish a case, change the facts slightly and then defend your arguments for the same or different outcomes. The more you practice successfully answering hypos at home or in a study group, the more confident you'll feel about answering them in class.

Reading Cases Like a Pro

A large part of what many lawyers — especially litigators (trial lawyers) — do is read cases so they can distill the law and get at the subtleties that enable them to win their clients' cases. Cases are part of the law school curriculum so that students can see a court's reasoning in action. But reading cases isn't like reading a novel or even a textbook. Cases are often dry, difficult, and full of complicated concepts and terminology.

TIP

I always found thinking of each case as an exercise in its own right helpful. It gets you to focus on reading it in an active way (by asking yourself frequent questions).

Because reading cases is virtually all law students do (for homework), expect to read about 20 to 50 pages in your *casebook* (a thick book filled with appellate cases) per class per night. This reading will probably take you between four and six hours per night total. At the beginning of your first year, it'll probably take longer, until you get the hang of things.

The first cases I read for law school for torts, contracts, and criminal law took me *four* hours to get through, and I still didn't have much of an idea of what I'd just read! As you're reading cases, keep the following strategies in mind:

>> **Read each case twice.** The key to reading cases and getting plenty of information out of them, particularly the drier ones, is reading them a few times when you're first starting out. In fact, twice may be only a conservative estimate, especially during your first few weeks of law school. Getting the gist of complex cases often requires a few read-throughs, even for seasoned practitioners. And don't compare yourself to your classmates. If cases like *Pennoyer v. Neff, Korematsu v. US,* and *Palsgraf v. Long Island Railroad Co.* take you more reads than your friend, so be it!

REMEMBER

Reading a case twice enables you to initially give it a fast, understand-the-big-picture kind of read and then a more thorough, in-depth, comprehensive sort of read. Both reads are important to your overall understanding.

>> **Color-code your highlights.** Most people like highlighting the cases as they read them; I certainly found it helpful. But some take the highlighting even farther by color-coding what they highlight — for example, using pink for the facts, blue for the issue, green for the rationale, and yellow for the court's holding. (See the following section for more details on these terms.) Highlighting in this manner may help you to keep everything straight as long as you know your color system inside and out.

REMEMBER

At some point, if you're highlighting everything in the case, you aren't making distinctions that will help you.

>> **Write in the margins.** Another great way to remember important bits of a case, especially the next day in class when you need to recall information quickly, is writing notes to yourself in the margins of your casebook. I'd often create a brief summary of each critical point or significant fact and make stars next to key points. As an overall means of jogging my memory, I'd write a few short phrases at the top of each case about what the case was about and what the court's holding was. If you don't like writing in your books or may want to sell them after the term is over, use sticky notes instead.

>> **Take the material one step farther.** Has the professor recommended any law review articles that you need to check out? Go to the library and look them up. Are any points in the reading unclear to you? Look them up in a study aid or treatise.

>> **Talk the reading over with others.** If you're already a part of a study group (see Chapter 12), you may want to go over some or all of the assigned reading for the week with your group to clarify any confusing points. Collaborating with your peers and tossing ideas around is one of the best ways of getting the most out of your homework.

TIP

Checking in with your TA is also a solid way of ensuring you understand the material. TAs are students who did exceptionally well in a class and whom the professor has trusted enough to make their TA, so utilize their time and talent!

Briefing Cases: A Step-by-Step Approach

Most law students have a love–hate relationship with case briefing, mainly because it's important in your legal studies but a big old pain to do. *Briefing* means writing a short, well-organized summary of a case to use during class discussion, personal study, and outline preparation (covered in Chapter 13). The summary or *brief* (see Figure 12-1 for an example) ideally runs from half a page to two pages; any longer and it grows too unwieldy.

Vosburg v. Putney, 80 Wis. 523, 50 N.W. 403 (1891)

PROCEDURAL HISTORY:

P filed a complaint in the District Court alleging assault and battery by D. In trial, a finding for P was made, with a verdict for $2800. Judge granted award to P, and D appealed. Judgment was reversed for error, and a new trial was granted. In that trial, a verdict was awarded for P in the amount of $2500. D now appeals from that judgment.

FACTS:

P (Vosburg) is a boy just over fourteen years old. D (Putney) is a boy just under twelve years old.

In January, 1889, P suffered injury to knee that became inflamed and infected. Injury had almost completely healed when, on 20th of February, P was kicked by D on that same leg.

ISSUES:

1. Did the District Court err in allowing P to assert a cause of action against D for assault and battery?
2. Did the District Court err in denying Ds objection to a question upon examination by Ps attorney, ordering the expert witness to respond?
3. Did the District Court err in refusing Ds request to submit questions to jury?

HOLDING AND RULES:

1. Holding: No…
   Rule: In order to be held liable for assault and battery, it must be established that D had either unlawful intent, or was in fault. If action by D is unlawful, than intent is also considered unlawful.
2. Holding: Yes…
   Rule: Opinion of expert witness cannot be rendered until he has all the essential and material facts of the case.
3. Holding: No…
   Rule: D is liable for all injuries to P, whether foreseen or not.

REASONING:

1. D kicked P in a classroom, after class had been called to order. That is a violation of school rules and as such, considered an unlawful act. This being the case, Ds intent must also be considered unlawful, satisfying the requirements for alleging assault and battery.
2. Upon questioning the expert witness, P asks for the doctor's opinion regarding the cause of injury to leg. The doctor is not given the option of considering the first injury and how that may or may not have had implications on the condition of the injury as he saw it upon his first consultation with P. As a result of this fatal error, the jury may have been influenced in their judgment.
3. Although D may not have expected that kicking Ps leg would have resulted in such a severe injury or serious exacerbation of a previous injury, he is still liable.

JUDGMENT/ORDER:

- Reversed and remanded for a new trial.

FIGURE 12-1:
Typical first-year torts case brief.

Until you become a well-seasoned law student, case briefing is likely a tiresome activity, ranked right up there with getting root canals and flu shots. But it can help you move closer to your goal of thinking like a lawyer because it forces you to genuinely consider the legal principles involved in each case.

Putting the brakes on briefing

Although professors generally don't advise it, many 1Ls stop briefing around the second month of law school, after they think they've gotten the hang of reading cases. Some stop out of laziness (writing those briefs tacks on additional time to your nightly reading assignments); others feel that after a certain point, they get diminishing returns. Other law students keep doing it until the very end; it's totally up to you. You can also adjust for the courses where you feel like it comes to you easily. It's great when you can read the cases once and just get it.

I felt like I needed to brief the majority of my first year, especially if the case was extremely confusing or I thought I'd be called on. Briefs are downright crucial when you're called on as a first-semester 1L. Writing them means less of a chance you'll end up floundering around, trying to hunt down parts of the case when you need to be formulating your argument. In fact, when called on, most first-semester 1Ls just recite directly from their briefs, mainly because holding so many facts in your mind is harder when you're just starting out.

Case briefing is a step-by-step process. It works best when you do each step in a particular order because each new part builds off the previous. Keep in mind that you don't need to write a novel; a few sentences for each of the main briefing steps in the following sections is perfectly fine.

1. Identifying parties

REMEMBER

Cases don't have names like "The Exploding Fireball Case" or "The Man Who Slipped on the Icy Sidewalk Case." Instead, their official names are the names of parties suing one another. Each case has two parties:

>> The *plaintiff* (the party that's suing)

>> The *defendant* (the party that's being sued)

The parties' names are separated in the case name by "*v.*" (which stands for *versus*). Don't worry if you keep mixing up the definitions of *plaintiff* and *defendant* or *petitioner* and *respondent.* You get the hang of it soon enough.

>> Petitioner = plaintiff at the trial level; appellant at the appellate court level

>> Respondent = defendant at the trial level; appellee at the appellate court level

At the top of the case, beneath the case name, is the name of the court and date. The date is self-explanatory, but figuring out which court the case is originating from is often tricky for a 1L. All the cases in your casebook are (usually) going to be at least *appellate-level cases*, meaning they've already been through the *trial* (lower) court and now one of the parties is appealing that court's ruling.

2. Discovering procedural posture

The *procedural posture* is a short summary of how the case made its way through the court system to end up where it is today. For example, your procedural posture may state that the case was tried in the lower court and appealed to the appellate court. Although this information isn't usually particularly important to the facts or the ruling, your professor is nevertheless likely to ask you about it when you're called on, so figuring it out sooner rather than later is best.

3. Finding the facts

Basically, the *facts* are a description of what happened in the case. They're usually described in the first few paragraphs of the case, where you find out which party is suing the other and why. A broad range of facts is likely to be included in describing the case. Some facts are more important than others to the court's ruling.

REMEMBER

Part of the reason for using the *case method* (the way you learn to think like a lawyer) is to help you determine which facts are important so that when exam time comes around and you're given a *fact pattern* (a set of facts arranged in a similar way to the ones you read in your cases), you know which ones to take a closer look at and which to pass over.

The case method involves you reading a case, identifying the facts, the legal issue, the holding, and the reasoning. This will allow you to participate and engage in the Socratic method in class and discuss both sides of the case.

4. Identifying the issue

The *issue* is anything debatable confronting the court. For instance, if in the case you're reading, a child drowns in a swimming pool, the issue may be whether the pool owner was negligent for not installing a higher fence around the pool. Often, the issue is framed by a "whether" and can be answered "yes" or "no." Spotting or seeing the issue is one of the key elements of lawyering that law school teaches you. In fact, you need to make a point to become good at it because it's one of the main things you do on exams.

5. Reeling in the rationale

The *rationale* is the reasoning that the court uses in reaching its decision, or *holding* (see the following section). Besides using cases as teaching tools to identify the issues, law schools teach the case method so you can see and understand the reasoning courts use in reaching their conclusions. You discover the court's rationale so you can apply a similar (or dissimilar) one in your own analysis.

6. Homing in on the holding

Thankfully, courts at least make finding the holding easy for law students. It's typically the last sentence of the case and often is preceded by the words *We hold*. The holding describes the court's final decision on a matter and answers the question raised by the issue. For instance, in the example of a child drowning in a swimming pool, the court may say, "We hold that the homeowner was indeed negligent for not installing a higher fence around the swimming pool."

TIP

You also want to read dissenting and/or concurring opinions whenever they're included.

>> A *dissent* is written by a judge or judges who don't agree with the majority's holding and want to make their opinions known.

>> A *concurring opinion* is written by a judge or judges who agree with the outcome of the case but don't agree with some or all of the rationale of the majority's opinion and want to explain their views.

Reading these opinions can help point out flaws in the majority's reasoning that you can bring up in class or later in court. However, briefing dissenting and/or concurring opinions isn't necessary because they don't represent a majority opinion (one agreed to by more than half the judges). Professors commonly want to home in on the dissenting opinion in class because they believe the majority opinion is wrong or has serious flaws.

Recognizing the Importance of Class Participation

Generally, you need to have exceptional participation or exceptional nonparticipation (such as being continually unprepared or never once saying a word) to make a difference in your grade. The students who contribute once in a while usually don't have their grades affected at all.

Although class participation typically doesn't make or break you, in some rare instances it can raise or lower your grade a small amount after you've taken the final exam. Some professors call these extra points *push points* or *participation points*; you can usually find this information in the syllabus. Rarely do professors move grades up or down by an entire letter grade; more often, the adjustment is only one increment — say, from a B to a B+ for exceptional participation or from a B to a B– for missing too many classes, never volunteering, or continually coming to class unprepared.

TIP

Participate every time your class meets, don't miss many classes (pay close attention to the attendance policy), and continually ask thought-provoking questions.

Class participation becomes more important, however, when you're applying for a clerkship, you need reference letters, or you want a particular professor to serve as a reference in your job search. When a professor can comment profusely on your excellent participation and reasoning skills after hearing them firsthand in class discussions, you're likely to benefit.

REMEMBER

Most professors want you to tell them at the beginning of class whether you're unprepared so that they don't waste time calling on you. In fact, some professors grow annoyed when you fail to tell them, and they end up calling on your clueless self. Some of the more blunt ones even comment out loud on this unfortunate circumstance in class.

IN THIS CHAPTER

» **Figuring out how to be your most productive**

» **Preparing for exams**

» **Creating outstanding outlines**

» **Discovering the benefits of practice exams**

» **Snagging a study group**

Chapter **13**

Making the Most of Your Study Time

S uccessfully getting through law school is no easy task. It requires plenty of hard work, motivation, and discipline, not to mention first-rate time management and study skills. A healthy sense of humor also helps out tremendously.

Unfortunately, few schools provide first-year students (1Ls) with fundamental study or time management skills. At some schools, new students are left to flounder, having no idea how to tackle the enormous amount of information they're expected to absorb in a single semester. Because of this lack of traditional instruction, you may feel overwhelmed and frustrated.

In this chapter, I try to ease your fears by helping you get the most out of your study time on a daily basis and while preparing for final exams so you can manage your coursework with more ease and greater confidence. I discuss exactly what you can do to conquer the immense amount of material and successfully prepare for exams. I also explain how to create an outline that summarizes your entire course in one succinct document and why taking practice exams is the perfect way to hone your skills for the real thing. Finally, I cover study groups and why they can make a big difference in your comprehension levels. (For more on the time management aspect of things, head to Chapter 11.)

Maximizing Your Study Time

People in law school are certainly bright; they're often used to being at the top of their classes in college or other graduate study. However, even the brightest student can't get through law school purely on innate ability alone. They, too, fall flat on their faces come exam time without the right work ethic and time management skills.

That's why the key to success in law school is working *smart*, not necessarily running yourself ragged. You don't have to log 60 hours of studying per week to get top grades, but you must find a productive study system that works for you.

Creating a study schedule

Because most full-time law students take four to five courses per semester (or three to four, for part-time students), you'd still be studying most of your waking hours even if you had no other obligations (such as sleeping, eating, or working out). That's why making a study schedule for yourself, one week at a time, is always a good strategy.

REMEMBER

A study schedule differs from the activity checklist I discuss in Chapter 10 in that the latter's purpose is to help you figure out exactly how you spend your time. With that productiveness log, you may find out, for example, that you spend four hours cooking per day or two hours practicing the guitar. This information is valuable for when you sit down each week to compile your study schedule.

Your study schedule, which you can conveniently add to a planner or your wall calendar, lets you know exactly when you've carved out time to study. On your schedule, you can note the blocks of time when you're free for studying and then pencil in what you plan to study or accomplish during those times. All this planning helps you avoid wasting time because you know when you're supposed to study, and nothing else is planned for that time.

TIP

The standard ratio of time that you're supposed to spend on each course is three hours outside class for every hour in class. In other words, for a three-credit course, you spend at least nine hours a week studying. Now, I don't know anyone who actually sticks to this formula, but recognizing it generally helps you remember that you need to spend more time on your five-credit constitutional law course than you do on your three-credit contracts class. Of course, if you have a two or three-credit class that's really kicking your behind, you may want to up the ante on the amount of time you spend on that class, no matter how many credits it carries.

Scheduling ample study time is a great start, but it isn't 100 percent of what you need to do to get the grades you want. The other part of the equation is getting a good handle on what is — and isn't — important. Spending most of your study time learning obscure material the professor doesn't even cover in class isn't productive. Instead, use your class notes as a guide, and put your emphasis on those topics and points the professor stresses in class.

Flying your night owl or early bird flag

Some people are chipper, wake-up-early-and-watch-the-sunrise types. They sing in the shower and feel refreshed and energetic when they first wake up. Others, however, are creatures of the night. They stay up until all hours, wake up at noon, and feel most energetic in the late afternoon and evening (that's me).

Whatever type you are, don't try to fight Mother Nature. She generally wins. Instead, just plan your study habits around when you feel most awake and ready to go. For example, an early bird won't get much studying done after 10 p.m., and a night owl will probably be too out of it to study well at 7 a.m. Otherwise, you're working against your body's natural biorhythms, and you're not likely to do your best.

Improving problematic productivity

How many times have you been studying, looked at a clock, and said to yourself, "Where did all the time go? I didn't get a thing accomplished!" Whenever these thoughts are frequently racing through your mind, you may have a productivity problem.

A *productivity problem* just means that you're not being as productive as you can be when you sit down to study. Everybody's productivity level naturally waxes and wanes (studying for your property final is awfully hard when the weather's warm and sunny). But for some people, not getting their studying done becomes a chronic issue, and that's when you need to take action.

People with productivity problems can't focus easily on the tasks at hand or sit quietly for a period of time without feeling restless (which leads them to take too many distracting breaks). They usually get up from their study session feeling like they barely accomplished any of their goals; sometimes those goals are so lofty that no mortal could ever achieve them anyway. As a result, these people often feel frustrated and angry with themselves. Several ways that you can increase your overall productivity include the following:

>> **Avoid distractions.** You can do this by:

- **Finding a quiet space to work in:** Your apartment, the law library, or a cozy coffee shop may fit the bill. (**Note:** Some people find the law library stressful around exam time, as I explain later in the chapter.) If you want maximum concentration, head to an undergraduate library on campus where you're unlikely to see law students you know who want to hang out. I typically studied at a coffee shop away from the law school, so I'd rarely run into anyone I knew who wanted to chat up a storm.

- **Getting tested for conditions like ADHD, anxiety, and so on:** Your focus issues may have an underlying medical component that you can't address by simply pushing harder.

- **Making your study environment conducive to studying:** That means turning off the TV and music (unless they help you focus), putting your phone on silent or do not disturb, and staying off social media except for hard-earned breaks.

REMEMBER

  The last point is crucial, because what starts as quickly checking your friend's update can become a 30-minute rabbit hole of world news and dance trends very easily. Then you're off schedule and potentially feeling bad, guilty, and distracted.

- **Getting a significant other or friend to keep small children occupied for a portion of each night:** Going to law school and taking care of small children isn't easy, particularly when they're not yet school-aged. Finding someone to look after them for a few hours while you get your studying done helps you concentrate. If doing that is impossible, try to arrange your schedule so you get maximum studying done while they're asleep. Also try to connect with classmates who have small children. You may be able to share connections, resources, and maybe costs.

- **Separating work and school:** If you're a part-time or evening law student, putting away work-related concerns when you buckle down to study can be difficult. But doing so is essential if you're going to give your law school work the undivided attention it requires. Keep a planner with you so you can immediately jot down any work-related meetings or issues that pop into your mind as you study, and then put it away.

>> **Make a priority list for every study session.** Write down the goals you have for your study time and try to meet them. This simple act helps you subconsciously reinforce your goals (and feel accomplished when you can check them off your list). When one of your goals is too lofty, such as reading four

chapters of environmental law in an hour, break it up into smaller pieces to work on through the week.

>> **Set a time limit.** Sometimes making a regimented study span for yourself is a great way to make sure you've put in your time for the day without getting sidetracked by other things. Plus, you feel really good when you have "study 4 p.m. to 6 p.m." on your calendar or planner and you're actually able to meet that goal, undistracted. As simple as this step sounds, I found it was one of the most important things I did to keep my studying on track all through law school. For those who are easily distracted, breaking things up into one- or two-hour time blocks is much more manageable.

>> **Avoid zoning out (daydreaming).** If you find yourself frequently drifting off into a daydream when you know you need to be studying, resist the urge. Try getting your mind back on track by shutting out all extraneous thoughts and instead focusing your attention like a laser on the task at hand.

TIP

If you still find your mind racing with thoughts other than studying, write them down and schedule time to take care of them later. Then put the note away. The "out of sight, out of mind" concept really works! (Of course, if you're like me, you may end up with sticky notes and random musings that you texted yourself as reminders, but you'll get around to dealing with those another time.)

Tackling a Wealth of Information

Although studying a little every day is crucial for keeping pace throughout the semester, your study habits become especially important when exams roll around. (I talk much more about exams in Chapter 15.) In fact, most law students begin feeling the heat of impending finals when they're about a month away. At that point, in spite of all your efforts to stay on top of things, you may feel hopelessly behind after realizing just how much more information you must learn.

REMEMBER

When the going gets tough (and believe me, it will), keep in mind that generations of law students before you have successfully passed their law school exams, and you can, too. All you need are the following strategies (and sleep, some healthy snacks, and a month's supply of caffeinated beverages).

Realizing the value of memorization

Law school courses aren't like science courses, in which you memorize everything, but they still involve a good deal of memorization. You must be familiar enough with the law to spot issues well. (See Chapters 12 and 15 for more on issue-spotting.) You must also know the court *holdings* (decisions) of the cases you studied and the legal principles those cases take up. That's where the bulk of your memorization comes in. You generally don't need to remember specific case names, dates, or party names, though.

Most of your fellow classmates will know the law (the most basic level of studying), but the students who really distinguish themselves on exams are the ones who are able to work through the reasoning behind the law. In other words, they can not only distinguish that a tort has occurred but also analyze the type of tort and show why a given party should or shouldn't prevail. (Chapter 15 has more on answering specific exam questions.)

But why bother memorizing, you may wonder, when the exam is probably open book? (Chapter 15 explains why open-book exams tend to be the rule rather than the exception in law school.) Isn't just having your notes in front of you enough?

REMEMBER

You should use notes in open-book exams as a last resort to clarify a particular point or briefly refresh your memory. Trust me, you probably won't have time to flip through your books and notes; even if you do, that tactic slows you down significantly. You need to know the law well enough *before* you set foot in exam room so that you don't waste time digging around in your notes.

Learning small chunks at a time

Studying throughout the entire semester is the best approach. Leaving all the studying for your exams until the last minute is stressful and unproductive. You have little chance of learning everything you need to know when you start studying only a day or two before the exam. Additionally, as a 1L, you're just discovering the format of a law school exam, and getting into the swing of things takes time.

TIP

Reviewing after a unit or chapter has ended in class is a fruitful way of keeping up with your studies and avoiding some of the last-minute panic before an exam.

Attending review sessions

When exams are closing in, nothing sounds better to a law student than the words *review session.* Review sessions are prime time for:

» Asking pertinent questions

» Clarifying any issues, concepts, or rules you're unclear about

>> Discovering last-minute changes or additions to an exam

>> Finding out once and for all what your professor wants out of an exam

TIP

Because review sessions in law school are few and far between, attend any and all of them that your professors — and TAs — decide to conduct.

REMEMBER

You have the most luck finding review sessions when you're a 1L. Few professors offer them for 2Ls and 3Ls, probably because by that stage they figure you're an old hat at taking exams. When your professor decides against offering one, you have two options:

>> **Petitioning the professor to provide a review session (perhaps by coaxing several people in your class to send email requests).**

>> **Staging your own mini-review session by attending your professor's office hours prepared with a list of your own questions.** While you're there, ask the professor for thoughts on the ideal way of organizing your exam response. Because each professor has their own ideas of how an exam needs to be written, this tactic is guaranteed to put you head and shoulders above the people who never bother to ask.

Instead of having a bona fide review session, some professors devote part of a class period toward the end of the semester to a discussion of what they look for in their exams. Perk up your ears while the professor is talking about this information because you can get some valuable insights into their grading persona. A professor's wish list may include the following:

>> Writing on every other line

>> Emphasizing a particular approach to the course (such as economics or political theory)

>> Organizing an answer in a specific way (such as by party or by cause of action)

Take the most detailed notes of your life during these discussions because following your professors' explicit instructions to a T means you're likely to reap the resulting benefits when they grade your exams.

TIP

Some law schools offer general exam-strategy programs for 1Ls (or other interested students). Nowadays, the academic support/success team, professors, and/or TAs hold these sessions throughout the fall and spring; they may take the form of an ongoing series of workshops, sessions, or seminars. In some instances, professors explain what they generally look for in a law school exam and give examples of universal do's and don'ts. These events are usually very helpful, and

I encourage students of all years to attend to ensure they get the best grades possible.

Posing hypotheticals to boost understanding

Hypotheticals (or hypos) are one technique your professors rely on heavily in teaching the law. *Hypos* are bits of facts taken out of the case you're studying and twisted around to illustrate how the same rule of law may apply to a brand-new situation. (You can see some specific examples of hypos in Chapter 12.) Hypotheticals are one of the most valuable ways of learning the law because no two factual situations are exactly the same. After all, as a practicing attorney, you'll rarely have two clients come to you with the exact same problem and the same set of facts/circumstances.

You can vastly improve your understanding of a concept by using hypos when you study. Here are a few ideas:

>> **Study group practice:** The best way of incorporating hypos into your studying repertoire is by posing them to other people in your study group. One person can think up the hypos, and the rest can take turns answering and critiquing them.

>> **Asking the professor:** Visit your professor during office hours and request a run-through of some of your hypos. You can also try this out with your TAs.

>> **Flashcards:** Practice with store-bought or homemade flashcards that have a hypothetical on one side and answers on the other. (Flip to Chapter 14 for more information on flashcards.)

Getting the Skinny on Outlines

Before law school, you'd probably never heard of the concept of outlining for a course. I sure hadn't. However, in law school, many people believe outlining is as essential to success on exams as air is to breathing. In fact, some law students don't feel completely prepared for exams unless they've created their own outlines. They can go to class and meet with their study groups, but unless they wrestle, grapple, and pin the course material in a half nelson, they never truly know it well.

So what exactly is an outline? An outline *compiles* whatever you think can help you understand the rules, case holdings, and principles of law from the course you're taking. Another take, from Tajira McCoy, author, law school consultant, former law school admissions dean and director, is that an outline is a synthesized version of the core principles covering a specific set of the rules, cases, and so on that are sectioned into broad topics of rulings and rationales, which then can be applied to a variety of *fact patterns* (the legal education equivalent of story problems).

Another helpful tip from Allana Forte Branch, general counsel, former law school admissions dean, is that the outline should follow the syllabus. It should allow you to read the topic or issue and be able to quickly apply the rules or law to a different set of facts.

The point of the outline is to turn the enormous amount of material you absorb in a course into a more palatable and digestible amount (most outlines are anywhere from 20 to 50 pages long). In a typical course, you probably:

>> Read close to 500 pages of text

>> Sit through approximately 50 hours of the Socratic method (which I cover in Chapter 12)

>> Debate with your study group for 25 hours

>> Read 200 pages of a commercial outline

>> Take 150 pages of notes (class and reading)

That's a heck of a lot of information to study buffet-style in preparation for exams. Your new ally, the outline, makes your life a whole lot easier by condensing all of that material into one (hopefully) coherent document.

An outline usually includes the following:

>> Your class and reading notes

>> Study group materials

>> Bits and pieces of commercial study aids

>> Chunks of upper-class students' outlines

>> Your thoughts and interpretations

>> A table of contents (this element is optional, but it may make the outline easier to navigate)

Ideally, you eventually pare down your 20-to-50-page outline into a 10-to-15-page outline, a 5-page outline, and then a 1-to-2-page outline. Your understanding of the concepts and principles you've learned throughout the term will easily conjure up the black letter law (basic legal principles or the law as it is written or it says what is says and it means what it means), while allowing you to look at a concept, principle, or case name and articulate why a court should rule a certain way.

TIP

Outlines are particularly useful for open-book exams. Having the information you need neatly organized in a document you created is much easier than digging through your books and notes for an answer. Some professors allow you one two-sided sheet. The creativity that goes into getting a massive amount of information into a document that size with legible font is amazing!

Outlining to promote active learning

Outlining takes a lot of effort, so why bother doing it at all? Can't you study for exams as well — or better — just by rereading your notes and glancing at commercial study aids? Well, maybe, but experience shows that tons of law students before you have been successful when using the outlining method, so you at least need to *consider* outlining as part of your exam preparation. No sense in reinventing the wheel.

In general, reading your notes, commercial study guides, or other people's outlines is *passive studying,* which means you sit there with the book and try to absorb the material without doing much else in the way of reinforcing your efforts. Passive learning is okay, but many people believe that it isn't quite as effective as active learning.

REMEMBER

Outlining is 100 percent active learning. Proponents of outlining argue that it enables you to actually organize the material in your own way and in a format that makes sense to you. Instead of reading what someone else writes about your course, you actually roll up your sleeves and dig into the material yourself. You're engaging in a *synthesis* — pulling all the material together, drawing connections between concepts, and highlighting those connections. You're also linking cases together, forming conclusions, and seeing the big picture. Most law students say that synthesizing the material makes all the difference between a high exam grade and an average one.

REMEMBER

If making an outline doesn't help you learn, you don't have to do it; outlining isn't required. But trying outlining for least one semester so you can determine that it really doesn't work for you is a good idea.

Finding a workable outline format

Outlines get their name because they're usually constructed like an undergraduate or law school syllabus is: with roman numerals and sub-letters denoting each topic and subtopic.

For instance, you start with a main heading under a roman numeral, list subheadings 1 and 2 under that, and so on. You can see an example in Figure 13-1. When I was outlining, I used the samples from my mentors and the class syllabus to ensure I had the correct headings, subheadings, rules, and case law. However, if the traditional outline format turns you off, feel free to experiment with whatever setup works for you. Some people make straight lists; others write up their thoughts in paragraph form.

TIP

If you're having trouble with the outline format concept, try using your law school course syllabus or the table of contents of your casebook (see Chapter 8) as a starting point. That way, you can see exactly how your professor or the casebook author outlined a topic — perfect for tailoring your own outline.

REMEMBER

Above all, keep in mind that no one lays eyes on your outline except you. Your outline doesn't have to be fit to publish in a law review. All it needs to be is something that you can use to study the material and/or to help you during an open-book exam. Use whatever acronyms, shorthand, and terminology make sense to you and help you learn and retain the information.

Deciding what to put in your outline

Most outlines total between 20 and 60 pages, but they can be as short as 1 page or as long as 120. The key word to remember in outlining is *summary.* You don't want to write a book; you just want to condense the immense load of information into more manageable chunks.

Good outlines need to have a rundown of the following items:

>> Every important principle or rule you studied

>> A short summary of the relevant cases

>> Any *tests,* or specific conditions when a rule applies, that courts have devised to explain a principle or rule

>> Any exceptions to the rules

>> Any policy issues that are brought up in your course

CIVIL PROCEDURE I
I. Purpose and Due Process

A. Goals:
1. Show development of lawsuit in federal court to time of trial.
2. Explore values implicit in procedural choices...purpose of process is to reach correct decisions under substantive law in manner that protects dignity of litigants as well as society's interests in efficient and inexpensive resolution of disputes
3. Constitution recognizes interest in fair procedures (Due Process cases)
   - Nature of interest
   - Possibility of error
   - Cost of additional procedures
   - Dignity interest of individual/power of government

B. Courts Powers
1. **Injunctions:** Court may hold parties in contempt for violating its orders, and it can also hold non-parties in contempt for interfering with the court orders if they are involved with parties. (US v. Hall 5th Cir. 1972). See Rule 65(d) injunctions binding to parties, their agents, officers, servants, attorneys and employees.
   a) Court plays loose with Rule 65, well if our court order doesn't apply to you, then Rule 65 doesn't apply to us.

C. Due Process Rights
1. **Property Interests**
   a) Termination of benefits:
      - notice in advance,
      - access to counsel (not pre-termination),
      - opportunity to testify yes, orally, not only by written statement,
      - opportunity to cross examine witnesses: there is a right to confront adverse witnesses and evidence,
      - no requirement of formal written record,
      - requires a statement of reasons for termination of benefits and case/hearing decision.
      - Independent judicial review by impartial decision maker (i.e. not a board composed of the same bureaucrats who cut you off in the first place.)

      i. protected so that people are not put in desperate situations by erroneous benefit termination and government cost cutting. Weighs this issue against maximizing government efficiency.
   b) **Termination of Welfare benefits:** Goldberg v. Kelly (US Sct. 1970) Welfare is a protected property interest and cannot be taken away w/o due process. Court requires stuff listed above.
   Test: does the person's property interest outweigh the govs interest in efficiency via simple procedures? Is the recipient in an immediate situation that could threaten their survival or subsistence? Yes in Goldberg.
   c) **Termination of Disability benefits:** Court comes out opposite of Goldberg. They draw a distinction by saying that people on disability have other income, and if they don't, they could just go on to welfare and fix the situation later if a mistake was made in terminating the benefits. (Mathews v. Eldridge US Sct. 1976) H: **No pre-termination hearing is required.**
   d) **Seizure of property:** constitutional due process rights require state to give notice and an opportunity to be heard before seizing property. See Fuentes v. Shevin (US Sct. 1972), where a person puts down a bond for a writ-of-replevin. Sheriff goes with party and takes the property=unconstitutional.
      i. **opposing argument** is that people will give themselves the right to do this by including it in contracts for car payments, etc. Creates a repo-man situation that endangers people. Private parties are not restricted by the due process requirements.
2. **Access to the Courts:** if a party cannot afford to pay court filing fee to exercise fundamental rights, they can file to have the fee waived. See Boddie v. Connecticut (US Sct. 1971) where welfare recipients sued state to make them waive filing fee to get a divorce court sided with them, marriage (and dissolution of one) are fundamental rights.
      a) **To waive filing fee:** Use 28 USC/1915(c&d) which requires you to make a motion and affidavit stating why you cannot pay and that you have nothing to give for security. See Rule 7(b) and 10 for info on basic motions.
3. **Access to a lawyer**: indigents right to counsel exists only where the litigant may lose his physical liberty if he loses the litigation.
      a) No right to counsel in a hearing for termination of parental rights. (Lassiter v. Dept. Soc. Serv. NC (US Sct. 1981). State courts should determine this in a case by case basis. Ironic that one is entitled to counsel for a two-day marijuana prison term, but not for a hearing where gov seeks to take ones child away. Court basically said that if you have a bad case, you don't need a lawyer anyway waste of state $.

FIGURE 13-1:
Sample outline.

REMEMBER

Your outline needs to be tailored to your particular professor's approach, which you can figure out from class discussions, lectures, old exams, your teaching assistants, and study-group sessions. For example, when your professor regularly mentions economics policy preferences in class, you want to develop your outline with this tendency in mind. Glancing over some past exams may further help you tailor your outline to your specific professor.

Many law students struggle to figure out what's important enough to include in their outlines and what isn't. Most students seem to err on the side of including too much rather than too little. I, too, fell victim to the problem of including too much the times I made my own outlines. I was so worried about missing something critical, especially in my first semester. The dilemma is that you don't want to exclude something important that can potentially appear on the exam, but a 50- or 100-page outline is way too much to be useful as you get closer to exam time.

The solution to figuring out what to put in and what to leave out is remembering that exams can test only so much. All professors cover the main points. After all, that's all they have time to assess during a three-to-four-hour exam. Because most professors don't test minor concepts, you don't need to waste your time focusing on those to the exclusion of material that's more likely to be tested. So when you're in conflict about whether to include concepts your professor discussed for five minutes in one class period, remember the wise saying "When it doubt, leave it out." Then your outlines become a much more manageable length.

Condensing your outline even farther

Some people firmly believe in the benefits of whittling a big, unwieldy, 20-to-50-page outline into something more compact. In fact, many law students aren't content with leaving things as they are when they finish their main outlines. Instead, they condense their original outlines into one-third of their original size and may even create *checklists* (1-to-5-page summaries of the most important points).

A checklist can take the form of a flow chart, a condensed outline, or a simple list with no particular order of the most important issues your professor is likely to test and information that you shouldn't leave out in your essay answers. Instead of flipping through an immense outline and hunting down a particular point, you've boiled down the key issues to fit within your one-to-five-page checklist.

REMEMBER

Some students find condensing all that information an integral part of the studying process. After mastering the material in their original outlines, they feel like such an enormous document has become like excess baggage. So they pare it down to the bare bones to make it more user-friendly. I often found myself feeling pretty good about a course after I was able to whittle my 30-to-50-page outline down to a 10-to-15-page outline and then to 1 or 2 pages. It meant that I had mastered the major concepts and could use cases and specific facts to instantly recall the rules and policy issues.

TIP

Here are a couple of ways you can keep your outline focused on the main points:

>> **Select the three most important concepts from each class session to include in your outline.** Three points per class is plenty. And when you figure about a third of a page devoted to one point, your outline will run about 50 pages total, a manageable size.

>> **Flag key points as you go.** I always read my outlines with a highlighter and colored tabs in hand so I could mark them up and tab the most important parts. This process helped me cut down my outlines from 15 to 20 pages to 3 to 5 pages.

Adding to your outline each day (and getting back on track if you fall behind)

When you decide to bring your laptop to class each day, you're far ahead of your computerless peers because typing class notes each day can lay the foundation for your outline with minimal effort. You're already typing your class notes, so all you need to do to create a gourmet, full-length outline by the end of the semester is add in your reading notes a little at a time each day. You can begin synthesizing the material immediately, or you can wait until after each main section or chapter if that feels more natural for you.

Even if you don't (or aren't allowed to) bring a laptop to class, you still can work on your outline every day from the beginning of the semester. All staying on track takes is a good dose of motivation.

When exams are looming and you've finished only the first page of your outline, you may be tempted to forget it entirely. However, I advise you to catch up and finish it, even if it's only a bare-bones model. Mustering only a one-sentence summary of each case, all in chronological order, is far better than nothing. When your exam is open book, having some semblance of an outline is especially important.

Putting your outline to work for you

Your outline finally is finished — hooray! Take a step back and admire all your hard work. Now that you've your completed outline, you can:

>> **Study it:** Cross out parts that no longer seem relevant, and highlight the ones that seem especially important. Make notes in the margins regarding any additional points you may have left out. Meet with your study group to talk over your completed outlines and note any issues that come up in these discussions.

>> **Read it over many times:** Five is great, ten is better, and even more is best. You want to become as intimately familiar with your outline as you are with your journal. Try to sear the concepts into your brain. After you're familiar with it, close your eyes and try to see it in your mind's eye. More often than not, after reaching this level of mastery, you start having dreams about your outline!

>> **Compare it with classmates' outlines:** One good way of knowing whether your outline measures up to the ones prepared by others in your class is to get together with a classmate or your study group partners and compare. Find out whether you phrase case holdings and legal principles similarly, what your friends emphasized and deemphasized, and which of the professor's particular approaches everyone incorporated. What policy issues did they highlight? Were there any dissenting or concurring opinions that the professor was particularly fond of or focused on and/or referenced frequently?

>> **Sleep with it under your pillow:** Hey, it can't hurt, right? Maybe you'll be the first to learn law by osmosis.

Taking (Many) Practice Exams

Practice exams are to studying what yeast is to baking bread. If you leave out this crucial step, your grades don't rise. Pun intended. Reviewing old exams highlights what issues, cases, and rules the professor focused on in previous exams.

REMEMBER

The purpose of taking (or at least reviewing) practice exams is to find out what kinds of questions your professor has asked in the past and what they deem to be a good exam. Professors don't often dramatically revamp their exams every year. Instead, they're far more likely to stick to a tried-and-true method. Their predictability works in your favor. If you have a good grasp of what they've done in the past — trends and themes they've leaned into, how well-scoring responses are formatted — predicting what your own exam will be like becomes easier.

You usually can find practice exams either on reserve at the library under your professor's name or in your course portal (check with your law library team for the password). After you print or photocopy as many practice exams as you can, lay them side by side. What do you see in common? Do fact patterns highlight the same issues year after year? Does every exam emphasize certain course topics? What do the policy questions have in common? Chapter 15 has more about fact patterns and policy questions.

Some, but not all, practice exams include model sample answers. When they do, that's a big bonus, so you need to study the answers as thoroughly as you do the questions. Answers show you things like the following:

>> How in-depth your professor wants you to go

>> How your professor wants certain issues treated

>> How you need to structure and organize your answer

>> What policy issues the professor prefers you include

All my law school professors made practice exams and answers available. I spent more time extensively studying those answers than doing any of the practice exams, and it paid off. By critiquing each answer, I found buzzwords that my professor liked to use, saw what they wanted in their answers, and noticed what structure they were looking for.

TIP

If your professors don't provide answers, see whether your study group can get together to puzzle them, perhaps with your teaching assistants.

When time allows, sit down and take as many full-length practice exams as you can instead of merely reading through the questions. Do this prior to midterms (if offered) and final exams. Although actually completing a practice exam takes a lot of motivation, it enables you to find out whether you can answer the questions in the allotted time and how fast you're able to spot issues. This point is often where students begin to identify potential problems with their study habits, study schedule, ability to follow along in class, and/or ability to spot the issues their professors are looking for.

Don't worry that the practice exams seem much too hard when you first sit down with them because it's all a matter of perception. It's your first time, and the stakes are very high. The difference in your level of concentration while casually taking practice exams during your study time versus taking the actual exam is a big one. Likewise, unless you're taking your practice exam the day before the real final, you're likely going to have much more time to study. So be sure to give yourself a break when you're feeling in over your head. It's perfectly normal.

A PROFESSOR'S TAKE ON PRACTICE EXAMS

The following advice comes from Kathy Northen, Associate Dean/Robert M. Duncan/Jones Day Designated Associate Professor of Law.

An athlete wouldn't go into a game without practice, nor a musician without rehearsing, and a law student should not take an exam without taking multiple practice exams. The first one or two practices, get comfortable with spotting issues and the applicable legal rules-to develop a strategy for organizing your answers. Then, take one or two under timed conditions. Finally, don't be complacent — your professor may change the structure of the exam. Practice short answer, multiple choice, and extended fact patterns. Preparation provides the competitive edge.

Understanding the Science: Law Students and Study Groups

Even when you're a lone eagle type, you may find that participating in a study group improves your course comprehension more than anything else you try. A *study group* is essentially a group of any size (but typically two to eight people) that forms to study regularly throughout the semester; to cover one, some, or all courses; or to study at the very end of the semester in preparation for exams. Although you probably never encountered many study groups in college, they're a mainstay in law school.

Here are few things to consider about why study groups can be so instrumental in student success in law school:

>> Sharing resources (such as notes)

>> Building relationships and making connections

>> Learning by teaching and repetitive conversations

>> Forcing accountability and staying on task

>> Providing additional assistance with outlining and exam prep

>> Helping students better understand complex material, improve their issue-spotting abilities, and articulate legal concepts

On the other hand, study groups can have their downsides, such as groupthink, personality conflicts, and failure to accommodate different learning styles.

Looking at different types of study groups

REMEMBER

Study groups run the gamut from the ultra-disciplined to more laid-back and casual. (I knew of one that sponsored potluck dinners at most meetings.) Regardless of the atmosphere your study group provides, make sure the people in it can get the job done.

Some law schools now require study groups; in fact, they assign them and designate a TA to help keep you organized. But at other law schools, students arrange the study groups informally themselves. Although most students form groups with people in their same classes, you can join or form study groups with anyone.

Each study group decides on its own what it wants to accomplish. Some groups assign each member a portion of the course to present, and then all members discuss those presentations. Other groups review practice exams or pose hypotheticals to each other.

Forming groups with strangers and friends

As a new 1L, you may not know anyone well enough to feel like you can simply join their existing study group. That's why many law schools help facilitate the creation of the study groups based on your track or section. But if your law school doesn't set the group up for you, bite the bullet and form your own study group. Identify a few classmates you believe you can work with. You don't know any of them? Great! They probably don't know many people either. Just remember, you're all in this together.

REMEMBER

You may end up meeting some of your closest friends during your first year. I was lucky to have met lifelong friends during that period. When you're meeting on a regular basis and discussing such difficult issues, you can't help but get to know people well.

Another approach is starting a study group with your friends. However, bear in mind that study groups consisting of friends can often get off track, and conversation can quickly move to more fun topics. Although chatting with your friends is enjoyable, you won't get much studying accomplished when it's a regular occurrence. You may find that you're more productive in a group with strangers.

Ousting unproductive people

You may find that someone in your group is dragging you and the others down — constantly showing up unprepared, never contributing to the discussion, or regularly asking questions that are too basic. Of course, when it's one of your friends, finding a nice way to ask them to find another group is difficult. But you sometimes, you just have to put it out there. You don't have to embarrass them; just be honest and check in. They may be feeling the same way, and you may give them out.

When the unproductive member is merely some random person in your group, the rest of you may decide that member just isn't working out. Perhaps at your next meeting you can say something like, "Everyone in our group is putting in a great deal of time and effort, but we feel you aren't always as prepared. If you're not willing to put in the necessary work, maybe you need to try another group." This ultimatum makes that person either reform or voluntarily leave.

REMEMBER

Be mindful of how you'd want to be treated, but also remember that making sure everyone feels respected and valued and like they're investing the same amount of time is key to the group's success. Communicating what you need and why you're making changes can help maintain your professional relationships with your classmates. The legal profession isn't that big. You don't know when you may end up in the same agency, firm, or organization or on the other end of a hiring committee. So be kind, thoughtful, and direct.

Chapter **14**

Assembling Your Study Aid Arsenal

Despite all the hard work you do in your classes, sometimes you just don't get certain parts of a course. And when that happens, you're not in the mood to grapple further with legal concepts on your own; you just want to be *told* the law, plain and simple. Don't be too hard on yourself because you don't understand a particular concept; instead, turn to the myriad study aids that are available.

This chapter helps you sift through the myths and realities of study aid use so you can determine which of them meet your needs. Besides traditional study aids, plenty of other tools — from flashcards to online legal databases — can help you pull together everything you're studying. Don't forget the law library, which can make your life loads easier by providing you with study aids on reserve, legal encyclopedias, and law review articles to boost and speed understanding.

Improving Your Comprehension with Study Aids

Study aids (otherwise known as commercial outlines or summaries) are any items outside your assigned course books that help explain legal concepts. (See Chapter 13 for more information on self-compiled outlines, which aren't considered commercial study aids but are nonetheless a helpful tool when studying for exams.) More specifically, a study aid ideally takes everything you learn in a single course, explains it in plain English, condenses it, and organizes it in a user-friendly way.

Many people think study aids are essential to law school success because they help you become familiar with unfamiliar language, fill in gaps in your knowledge, and take the mystery out of case briefing (which I cover in Chapter 12). Students appreciate the ease of navigating study aids because, unlike casebooks (see Chapter 8), they summarize the cases for you and explicitly tell you each case's rules or principles (*holdings*).

Study aids are most helpful to get an overview or some background information on a topic when your casebook or class notes are unclear or vague. When you're just starting out, you'll find many times when your class notes (or the class discussion) don't make any sense. So as you're trying to figure out how a particular concept fits in with the unit you're studying or what the holding of a particular case is, just whip out your good friend the study aid. Everything you need to know will be in there.

You have countless study aids to choose from, but *National Jurist* ranked these as the top 10 in 2023:

>> Examples and Explanations

>> Quimbee

>> Emanuel Law Outlines

>> Nutshells

>> Emanuel Law Crunch Time

>> Law in a Flash

>> CALI Lessons

>> Short & Happy Guides

>> Glannon Guides

>> Crushendo

TIP

Keep in mind that each series has titles for individual courses. For instance, Quimbee is the product name; that line has study aids, flashcards, and so on broken down by course (such as property and torts).

All first-year (1L), and many upper-division, courses are covered by commercial study aids. Some even cover the more focused 2L, 3L, and 4L courses such as business associations, federal income tax, Native American law, or white-collar crime. But if you can't find study aids for a specific course, you're better off compiling your own outline or finding an upper-division student's to use as a model.

REMEMBER

Though many students end up using study aids at the last minute for midterms and finals, working with aids consistently throughout the semester can help you stay on top of your coursework, get a better grasp of class discussion, and develop questions for further study.

TIP

If you're considering law school or have yet to begin your first year, consider browsing in a law school bookstore or perusing the study aid section of a law school's library to get a feel for what study aids are all about. Actually purchasing a study aid at this point probably isn't productive, but by looking through a couple, you can get an idea about what the content of your first-year courses will be like.

Boxers or canned briefs?

Canned briefs are a subgroup of commercial outlines dedicated to summarizing case facts, rationales, and holdings and providing you with *black letter law* (well-settled law). Books with canned briefs are often keyed to your casebook (author and edition), so they present material in the same order you read it in your casebook. Canned brief books give you a short overview of every major case in your course; however, many times not every case that you study is included.

Many first-year (1L) students like to keep their canned briefs open to the right pages during class in case they're called on and need to recite the facts quickly. Professors, as you can imagine, don't like students using canned briefs, because you end up reading someone else's brief rather than writing and digesting your own.

When to procure study aids

Many law students probably agree that you need to wait a few weeks before plunking down money or searching the library for study aids. The following are a few good reasons for waiting a little while.

>> **You need time to decide where and how you need help.** Take a few moments to write down problem areas you face in each of your classes. For instance, you may not have enough examples or hypotheticals (covered in Chapter 12) to work from; maybe you can't write fast enough in class to take down all the hypotheticals, or your particular casebook doesn't provide any at the end of particular sections. If that's true, you want to look for a commercial study aid that emphasizes what you're missing.

Or say that your weakness is that you don't know how to organize your notes into a coherent outline. In that case, you want to look for an outline-format study aid, one with similar emphasis on topics to the course you're taking, so that you can use it as a model for your own outline. (Check out Chapter 13 for more on preparing outlines.)

>> **You want to be able to make an informed decision.** Consult with a few students who've had your particular set of professors to determine which study aids can benefit you the most. For instance, your upper-class buddies may inform you that Gilbert's is great for one of your courses but that Emanuel's is far better for another. Instead of going out and buying or searching the library for a bunch of different outlines, you'll have first-hand advice from students who've been in your professor's class.

When you're feeling brave, you may even ask your professors for their opinions. If you talk to them about the problems you're having in their courses, some professors don't hesitate to recommend a particular study aid or hornbook. (See the section "Hornbooks versus commercial study aids" later in the chapter.) Professors of 2L and 3L courses seem more open to offering recommendations than the 1L profs do, but you never know until you try. Another great reason for getting direct recommendations from professors is that they may recommend a particular study aid because it stresses the same topics they focus on in the class, which you otherwise may not pick up on if you were to select them on your own.

>> **You don't want to risk information overload.** You don't need to buy or borrow one of every study aid available. Trust me, one study aid per course suits you perfectly well. Too many study aids per course can often hurt more than help because you have too much information there for you to digest.

Here's an example of the pointlessness of stocking up on too many study aids. For my corporations course, which I was highly worried about as a 2L, I bought and/or borrowed five study aids. Doing so was a mistake because study aids contain so much material that I never got my money's worth. I ended up using only one; the others grew mold in my locker. At least I was able to sell some back to the law school bookstore (for only a fraction of what I paid for them, of course).

> **》 You don't want to drain your life savings.** Because study aids aren't cheap (they average between $15 and $40+ each; hornbooks are often $35 to $50), saving your money for when you really need them is your best bet.

Where to find study aids

The decision about whether to buy or borrow study aids depends in large part on what you plan to do with them. For instance, buying study aids is useful if you're looking to take the study aid to class with you each day, highlight it, or incorporate your class notes into it. But if you just want to read a study aid for background information or need a little extra help in one or two areas of a particular course, purchasing study aids may not be your best option.

Also keep your budget in mind. The law school bookstore isn't your only option for *purchasing* study aids. Many law schools feature student-run used bookstores, where you can pick up used study aids at discounted prices. If you do enough digging, you'll probably be able to get two or three used study aids for the price of one new one. Alternatively, you can post a want ad on your law school miscellaneous bulletin board; students will line up in droves to sell you their used study aids.

If you don't have the inclination or the cash to buy study aids, you can often find some of them behind the reserve desk at the law library, just waiting to be checked out. (Some libraries may also keep study aids in the stacks.) Although it differs between law libraries, many have study aids available for nearly every course the law school offers. However, many libraries offer only one to a few series of study aids. For example, your library may offer the Nutshell series and the Hornbook series, but no others.

WARNING

Just remember that if you get study aids from the library, you can probably check them out for only a limited amount of time — usually between 24 and 48 hours. Around exam time, that window may be even narrower, such as a two-hour block. Plan accordingly so you're not desperate for a study aid only to find that the waiting list is a mile long.

The Internet is another extremely valuable resource for finding study aids. Although you don't find commercial study aids reproduced in their entirety online, you can find some great websites that offer:

>» Study tips for particular courses

>» Overviews of particular subject areas

>» Links to individual students' outlines for specific courses from other law schools

Why some professors discourage using study aids

Professors' reactions to study aids range from enthusiastic encouragement to tolerance to adamant discouragement. Although most professors generally think study aids are helpful, they don't want you to use them as crutches. Doing background reading about a subject or getting help illustrating how a particular case or topic fits into a course's overall picture is one thing, but professors want you to first learn the law on your own instead of by reading how someone else analyzed it. Study aids should be a supplement to your casebook, not a substitute.

At the beginning of the semester (particularly in your first year), your professors are likely to share their thoughts on the evils of study aids. They caution you about how study aids do law students a disservice and how, if you rely on them, you won't learn to think like a lawyer.

Many professors also advise against using them because they believe you won't learn the course the way they teach it when you use study aids. Each professor's course is unique to that professor, and commercial outlines, by their broad nature, are meant to be applicable to as many professors' courses as possible. Your professor may teach criminal law differently than the study aid outlines it by emphasizing or deemphasizing certain parts. Your torts professor may focus on an economic perspective that your study aid doesn't.

REMEMBER

As long as you know what topics your own course covers and doesn't cover and you have a firm understanding of your professor's approach to the course, overreliance on a commercial outline doesn't have to present the kind of catastrophic problems that many professors want students to believe. Use your course syllabus to easily figure out which sections of the study aid you can use and which ones to ignore. The goal is to use these tools to enhance and solidify your understanding of the materials.

Hornbooks versus commercial study aids

As I note earlier in the chapter, commercial study aids are aimed at giving you maximum information in minimal time. *Hornbooks* (also called *treatises*), on the other hand, are more scholarly treatments of a particular course topic. Similar in content (and size and weight) to a textbook, hornbooks aim to provide an in-depth, heavily footnoted discussion of your course.

Although commercial study aids (with their outline formats) are often more user-friendly than hornbooks are, you may find that hornbooks cover your course topic more thoroughly. You can find hornbooks at the bookstore or online, but they're quite expensive. They're also available at the law library (usually on reserve); many commercial outlines are not.

Loading Your Study Kit with Other Essential Tools

Besides the hornbooks and commercial study aids I discuss in the preceding sections, several other important study resources can make your life as a law student much easier, provide you with additional practice, and guide you to resources for your legal research and beyond. Among them are:

>> *Black's Law Dictionary:* *Black's Law Dictionary* is an important resource for all those new words you'll be looking up on a daily basis. Get one to always carry with you; you'll find it especially helpful for looking up foreign-sounding tidbits of legalese in the nick of time during class. (Chapter 12 has a discussion of legalese.)

>> **Lexis and Westlaw login information:** Lexis and Westlaw are competing online databases that attorneys and law students use to conduct legal research. During orientation or during the first few weeks of law school, you receive free subscriptions to these services that last until you graduate. Keep your login info for these sites handy (don't worry; you'll come to have these numbers memorized soon enough). Typically, these free subscriptions provide you with unlimited use of their respective databases, but only for educational (not on-the-job) use.

   You use them most heavily during your legal research and writing course during your first year, but don't overlook their usefulness for studying other courses. The cases often provide links to other cases that may help put the one at hand in better context. Other links to law review and other articles discussing your case also are accessible with a click.

>> **Flashcards:** Flashcards present short hypotheticals (similar to the type you get in class) and are great for reviewing legal concepts in preparation for exams. Grab a friend or study-group member, sit down with a stack of these premade cards (like the Law in a Flash series), and start quizzing each other. Because flashcards generally have a hypothetical on one side and possible answer choices on the other, you have plenty of material to discuss and debate with your partner for hours! You can buy these cards online and in your law school bookstore, among other places.

>> **Upper-division students' outlines:** No law student's study aid arsenal is complete without a bevy of outlines from upper-division students. These outlines are invaluable because students who actually took your course wrote them.

TIP

Whatever you do, don't pass through your three to four years of school without becoming intimately familiar with everything the law library can do to help you. Make a point of meeting and greeting your law librarians, who want to help you get the most out of the law library. They're well equipped to point you toward resources you never knew existed, give you a head start on your legal research, and show you how to use the many online databases your library subscribes to. At many schools, you can even make personalized appointments to sit down with the librarians for help devising a research strategy for a paper or brief. The librarians can help you expand your search terms and lead you to obscure old-school sources on microfilm or microfiche (or they can at least show you how to use these complicated-looking devices).

Chapter **15**

Acing Your Law School Exams

You've taken copious notes, attended class (most of the time), and met with your study group religiously. Now the heat is on, and it's time to show what you know! Of course, no one particularly enjoys the stress, nail-biting, and all-nighters that inevitably surround law school exams, especially if they're all one-shot deals. But if you follow the tips and advice in this chapter, you can pass your finals with flying colors. So whip out that outline, charge your laptop, and get your notepad ready, because Dean's List, here you come!

Mastering the Most Common Exam Types

After the Socratic method (which I cover in Chapter 12), the second most universally feared aspect of the law school experience is an exam, the three-to-four-hour test given at the end of all first year (1L) — and most 2L, 3L, and 4L — courses. Although you probably experienced essay, multiple-choice, and short-answer exams in college, you've probably never had anything quite like the tests given in law school.

That's because law school exams are a unique breed. Their uniqueness lies in the fact that instead of merely asking you to regurgitate information, they test your ability to issue-spot, which refers to identifying the conflicts between rules of law. Issue-spotting is hardly an innate skill; it's what you've been exposed to in class and in your own studying throughout the semester. (That's probably why law schools test it.) I get into this skill in the "Issue-spotting: The name of the game in fact patterns" section later in the chapter.

REMEMBER

Regardless of which exam format ultimately confronts you (and I describe each of them in the following sections), keep in mind that you need to approach all your studying in the same way: by creating an outline and doing practice exams (both of which are covered in Chapter 13). You also need to divvy up your time to adjust for exams that weigh more heavily in your GPA. The general rule at most schools is that you have one hour worth of exam per credit hour of the course. For example, if your civil procedure class is three credit hours, you'll have a three-hour final exam.

TIP

One of the more important resources you have at your disposal is other students. The ones who have taken your course in the past can give you the lowdown on the exam (whether it's closed- or open-book and the difficulty level), tell you what sort of questions your professor favors, and explain how your professor wants the exam written.

Essays

Essays are by far the most common type of law school exam, which is comforting in one respect. Unlike all-or-nothing multiple-choice tests, essays at least give you the chance to earn partial credit. On the other hand, the sheer amount of writing you do in a semester's worth of essay finals isn't so comforting. I hope you came to law school liking to read, write, and type, because you do a heck of a lot of it.

A typical three-hour essay exam usually consists of three essays. You write all the essays in a *blue book* (test-taking booklet) or in exam software on a computer. Most professors don't give you a page or blue-book limit; however, I've never needed to use more than three or four blue books for a single exam. Professors also vary on whether they want you to use a fresh blue book for each essay.

Introducing the fact pattern format

Describing these tests as essay exams is kind of misleading. You certainly don't see the typical essays that you had in college, such as "compare and contrast the U.S. Civil War with the French Revolution." After you set eyes on your first law school exam, you know you're not in Kansas anymore. That's because rather than a normal essay you have what's called a fact pattern.

Think of *fact patterns* as a variation on the story problem (like the kind you had to solve in high school algebra). The purpose of this traditional law school exam approach is to highlight the overlapping subtleties of various legal principles. Basically, your professor takes a bunch of (sometimes outrageous) facts and puts them into a hypothetical story format. Recall the types of facts you've read in cases all semester. When you weave six or seven of those fact patterns into a story (liberally embedded with issues), you come up with something that resembles a law school exam.

WARNING

Fact patterns run quite long. In a three-hour essay exam, they're each generally a page to two pages. But despite their length, not every fact in the fact pattern is important in your answer. Keep in mind that your professor purposely inserts a few *red herrings* (extraneous facts) to throw you off track. Top students can spot these red herrings, briefly identify them as irrelevant in their answer, and move on with the rest of their discussion.

Issue-spotting: The name of the game in fact patterns

The point of having a fact pattern as an exam is to test your skills at issue-spotting. *Issue-spotting* is exactly what it sounds like: identifying an *issue* (the conflicts between rules of law) in a fact pattern. You've had plenty of practice spotting issues in fact patterns all semester because that's what your professors help you discover when giving you hypotheticals (which I cover in Chapter 12) in class.

When you spot an issue in your fact pattern, point, you want to do the following:

>> State the issue.

>> Specify the relevant rule(s).

>> Apply the law to the facts and analyze why the rule should or shouldn't be applied to those facts (arguments for and against).

>> Provide a conclusion (take a stand) on how the issue should be resolved.

Professors allot points based on how many issues you spot. In a typical one-hour single fact pattern, you can find as many as 10 to 20 separate issues. Professors also award points for how well you discuss the issues and how well you view the complexities (such as subissues and exceptions) that are involved.

TIP

Most essay exams are structured so that almost all students can spot basic issues. From there, however, your professor inserts subtler issues. Students who score high grades successfully spot more of these subissues than their peers.

TIP

As you're working through a fact pattern, you may find that physically crossing out issues that you've already spotted and discussed can help you stay on track and avoid redundancy. Another helpful tactic is having a *checklist* (an extensively whittled-down outline) handy. Your checklist can show, in abbreviated form, all the possible issues for the course. When you're taking the exam, you run down your checklist and ask yourself, "Does this question touch on any of these issues?" Flip to Chapter 13 for more details about outlines and checklists.

Watching out for the policy question

A *policy question* asks you to evaluate a particular court's stance on an issue, discuss a legal idea or theory, or comment on a recurring theme of the course. Many law school essay exams include a policy question in addition to two or three fact patterns. Nearly all my law school essay exams (and most take-home tests) had them.

A typical policy question could be something like this: "Choose three cases we read over the semester and discuss how you'd rule differently." On some of my law school exams, professors would take a quote that we'd never talked about and make it the policy question by saying, "Discuss how this quote applies in the context of this course." In other words, it's more like a typical college essay question.

Policy questions may cause you to breathe a huge sigh of relief, because it's an area on the exam where poor issue-spotters can redeem themselves. Because your answer can be more touchy-feely than a typical fact pattern answer, you may think you have more freedom to experiment; however, don't make the mistake of thinking that you don't need to study for the policy question. After all, in a three-hour exam, a policy question may count as one-third of your grade. So when you want to earn maximum points (and who doesn't?), giving some serious thought to what your professor may ask actually pays off.

Predicting the policy question doesn't need to be a daunting task. Just think back to what your professor stressed during the semester. Were they keen on feminist or economic theories? Make sure you review your notes about these areas thoroughly. Did they assign outside articles on a particular topic? Find those articles and reread them before the exam. If you need help brainstorming possible policy question topics, get together with a classmate, your study group, or your TA and start throwing around possibilities. (You can read more about study groups in Chapter 13.)

In writing your response to the policy question, you depart from the traditional law school exam writing approach I outline in the following section. Instead, try writing it the way you'd respond to a college essay. Concentrate on making as many points as possible and tying different aspects of your course together. Organization is key; sketching out a rough mini-outline of the points you want to make is always a good bet.

Writing the essay answer

Simply knowing the material cold isn't enough to score a top mark in law school. In addition, you must master the art of analyzing and writing the law school exam. The majority of law school professors are quite particular about how they want their exams written. Here are some key factors to keep in mind as you write your answers.

>> **Organize, organize, organize.** Your professor doesn't want to wade through a hodgepodge of random thoughts and observations; instead, you need to state each issue in a topic sentence and then arrange your discussion of that particular issue underneath. In other words, if stream of consciousness is your writing trademark, you need to find a new style during exam season. One of the best ways to ensure top-notch organization is to sketch a rough outline of the issues and subissues you want to cover, in order, in a scratch blue book or inside your exam itself. This way, you can continually check against your outline that you're heading in the right direction.

The reason professors stress good organization is that they don't want to see anyone changing gears mid-paragraph or switching their stand on an issue halfway through the discussion. That signals to them that you don't have a clue what you're talking about. And on an exam, being perceived as incompetent is the last thing you want.

>> **Write clearly and plainly.** This isn't a literature exam; you aren't being graded on your literary skills or your grasp of difficult nonlegal vocabulary. The simpler and more pared-down your writing style, the better. Get to the point in as few words as possible and leave the flowery language for your career as a novelist.

>> **Do a thorough analysis.** Lawyers are precise; they don't make blanket statements without explaining them. Thoroughly explore each assertion you make by applying the law to the facts. If you merely state the relevant law without explaining how that law applies to your particular situation, your analysis is incomplete, and you'll be docked major points.

A good analysis always includes *counterarguments* — arguments that are in opposition to your main argument. Incorporating all counterarguments shows your professor that you can anticipate what the opposing side will do next, an impressive skill that shows mastery of the case's core elements.

>> **State your conclusion.** At the end of your analysis, always make sure to formulate a conclusion, such as "the situation suggests there was a battery." However, don't use definitive language in your conclusory statement, such as "this definitely was a battery." Nothing in law is black and white, and your professor appreciates that you're comfortable with uncertainty when you suggest rather than assert.

Multiple-choice

If you're like me, you view multiple-choice exams as a mixed blessing. Sure, you don't have to do any writing, but unfortunately, a question has only one right (or "best") answer. In general, you don't see many multiple-choice exams in law school; they're far less common than essay exams. Some professors, however, give you half and half — half multiple-choice and half essay.

Multiple-choice exams tend to fall into three camps:

>> Those consisting of mini-fact patterns (covered in the "Introducing the fact pattern" section earlier in the chapter)

>> Those consisting of short questions about *black letter law* (well-established legal rules)

>> Those consisting of mini-fact patterns and short black letter law questions

The frustrating thing about multiple-choice exams is that two of the answer choices often can be hair-splittingly close. Agonizing over which of the two answers is the right one can take a lot of time, and time is always at a premium on multiple-choice exams. In fact, on many law school multiple-choice exams, your time allotment averages out to between two and three minutes per question.

The trick to multiple-choice exams is understanding the format ahead of time. The best way to do so is by getting ahold of the professor's previous exams (like other types of exams, they're usually on reserve in the library under your professor's name or on the course's website) to see what the questions were like and to practice with them.

Short-answer

Short-answer exams give you either a mini-fact pattern to answer, as in a regular essay exam, or questions about black letter law. They differ from multiple-choice exams in that you're writing out the answer in (short) essay form in a blue book or exam software. Sometimes these exams involve one- to two-sentence answers; other times, you write a few paragraphs.

These exams are relatively uncommon in law school, but you prepare for them the way you would for the other two types of exams: by creating outlines (see Chapter 13) and by finding past exams to look over.

Take-home exams

Yet another type of exam you may encounter at law school is the take-home. *Take-home exams* are a cross between an exam and a paper. Take-homes often require very lengthy answers. Having to type up five to eight pages per question isn't uncommon. How many questions appear on your take-home varies, but three-credit courses usually feature three questions. *Note:* You probably won't get any as a 1L because 1L professors tend to stick with essays and multiple-choice exams, but they're quite common from 2L on.

You may remember the take-home from college. Unlike papers, with a take-home you generally aren't required to use footnotes or endnotes and proper *Blue Book* style (a citation manual for the legal profession) or write in an overly scholarly way. But unlike in-class exams, you usually get a more generous time limit of 48 hours to a week for your take-homes.

In my opinion, take-home exams are the worst possible type, because they're long, drawn-out ordeals rather than quick and painless three-hour jobs. In fact, many students avoid classes that are known to have a take-home for the final because losing momentum is easy when you have an entire weekend or week to complete an exam. But if you enjoy the flexibility and the lack of time pressure they offer, you'll want to register for as many classes with take-home exams as you can.

Open versus closed book

One aspect of law school that genuinely surprised me is how many exams are open book/open note. One of the rationales for open-book exams in law school is that lawyers always keep their own books around so they can look things up. When a client walks into your office, you obviously need to have a certain level of legal mastery, but beyond that, you can always look up anything you don't know about in the case law or statutes. Open-book exams validate the idea that lawyers don't need to memorize everything.

REMEMBER

Even though you have your notes and books around for open-book exams, don't think you can locate everything you need to know while you're actually taking the exam. Most professors write their questions so that you can't find any "easy" answers in your books or notes. Many students taking open-book exams discover they don't even have time to peruse their materials. Only diligent preparation beforehand can adequately prepare you for these exams.

Regardless of the philosophy behind open- and closed-book exams, most students simply want to know which type is harder. Here is a rundown of their differences so you can judge for yourself:

>> **Some people find that open-book exams are more stressful.** Between your books, notes, and outline, you have plenty of material to sift through to find the answers in a short time period. However, psychologically, you may feel like you don't need to study that much before your open-book exam because you have everything right there. The presence of their notes and books makes some people overconfident; they think they'll have ample time to dig around for what they don't know. This rationalization may backfire, especially when you're confronted with questions that you didn't adequately prepare for (or your outline is a disorganized mess).

>> **Myth: Closed-book exams often don't go as deep.** Professors are human; they know you can recall only so much from memory. Nevertheless, closed-book exams can be very difficult. In my experience, questions on closed-book exams tend to probe at the same level of difficulty as the ones on open-book exams. Students who are good at memorization usually excel on closed-book exams.

>> **Some students freeze on closed-book exams.** They see a blank blue book and suddenly can't remember a thing they studied. Tensing up when you don't have your notes or books around as a comfort is pretty common, but I always found that re-reading the questions got me to relax and allowed me to look for even the smallest issues I recognized. Doing a *brain dump* — where you use the first ten minutes of the exam to write all the important things you can remember on your scratch paper — always helped me immensely on closed-book exams.

>> **In open-book exams, many students find the presence of their notes, books, and outlines immensely comforting.** For these students, the presence of these items helps them relax and perform better because they know their safety net is right in front of them. Additionally, when your outline is outstanding, you can easily find what you need.

>> **Some professors are stricter than others.** They may limit how long your outline can be or restrict you to a tax code book/list, a statutory supplement, a professor-approved cheat sheet, and they make check to make sure you

have no notes on the pages of your book. Please review the syllabus and notes about what is allowed very carefully. Some law schools will have the exam proctors review the materials prior to the exam start time to ensure there are not additional notes, tips, and so on in the book or on the document you are bringing into the exam room.

Understanding Your School's Exam System

Law schools across the country may have very different rules, policies, and procedures for exam taking. Your professors usually inform you about the school's policies, but when you're in doubt, see the academic dean and/or the dean of students.

Getting used to being anonymous

Most law schools use *the anonymous exam system*. The registrar or some type of university software assigns each student a randomly generated exam number that changes every semester. The *exam number* is your test identification. Instead of putting your name on the exam and/or blue book, you write only your exam number. That way, the professor has no idea who wrote what until after they submit the exam grades to the registrar. At that point, many registrars provide faculty members with a class list with the grades matched up with the names, thus enabling faculty members to adjust the grade up or down one notch to account for extraordinary class participation or lack thereof (or poor attendance).

WARNING

Be sure to keep up with your exam number. Ideally, you want to memorize it each time it changes. The last thing you need is to show up the morning of an exam and not have it. In some instances, someone onsite may be able to assist you, but even then, you may miss the start of the exam (and the proctors aren't going to give you more time).

Dealing with only one exam per course

Most law schools have just one exam that determines your entire grade in a course. Many law students find this one-exam concept nerve-wracking. After all, one bad exam day, and your GPA can be irrevocably damaged. Chapter 9 has more on the one-exam format.

As a 2L, 3L, and 4L, you may be able to find classes that offer a paper in place of an exam as the sole form of evaluation, or a class that offers a paper and a final. And some law schools now offer midterm exams. Sometimes these tests are graded, while others simply give you an idea about how well you're keeping up with the materials, how strong your notes and outline may be, and so on.

Preferring a paper to an exam

The one-exam format in the preceding section is the gold standard, and papers are more of an exception to the rule. Legal research and writing is usually the only "paper" class for 1Ls, but you may have more options for paper classes as a 2L and 3L. Third- and fourth-year seminars, for instance, may have a research paper, and potentially an in-person component, as their forms of evaluation. (Chapter 18 has more on seminars.) Many schools offer advanced legal writing and other classes where multiple short papers make up your grade.

Although your school likely doesn't offer enough paper classes to take three or four each upper-class semester, do peruse your course catalog or academic schedule if this option interests you. Realistically, you'll be able to find one or two paper courses per semester at most law schools.

The following are some reasons that you may prefer having a paper as your final evaluation:

>> **A paper enables you to work at your own pace.** You can work on it throughout the semester without any stress from cramming at the last minute. You don't need to methodically spill the contents of your brain during a three-hour time period; instead, you can refine your thoughts more or less at your leisure. The only due dates for papers tend to be those for turning in the topic selection, outline, and rough draft.

>> **A paper is more collaborative.** When taking an exam, you're completely on your own, but with a paper you can usually discuss your thesis and argument development with your professor. In addition, you can sometimes talk with other students and practitioners about the key issues when writing a paper. But different professors have different rules about whether and how much you can collaborate; check with your professor and the syllabus for guidelines.

>> **A paper allows you to conduct a more in-depth exploration of a subject.** Although you may yearn to cover all of trademark law in a three-hour exam, you probably won't even scratch the surface. In a paper, on the other hand, you usually have much more space to discuss the issues.

Coasting on the curve

Although all law school professors grade differently, they almost all use some sort of curve. Unlike in college, where you were graded on how you performed independent of your peers in most classes, the law school curve more or less pits you and your classmates against each other. For that reason (among others), law school sometimes has a cutthroat reputation. The good news is that because grading is anonymous, you can work with your classmates and study groups to ensure you all understand the topics the professor has outlined — and potentially force your professors to ask for an exception to the curve because you all did so well.

Preparing for Midterms

Think of midterms as a midsemester checkpoint. They're your opportunity to get a taste of what the final exam prep and experience are like and how much you know. They're also an excellent chance to determine whether you can communicate to your professor that you're grasping the material and can spot the issues, apply the rules, and provide thoughtful analysis in that professor's exam format.

Not all law schools offer midterms. But if they do, consider it a bonus!

Reviewing old exams

As I note throughout the book, looking over past exams is a tried and true method of preparing for exams and understanding your professor.

Evaluating your midterm grades

After you have completed your first law school exam or exams, you need to take some time to figure out what you did right and what, if anything, went wrong. Check in with your study group leader and/or professor for the following:

>> **If you did well:** Find out more about what else you could've done to earn an even higher grade!

>> **If you didn't do well:** You want to take advantage of their expertise, guidance, and wisdom. Especially if you thought you'd done well, they can help you figure out what went wrong, what you missed, and what you may need to do to improve your study habits, notetaking, and outlining to ensure you perform better on the final exam.

Embracing Exam Day Survival Strategies

The day you've been waiting for is finally here! You're prepared, and you know what's expected of you. Now all you need to do is spill the contents of your brain. Knowing the material is only part of the battle. The rest depends on how well you present your answers, follow your professor's instructions, and manage your time and stress.

Knowing what's allowed

Before the day of the exam, make sure you know exactly what you're allowed to take into the exam. You don't want to make the mistake of bringing in your books only to find out at the last minute that the test is closed book. Similarly, your professor may specify that bringing in, say, your statutory book is okay but your casebook isn't. Or that only outlines you prepare yourself (not commercial study aids) are acceptable. (Chapters 13 and 14 cover homemade outlines and commercial study aids, respectively.) Make sure to clarify any confusion beforehand; otherwise, you're bound for disaster.

TIP

Also check the rules on earplugs, drinks, snacks, hoodies, blankets, highlighters, and so on. You don't want to show up counting on stuff you can't have or fail to bring totally allowable items that would've helped you (like snacks if you need brain food to focus for several hours).

Updating your exam software

Work with your help desk, IT department, registrar's office, and/or academic success/support professors to confirm you know exactly what software you need to take your exams. Many law schools share this information before orientation so you can buy the laptop that is most compatible with the software you need. Don't make the mistake of just buying what you want without double-checking.

Ensuring your exam accommodations have been approved

If you had accommodations in undergrad or grad school, you'll likely need them in law school. Be sure to keep all your documentation and follow the steps and deadlines your law school outlines for securing those services. And don't hesitate to follow up with the appropriate office; depending on the school, accommodation requests may be handled by student affairs, the registrar's office, the office of accessibility, or a main campus's student affairs office.

If you aren't sure whether you need accommodations, get testing. Your dean of students and your academic success professors may be able to help you identify what issues you're having and what may help you become more successful in law school.

REMEMBER

The testing process can take some time and be very expensive, but it's important. You don't want to suffer through law school when you could have additional support, resources, and help. Plus, any accommodations you need in law school you'll probably need for the bar exam as well. Many bar examiners are more likely to grant your request for accommodations for the bar exam if you utilized those resources in law school.

Getting a full night's sleep

Although it sounds basic, getting a good night's sleep is essential if you're going to have enough steam to get through your exam. I know the night owls don't believe me, but law school exams are different. You need to be mentally and physically rested. Even the most well-rested student is going to feel a drop in energy somewhere toward the end of a three- or four-hour exam. If you've gotten only three hours of sleep the night before, you'll barely make it past the first question without your thoughts turning from criminal law to your comfy bed.

REMEMBER

Staying up until the wee hours cramming the night before can be counterproductive. If you don't know your stuff by the evening before the exam, you're never going to. Resting so you can focus and provide a thoughtful response leads to a much better outcome.

Understanding what professors love to see in an exam

Ask any professor what makes up a good exam, and you're likely to hear similar answers. I asked a bunch of professors what qualities they always find in A exams. Here's what I found, straight from the horses' mouths (so to speak). Professors suggest that you always do the following:

>> **Read the instructions, and then read them again.** Many professors lament that they read exams marred by one fatal flaw: Students fail to answer the question that's asked. Sure, you may write an A answer, but if you answer a different question (perhaps the one you wish your professor had asked), you're not going to score many points.

>> **Heed time limits.** Many professors do you the favor of specifying how long you need to spend on each exam question. If the instructions say to spend

30 minutes on the first, an hour on the second, and an hour and a half on the third, you do yourself an injustice by spending 20 minutes on the first two questions combined and two hours and 40 minutes on the last. Make sure you stick to prescribed time limits.

>> **Answer questions in the order they're presented.** The professor probably put the questions in a specific order for a reason. Often, the second question builds off the first, so if you start there, you miss some key issues that you may have seen otherwise had you answered them in the correct order.

>> **When you're running out of time, outline the remainder of your answer.** Professors understand that students sometimes run out of time on exams. When that happens (particularly on the last question of the exam), just write the remaining part of your answer in outline form. Although you'll probably receive only partial credit, you can at least get some points by letting the professor know that you spotted the issues and knew the right answer.

Typing versus writing (legibly)

Most law schools use exam software and strongly encourage — if not require — students to use laptops for their exams. However, proctors usually have blue books on standby in case of emergency (for example, your laptop dies or the software freezes).

WARNING

Illegible handwritten exams are law school professors' biggest and most universal pet peeve. Although the quality of your analysis is how you score the most exam points, professors subconsciously or even consciously subtract points when they can't make out your writing.

Imagine yourself as a professor reading the 50th student exam. You can barely decipher a single word of the chicken-scratch handwriting in front of you. Would you be likely to give credit for an almost-right answer, or to subconsciously mark the answer more harshly in a fit of annoyance?

Putting forth a little extra effort to write neatly can help you avoid any problems in this area. If you somehow can't find a way to improve your penmanship, you may want to try:

>> Writing in all capital letters

>> Writing on every other line and only one side of the page (which some professors prefer anyway because it makes reading your handwriting easier for them and prevents your ink from bleeding through to the other side of those thin blue book pages)

>> Simply printing (because cursive can be hard to read when you're rushing to get your thoughts on paper)

TIP

During the course of writing an answer, everyone occasionally needs to cross out passages or make additions. Whenever you cross something out, make sure you're thorough so your professor knows not to read it. Likewise, when you need to add something, make an asterisk or a *caret* (∧) symbol and write your addition neatly in the margin or on the line above or below. Just make it clear where exactly the additions need to go. The last thing you want is your professor having to decipher a mess of arrows pointing every which way.

Notifying the proctors if you have special needs

Whether you have medication you need to take or have to take breaks to stand because of back issues, be sure to arrive well before the start of the exam to ensure your proctor knows what you need. Managing expectations and communicating are key to reducing your anxiety and making your exams go smoothly.

Keeping an eye on time

Keeping track of time during your exam is as important as having pens that work or your laptop charger. The last thing you want to hear your test proctor saying is "Okay, time's up," especially when you've just started on the second question. That's why you need to watch the clock (or whatever devices your law school allows) at all times.

One way to ensure that time's on your side is by heeding the suggestions your professor makes regarding the amount of time to devote to each question.

Similarly, whenever you finish your exam early, don't be one of those triumphant people marching up to the front of the room and smugly depositing their exams in the box with an hour to spare. Use the remaining time to check your grammar, punctuation, and overall clarity. In fact, you can always go back and add something to your answers or cross out irrelevant passages because doing so may make a noticeable difference in your grade.

Chapter **16**

Starting Your Second Semester

One semester down, five (full-time students) or seven (part-time students) to go! Now is the time to take what you've learned and apply it to your second term.

You now have lots of experience under your belt. You know your strengths and your weaknesses, so pause for a moment and take stock of what has worked and what you need to change for the semester ahead:

» Who do you need to meet with?

» What if any adjustments do you need to make to your sleep schedule or diet?

» What questions do you need to ask your professors, your support team, and your mentors?

» What do you need more of, and what do you need to eliminate or change altogether?

» Have you managed your funds properly to last this semester?

Managing Your New Schedule

For many American Bar Association (ABA) law schools, the spring semester of the first year is a bit busier and more hectic. You add another course or two, and the unit count is slightly higher. You'll be busy, but you can handle it. Get and stay organized, and prioritize accordingly.

REMEMBER

More is at stake because now you're eyeing the end of your first year and your first-year class rank. Your cumulative GPA is also in sight for the law schools with yearlong courses. Many of the jobs and internships you're looking at have class rank or GPA criteria, so this all matters a bit more than it did in the fall.

That's why you need to take some time to get readjusted. You may need to tweak your study schedule and your study habits. You may need to incorporate more time for things like office hours, study groups, and meetings with your TAs. You're also ramping up your job search, figuring out which student organizations you want to join, thinking about which journal or competition teams you're interested in, and considering which professors you may want to be a TA or research assistant for.

Making the Most Out of Reorientation

So much happens during your orientation that most 1Ls are completely overwhelmed. No one can remember where every single person's office is, their email addresses, or even their names.

That's why some law schools offer reorientation for the second semester. These programs give you a chance to actually reorient yourself — figure out what you may have missed, what you need to focus on during the spring, and when upcoming deadlines, assignments, and programs are. You may hear from faculty members in various departments (such as student affairs, career services/development, financial aid, academic affairs, the registrar, and academic support/success) and find out more about things like clinics and their application process, scholarships, on-campus interviews, and academic assistance/support.

TIP

Not every law school hosts a reorientation, but be sure to participate if yours does, especially if it isn't mandatory. Take advantage of this opportunity to refresh your memory about where to go and who to see for all the administrative issues and tasks you must take care of. Because you have so much experience, much of the information will sink in and be much more applicable to your life as a law student.

Understanding the Importance of Your First-Year Grades

Your first-year (1L) grades tell you where you stand compared to your classmates. But they also show you understand how you performed and what that means for your cumulative GPA, academic standing, and class rank. These stats matter because employers often use your first-year grades as an indication of your skill level and work ethic. (Many often count your previous work experience/résumé, interview, writing sample(s), and so on, too. But the one thing that you'll have in common with every other law student applying for those positions is a first-year GPA.)

REMEMBER

If your grades aren't what you hoped for, take a deep breath and remember that you are not your grades. Everyone always has room for improvement.

By the same token, don't bury your head in the sand. You don't want to ignore the fact that maybe you didn't understand some of the concepts or rules as well as you initially thought. Or that you now recognize you may have, say, a time-management or anxiety issue and need to be tested.

TIP

Seek help so you can perform at the level you expected. Your student affairs office, office of accessibility, and/or academic success office can provide you with guidance, reassurance, and direction.

Meeting with Your Mentors

When you have time to process your GPA and your grades for each course, connect with your mentors. They can give you some insight into how they think you did, why, and what they think you can do to improve or maintain. They can also provide you with emotional support and perspective if you're being too hard on yourself. Level setting (clarifying your needs and expectations) is important, and understanding how to move forward is critical to your success.

REMEMBER

Everyone gets in their own head sometimes and ends up bogged down in the things that don't actually help. Your mentors have been there and have already been through that. They want you to benefit from their wisdom and experience so that you don't make the same mistakes. They can also give you advice on who you should connect with next.

TIP

When you find a good mentor, keep in touch with them. Law students who volunteer to become mentors do so because they want to help. They want to share what they've learned. Most often, these folks are disappointed when they don't hear from their mentees. So take advantage of their time, care, and concern. They want to be there for you. Let them.

Putting in Time with Your Professors

When you have your grades, connect with your professors as soon as possible, especially for the yearlong courses. Whether you did well, so-so, or poorly, you want their insight and feedback — and to demonstrate that you're receptive to their suggestions and guidance.

Your faculty can provide you with valuable insight to understanding what you did correctly and what you missed. *Remember:* Your professors are the ones with the secret sauce. They created the exam and the grading rubric and knew exactly what they were looking for. Talking with them may change how you take notes, prepare for class and exams, and create your outlines.

Bringing in Your Academic Success/ Support Professor(s)

If your grades aren't what you expected, your academic success team can help you assess what steps you need to take to study differently; whether your outlines were on point; and why you may have missed the mark on a certain question.

REMEMBER

Most importantly, your academic support team can help you figure out whether you need to be assessed for a learning difference or learning disability, whether mental health is interfering with your ability to focus, and so on.

Recalibrating Your Approach

Armed with your grades and input from your mentors, faculty members, and academic support professors, you may be ready to make some changes. Consider the following:

>> Do you want to take a different approach this time around?

>> Have you set new goals for yourself?

>> What new self-care habits are you incorporating?

>> What things do you want to change?

>> What things worked that you should keep doing?

REMEMBER

As you rework your approach, you want to find the balance between being realistic and taking advantage of this opportunity to do some things differently.

Preparing for the Summer

How do you make the most of these two to three months you have off? Besides getting some rest and sleeping in, you need a game plan. What are your goals for the summer? Do you want to get ahead in terms of units and credit? Do you want to get experience as well as travel? Do you want to move back home?

Whatever your plan, take the advice and guidance your mentors, career services professionals, professors, and so on have given you. Do everything you can to have a successful second semester so that you can go into the summer feeling like you've done everything possible to ensure the next two to three years are exactly what you need to become the attorney you want to be.

REMEMBER

Overall, you want to make sure you put yourself in a position to relax and also gain invaluable experience to add to your résumé as you begin applying what you learned throughout the year.

Attending summer school

With summer school, you have to think through financial aid issues such as loan eligibility. If you have a full-time summer internship, can you take summer courses virtually? And consider how much per unit those courses cost, because as I discuss in Chapters 5 and 17, scholarships at most ABA law schools often don't cover summer school. (Some law schools allow you to cover any units up to the graduation requirement unit count, but that's rare.)

TIP

If you take summer courses, you want to make sure you keep your grades up because they impact your cumulative GPA. Some students take one difficult course during the summer to ensure that it's the only course they have to focus on.

Doing an internship/externship

You want to make sure you make a great impression on your internship or externship. The goal is to be invited back. Position yourself to be as competitive as possible by completing your assignments on time, understanding what's being asked of you, asking thoughtful questions, dressing professionally, understanding the organization's culture, and conducting your research (and then citing it correctly).

TIP

As you make new connections, ensure you keep in touch with everyone you meet.

Chapter **17**

Making the Most of Your 1L Summer

You might think that summer vacation is the time to, well, take a vacation. When you're in law school, that's not exactly true. While you should take some time to decompress, you should also be looking to improve your academic standing, take part in additional coursework, and maybe even get a summer job in the legal profession. This chapter covers those options.

Focusing on Academic Endeavors

During the summer, you have a variety of opportunities to learn and explore the law in different settings, including potentially taking law classes. I discuss a few of those options in this section.

Studying abroad

Studying abroad is a great opportunity to explore a new country and city while also learning international principles of law and gaining credit, legal experience in another jurisdiction, and a global perspective.

Many American Bar Association (ABA) law schools have their own study abroad programs, but the beautiful thing is that you can attend a study abroad program offered by another ABA institution. It's a fairly easy process: All you have to do is be admitted to that program, ask your law school to verify which credits can transfer back to your home institution, and obtain a letter of good standing. Your home school processes your financial aid, and then you pay the other law school.

Exploring exchange programs

These programs allow you to study as a student at another law school. The exchange principle is similar to what you may know from undergrad: Two institutions One US and one International) agree on a program that allows students to participate in a program at another institution either internationally or domestically. A domestic exchange means you can focus on an area of law that your law school doesn't specialize in.

Exchanges often happen over the summer (though you can also find programs that take place during the academic year). You receive approval to attend another law school and take advantage of their courses, programs, and resources, but your home law school remains "your" law school.

Sticking around for summer school

Many law students want to get ahead of their required courses, so they opt to take them during the summer so that they don't have to mess with them during the academic year while they're trying to work.

TIP

Summer school is also a good way to get ahead on credits now so that during your last year of law school, you can focus on bar-related courses or take a lighter load as you begin bar prep.

WARNING

For most law schools, merit scholarships and even need-based scholarships may not cover the cost of summer school. Look into the terms and conditions of your scholarships so you know where you stand. One other thing to note is that to obtain financial aid during the summer, you must be enrolled as a student at your home law school (or in one of the study abroad or exchange programs I cover in the preceding sections). Most students use loans to cover their summer courses.

Reviewing Your 1L Grades and Class Rank

The time has come! You've completed your first year of law school. You're preparing for your first internship or externship or packing for your trip abroad.

Now it's time to figure out how you did and how you can improve.

Meeting with your professors and the academic support team

As you get ready to roll into your 1L summer, you're in a good position to check in with your professors and the academic support staff to address what went right and what (if anything) went wrong. These meetings are much like the ones I suggest you set up after your first semester; you can read about those in Chapter 16. But you now have an entire year under your belt. Now, your questions — what you may need to prepare for your summer courses and/or next academic year, and how to plan your schedule now that you get to make it — will be more nuanced and sophisticated because you are now a 2L!

TIP

If you implemented any changes after those first-semester meetings, these end-of-year chats are a great place to evaluate how your new approaches worked and adjust them if necessary.

REMEMBER

The students who do well in law school often seek out support from the academic success/support department. Their role is to guide you and to provide you with advice (and sometimes tough love and a reality check). They can help you diagnose what may be going on when you feel like you're struggling or just not getting a concept. Get to know your academic support team as soon as possible — ideally, during orientation if not before.

Updating your résumé

At the end of your 1L year, be sure to bring your LinkedIn account and résumé up-to-date. Be sure to include the following:

>> Your class rank (if your law school ranks the students), though most students only mention this info if they're in the top 20 percent or 25 percent of their class

>> Any extracurriculars you've signed up for, such as the following (you can find more on these activities in Chapter 19)

- Law review

- The mock trial or moot court team

- Any clubs or organizations

- Any TA or research assistant position you've been offered

» Any awards or recognitions you received, such as a CALI award (so called because it's presented by the Center for Computer-Assisted Legal Instruction) for earning the highest grade in the class

» Any scholarships you earned

Deciding Whether to Stay or Go

After your first year, you may face a decision about whether to stay at your current law school or attempt to transfer to another ABA school because of lifestyle changes, a spouse or partner that needs to move, or whatever. You may also consider visiting a school near home or a law school that has some specific courses or programs that you're interested in that your law school doesn't offer. (*Visiting* is taking a course or two at another law school.) The following sections cover some of the specific rules and parameters that can guide this decision.

Transferring

In short, a transfer means you become a new student at a new institution, and that's the institution you'll graduate from. For some, it's a unique opportunity to attend a school that they initially weren't admitted to.

WARNING

The decision to transfer is a significant one. It impacts your class standing and rank; your access to scholarships; and your ability to join law review, moot court, and honor boards, among other things, depending on each school's guidelines. Plus, the ongoing changes to on-campus interviews (OCI) and the earlier recruitment dates may impact your ability to be viewed for certain firms and organizations, depending on when you're admitted as a transfer student.

REMEMBER

Pay close attention to the deadlines and requirements. To transfer to some institutions, you have to rank at a certain place in your class at your home law school. For others, it depends on your GPA and LSAT score(s) and GPA after your first complete year at your home law school. Some law schools require a letter of good standing in addition to some type of Dean's certification, letter from a law professor at your home law school, and so on.

Visiting

When you visit another school, you basically spend a semester at another institution. Your home law school's academic affairs office or dean of students approves which courses can transfer back to that school. Note that some law schools allow you to visit only if you're taking courses that the home school doesn't offer. Your home law school serves as your base for financial aid and everything else. And after you receive your disbursement, you are responsible for paying the host law school. The remaining funds are to be used for your living expenses.

Doing Some Work During Your 1L Summer

How do you make the best impression on your new legal employer? How do you ensure that you're invited back for another opportunity — or make the most of the current one when you realize you don't love what you're doing?

TIP

The biggest piece of advice that I've heard from hiring partners and managers is that they expect you to show up and do the work. If you say you're interested in returning, you need to demonstrate that through your work product.

Legal jobs

REMEMBER

In legal jobs, you're working as a lawyer. They require a law degree and a bar license.

The way that NALP tracks these jobs is tied directly to jobs that require a license or require that you be barred to apply for the position, employer type, and funding sources. For statistical purposes, the ABA requires that the employment statistics are based on employment 10 months after graduation.

These roles include everything from an associate attorney to a judicial clerk to district attorney or public defender. You can find them in law firms/private practice, government agencies, and public interest organizations.

Nonlegal (or JD Advantage) jobs

Not to be confused with illegal (unlawful) jobs, *nonlegal* or *JD Advantage* jobs allow you to use your legal education and training but don't require you to have a license. These jobs do count in employment as statistics.

Nonlegal jobs may include the following (among many, many other roles):

>> Law school professor or administrator

>> Law librarian

>> Human resources or hospital compliance

>> Lobbyist

>> Law-enforcement

>> Nonprofit manager

>> Intellectual property analyst

Nonlegal jobs have been an exciting area of growth for the legal profession. (I know, the irony.) They've allowed grads to explore many more opportunities they're interested in.

4

You're Almost There: 2Ls and 3Ls

Select a course load and satisfy graduation requirements.

Take part in extracurricular activities such as law review, moot court, and more.

IN THIS CHAPTER

» Envisioning your ideal schedule

» Selecting the right electives

» Finding real-world experience somewhere other than a lecture hall

» Opting for non-law classes

» Understanding your study-abroad options

Chapter **18**

Choosing Courses, Concentrations, and Clinics

You've made it through torts, crushed your legal research and writing assignments, and aced your first year (1L) exams. Now that you're officially an upperclass student, you probably wonder whether that oft-quoted law school saying "The second year they work you to death; the third they bore you to death" is actually true. Guess what! It doesn't have to be when you choose your courses wisely.

REMEMBER

As a 2L, 3L, and 4L, you're in complete control of your schedule. With the possible exception of a few graduation requirements, you therefore have the freedom to mix and match your courses at will. Finally, you can focus on feminist jurisprudence or Internet law rather than the standard 1L fare.

So what are the *best* courses to take? That's the subject of this chapter. I walk you through the most important criteria to consider when creating your schedule and introduce you to time-honored strategies for choosing your electives. I also cover the frequently overlooked option of taking courses outside the law school and the adventure that awaits you through study-abroad options. With the right combination of advance planning and self-assessment, you'll remember your upper-class years as an intellectual smorgasbord for years to come.

Selecting a Successful Course Load

All law students choose classes in their own unique ways. Some students pick them based on what excites them at the time; others strategize based on an ideal schedule (such as no early morning classes or no Friday classes). And still others focus on packing in all the *bar courses* — classes that are highly recommended in preparation for the bar exam. (See Chapter 24 for detailed information about the bar exam.) A few try a different approach every semester of law school. The decision is all yours.

TIP

Because upper-division students take their classes together, you may find that some of the less-popular courses are offered only every other year. For optimal planning, review the most recent law school *course schedule,* which usually notes which courses aren't offered the following year.

TIP

Second-year law students may want to consider a lighter course load during the fall semester, when their time is nearly monopolized by interviewing, cite-checking for journals, and the moot court competition. Between the extracurriculars and the summer job search, you'll be very busy. This time often becomes overwhelming for some students and can feel like another high-stakes class.

During the third year and fourth year, academics notoriously take a back seat to job searching, studying for the bar, or sometimes just having a good time. Additionally, some students contract *senioritis* the day they accept a job offer, and they slack off the rest of the semester (or year). Professors tend to expect this reaction, but keeping up with your courses and putting in as much effort as you can is still a good idea. After all, you're paying good money for a legal education. Do your best to keep your grades up. You don't want an employer to ask to see your final transcript and see that you didn't finish on a high note.

But now that you get to decide what classes you take, you should try to take courses you're really interested in, like advanced secured transactions or international tax law.

Satisfying graduation requirements

For better or worse, satisfying graduation requirements is the most important aspect of choosing a good course load, because not doing so means you won't graduate. Before throwing down your course schedule in frustration, bear in mind that many law schools allow you to satisfy their graduation requirements with courses of your own choosing.

Some law schools will use an electronic *degree audit tool* to help you track your graduation requirements. The number of units required to graduate, required courses, upper-division writing requirements, bar-tested recommended courses, etc., are in the electronic program. The program uses the data from your registrar's office to determine what courses you have taken, which courses remain out of your required courses, and potentially what courses you need to take to satisfy a specific emphasis or specialization.

If your law school does not use degree audit software, you will track your progress the good old-fashioned modern way pen and paper or a spreadsheet! Don't forget to work with your Dean of Students and/or Registrar!

Most law schools have several graduation requirements, often involving professional responsibility (PR), several writing courses, and a research paper seminar course.

Law schools have introduced different courses into the first-year curriculum along with the required or suggested courses. The subjects include tax, federal income tax, and professionalism. The traditional courses on contracts, torts, property, and so on are still part of the first-year curriculum.

Many schools don't mandate that you take these required courses at any specific time during your upperclass years. Some require you to take, say, the writing course during the second year and the research paper seminar course during the third or fourth. Knowing that you often have a wide variety of courses to satisfy any writing or perspectives requirements is exciting.

Focusing on courses tested on the bar exam

Some courses come highly recommended as great preparation for students who plan on taking the bar exam. These classes may include the following:

>> Corporations

>> Evidence

>> Family law

>> Wills and trusts

>> Sales

>> Secured transactions

>> Criminal procedure

REMEMBER

Check your jurisdiction to find out exactly what appears on its bar exam; specific requirements vary from state to state.

Although taking these courses isn't a requirement for taking the bar exam (you'll learn everything you need to know about these courses later in your bar exam prep course), many law students end up signing up for them because of the extra confidence that doing so gives them heading into the bar exam. Some of the courses, such as corporations and secured transactions, can be more challenging, and some people believe they need the reinforcement that taking them provides before the bar.

If you decide that taking the bar exam isn't the right choice for you, you can still take any of the bar courses just for personal knowledge and/or a well-rounded legal education. If you don't take the bar exam, you still emerge from law school a JD like everyone else, but you won't be a practicing lawyer. And today, many positions prefer a JD but not a license. Just know that you have options!

Discovering the value of practice-related courses

Although law students don't have majors, if you know what area of law you want to specialize in, you may be able to find specializations, emphasis programs, or concentrations that suggest certain classes. For example, if you're set on being an entertainment lawyer, your academic dean, dean of students, or similar faculty member can provide you with some guidance on what courses may be most beneficial to you.

Making room for courses that interest you

After the graduation requirements are out of the way, you can really roll up your sleeves and dig into the fun stuff: whatever interests you. No longer limited to torts, contracts, and civil procedure as you were as a 1L, you can now try your hand at estate planning, trial process, environmental law, or health law. Your law school course schedule is full of thought-provoking courses, such as land-use controls and negotiable instruments. By your upperclass years, you've learned most of the basics; now you can find your true calling, if you haven't already.

Some people know right away what they're interested in; others, particularly students with minimal pre–law school exposure to the law, don't have a clue. Your second, third, and fourth years are the perfect times to take a wide assortment of random courses. Try family law, real estate finance, bankruptcy, international human rights, and federal criminal law all in one semester. A diverse schedule is the best way to dabble in different subject areas.

Another strategy is to take as many *survey courses* (those that introduce you to a broad overview of the subject matter, such as introduction to environmental law versus public natural resources law) as possible as a 2L. Then, as a 3L or 4L, go in-depth into some of the areas that you enjoyed most the year before. Doing so may help you understand the foundations and later augment them with more focused courses.

REMEMBER

Although finding courses that you're interested in as a 2L is pretty easy, during the second semester the third year, you may find that you've already taken all the courses you're interested in and are forced to register for the leftovers. Even in that situation, be bold and experiment. You may find yourself loving advanced corporate taxation law far more than you ever dreamed.

WARNING

Pay close attention to the course schedule. You don't want to plan on taking that last course for a specialty area to later discover that the faculty member is on sabbatical. And if you don't find what you're looking for, ask the registrar or academic dean about that specialty course you're interested in.

Working toward a comfortable exam schedule

Generally, law school exams are scheduled for the last two weeks or so at the end of each semester. Your exam schedule can make or break you. Whenever you have two exams scheduled on a single day, have two or more slated on consecutive days, or have all your exams squeezed in one week, you risk getting burned out faster than if your exams are scheduled at a more leisurely pace.

That's why some law students choose their classes based primarily on the exam schedule. I tried this approach for my 2L and 3L years by choosing only classes whose exams were at least two to three days apart. Doing so meant I'd have time to study for each exam with a slight break between them. This choice limited my course options, but it decreased my anxiety and stress levels.

TIP

Some law schools allow a student to reschedule an exam if they have two or three exams back-to-back or on the same day, especially if those are for required or recommended courses. But some law schools expect you to tough it out and get it done with no exceptions.

Revealing Strategies for Selecting the Best Electives

REMEMBER

Many factors come into play when you're choosing individual electives. For example, you may hear rave reviews about a particular professor and want to take their class no matter what the subject matter. Or you may hear that a particular course is super hard and want to stay away from anything that may destroy your GPA.

The following sections break down some points to consider as you're evaluating electives.

Casting a wide knowledge net versus concentrating in one area

Although no majors are awarded in law school, some students choose to focus on particular areas, such as intellectual property, environmental law, or criminal law, and therefore take multiple courses within those areas. Few schools have formal specialty tracks, so students simply decide on their own to take a bunch of classes in a particular area. The main benefits of this strategy are getting the best professional preparation for your chosen area of practice and convincing employers that you're serious about a particular field.

On the other hand, some students prefer taking a generalist's approach, getting the broadest education possible. If your aim is to be a general practitioner, this approach can work well for you. But if you're looking to specialize (which isn't required; see Chapter 22 for more information on choosing practice areas), you probably want to take at least two or three classes in your area to make sure it fits your personality and temperament.

A third approach, which you can mix in with the other two, is gaining as many practical skills for your professional plans as possible. (See the "Getting hands-on experience at law clinics" section later in this chapter.) Your specific career goals dictate how you decide to structure your course load. For instance, if you want to be a litigator, focus on trial process and advocacy courses and courses where you can work on your persuasive writing. If you're going to be a *transactional* (deal-making) lawyer, you want to try your hand at classes like negotiations, mediation, and arbitration.

Mixing case law and code courses

Some people flat out hate reading cases; they'd rather pore over statutes any day. If that describes you, try to avoid the *common-law* (judge-made law) courses, such as contracts, torts, and property, and aim for *code* (statutory) courses, such as sales, tax, or secured transactions. Although many law school courses generally require you to read cases and look over statutes, avoiding one or the other isn't terribly difficult after you complete your required courses.

Knowing what courses can make or break you (and your GPA)

Every school has its legendary professors, the ones you just have to take. They captivate you with their dynamic presence, their grasp of the subject matter, and make even the driest of subjects come alive. At the same time, every school has tough and boring professors who are infamous for giving plenty of C's, failing students, or being generally dull presenters. They're the ones who have the uncanny knack for making a fascinating topic fall flat. Of course, you need to take classes with as many of the truly amazing professors as you can while avoiding the dull ones at all costs.

Sometimes you encounter both types of professors purely by chance and not by word of mouth. Allow yourself to be surprised. Some professors may not be as popular but are experts just flying under the radar as they continue their scholarship in their field. You may end up with a wonderful mentor or an opportunity to work on a research project with that faculty member.

TIP

When your GPA is sagging, a good option may be finding the easy professors. They're the ones who give a disproportionate share of A's. If you're hoping to land a job at a large firm or a prestigious clerkship, taking an easy professor may factor heavily into your course-selection decisions. Find out about these gems through the law school grapevine.

Choosing faculty members who give strong recommendations

Some students, particularly the ones in their second years, often choose courses based on their perception of how good a reference the professor will be. If you've heard that a particular professor is connected to several judges, writes the best letters for judicial clerkships, or used to work at a firm where you'd be interested in working, obtaining a reference from that professor can be key.

Other students who need reference letters for jobs or clerkships choose courses where they know they can excel. That way, they're virtually guaranteed a sparkling reference from that faculty member. If you're going into tax law, for instance, you may want a strong letter of reference from a tax law professor who's particularly well known within the field. That letter may open doors for you, so doing well in the class and continually showing up for office hours (so the professor knows you) is wise.

Students who want to go into law school teaching also need dynamic references from faculty members; such students are especially advised to enroll in seminars, where you get more one-on-one interaction with professors. Having a professor who can eloquently speak to your academic gifts is crucial when you're applying for teaching positions. (See Chapter 23 for more information on law school teaching jobs.)

Another great path leading to a strong reference is to serve as a research assistant. (See Chapter 19 for more information on landing these positions.) This position enables you to delve into the professor's area of expertise, thus getting the inside scoop on a field and emerging from the experience with content for a sterling reference and a golden entry on your résumé.

Finding out what's expected of you

Before you sign up for Professor Smith's international securities regulation course, you may want to find out exactly what's expected of you. You can discover these juicy tidbits by reading the course syllabus, which alerts you to whether the class is primarily a paper or exam class, whether the instruction is Socratic versus lecture or discussion, and whether the course requires any short exercises or presentations. (The following section tells you more about how to judge the various forms of instruction.)

If you're the type of person who has a less-is-more mind-set, then avoid classes that require anything more than a final exam. On the other hand, when you feel more at ease with a class that offers multiple grading opportunities, you may opt for taking one with more than just a final.

Many law schools offer seminars for 2Ls, 3Ls, and 4Ls. Seminars are usually the same number of credits as regular courses and involve one long research paper and a class presentation element. Many schools allow students to sign up for multiple seminars, so if papers are your thing, this approach may appeal to you. Peruse your course schedule for more details on your school's specific guidelines and courses. And check out the "Surveying spectacular seminars" section later in this chapter for additional information on these types of classes.

TIP

Of course, your school may offer nonseminar classes that also have more grading opportunities than one final exam, such as advanced legal writing. Besides papers and exams, some courses such as negotiations, mediation, or a clinic (like the child advocacy clinic or the small business clinic) may involve an end-of-class simulation or oral argument rather than an exam or paper. The focus of clinics varies from school to school, so see your academic dean, registrar, or academic support professor, to find out which ones yours offers. These *skills courses* interest students who want more of a hands-on approach to legal problems, including the way they're graded at the end of the semester. See the "Getting hands-on experience at law clinics" section later in this chapter for more information.

Weighing lecture versus Socratic method

Although some professors tend to ease off on the Socratic method during the second and third years, some courses remain decidedly more Socratic than others. Relax; you have plenty of options if you're not a Socratic fan. (Chapter 12 has a complete explanation of the Socratic method.)

Consulting the course registration information and talking to upperclass students gets you the lowdown on which courses are Socratic versus lecture or discussion. The course information normally indicates the style of the presentation; however, you can also double-check during the *shopping period,* which is usually during the first two weeks of the new semester (the number of days varies by school). During this *add/drop* period, students can drop and add courses without penalty.

WARNING

One caveat regarding pure lecture courses, which I call the *slacking-off factor:* When you're taking a lecture course, you can go weeks if not months without reading, and no one will ever know. On the other hand, the Socratic method entails daily public and often humiliating interrogation when you're caught unprepared. If you need a kick in the seat of the pants to get your reading done, either find a friend who can be your taskmaster or stick with the Socratic method. Otherwise, you'll be cramming a semester's worth of materials the night before the exam.

TIP

Discussion courses are a nice compromise. Unlike in lecture courses, you're actively participating, and yet unlike in Socratic method courses, you're not being interrogated. Think of discussion courses as the friendly seminars you had in college, where everyone is encouraged to *share,* which in law schools may seem like a fresh breeze compared with your 1L boot camp days.

As an upperclass student, I avoided any classes that had Socratic-style teaching whenever possible. One of the ways I was able to do so was by checking on the size of the room where the course was being taught, based on the information on the course schedule. The smaller the room (I found), the less likely that the course was taught using the Socratic method. Smaller rooms tend to facilitate more of a discussion format. But as always, do your due diligence.

Surveying spectacular seminars

Seminars are intimate courses, usually with fewer than 20 students, that are often set up in a discussion format. Many schools offer opportunities to satisfy their research paper requirement by taking a seminar. Or they let you take one just out of interest.

Seminars are a refreshing change of pace because they don't always utilize case-books. They mainly use law review and other scholarly articles, individual cases, and other books, and they're graded on the basis of a final research paper and accompanying student presentation. However, some seminars require multiple short papers in addition to the long paper, which can become tedious. Others require selected students to present the day's reading during each class meeting.

WARNING

You may be tempted to load up on a semester's worth of seminars, because they:

>> Tend to have light reading

>> Often meet only once a week for two to three hours

>> Often end early in the semester (or have a lengthy break for students to work on research papers)

However, bear in mind that most seminars require a lengthy 25-to-35-page research paper, which in my opinion is much more work than studying for a single exam. That's because the research paper needs to include *primary* (cases and statutes) and *secondary* (scholarly articles and books) sources, and finding all that information is extremely time-consuming. For example, the research paper I wrote took around 80 hours to complete.

The seminars at many schools often are tailored to the particular research interests of their professors; therefore, you may find detailed and finely tuned topics such as law, morality, and community; law and society of Japan; and children and the law in modern America. In my upper-division seminar courses, I enjoyed the relaxed pace, the discussion format, and the emphasis on policy rather than pure case law. But you have to decide whether these qualities sound appealing to you.

Delving into directed studies

Most law schools offer students an opportunity to take several credits as *directed studies*. In other words, you find a professor in an area of the law that interests you; compile a reading list of cases, scholarly articles, and books; and create a syllabus. You read the materials on your own and meet with your professor once a week or so to discuss them.

Direct studies are a great way of satisfying a few credits, especially in your final year of law school. They can help you build a strong foundation in a particular area of the law and form a mentoring relationship with your professor. As an added bonus, they're normally graded pass/fail, so they should give you minimal stress.

Introducing independent research

In a similar vein to directed studies, some schools allow you to undertake an independent research project for course credit. Similar to a seminar's research paper requirement, you're responsible for the following:

>> Coming up with an idea or topic

>> Approaching the appropriate faculty member

>> Writing up an outline and rough draft

>> Turning in a research paper similar to the one required for a more structured class

Many students favor this option when they have specific research interests that existing courses don't meet. When your area of interest is somewhat obscure, seek out the appropriate faculty member and propose your idea. You never know when you'll be able to parlay your research paper into a writing competition entry or publishable note. (See Chapter 19 for more information on these opportunities.)

WARNING

If you choose the independent research option, make certain that you're a self-starter, because you're largely left to your own devices. No one's there to egg you on when you don't feel like researching. At least during a seminar, you have other students to interact with and carved-in-stone due dates for each stage of your paper: topic selection, outline, rough draft, and completed version. Without a professor breathing down your neck to submit these documents on time (they're related to dragons, you know), you may find yourself in over your head with a semester's worth of research to do during finals week.

Deciding whether to take morning, afternoon, or night classes

If you're a night owl, an 8 a.m. administrative law class is going to drive you crazy all semester. Similarly, if you're at your best in the morning, late afternoon classes probably find you dozing off.

REMEMBER

Whenever possible, take your own sleep/awake patterns into account when planning your schedule. After all, when you feel awful during class because all you can think about is taking a nap, you're not going to get much out of it. As a night owl, I tried to take as many late-morning and afternoon classes as possible. In fact, during one well-planned semester, I managed not to have a single class before 11 a.m.

Gaining Credit for Real-World Experience Outside the Classroom

Many law schools offer the unparalleled opportunity to gain credit, work on real cases and get hands-on experience doing legal research and writing out in the field. You can take advantage of these real-world experiences by participating in clinical opportunities, internships, or externships. These options are generally open only to 2Ls, 3Ls, and 4Ls, though most law students begin applying what they learned in their first year during their first summer.

These options especially appeal to law students who are tired of learning only about theory and policy in the classroom; in clinics, internships, and externships, you get to really show what you know by:

>> Writing memos and briefs

>> Interviewing clients (or assisting attorneys with client interviews)

>> Preparing for trial

>> Representing clients in court

REMEMBER

You won't be on your own entirely; in these opportunities, you work under the supervision of faculty, practicing attorneys, and/or judges.

Understanding the ABA's experiential learning requirement

One element of the American Bar Association (ABA) law school accreditation standards, adopted in 2014, requires at least six experiential learning credits.

The goal is to ensure that you graduate with actual legal experience. No one wants to go to a doctor who has never actually worked with patients in a medical setting with the supervision of nurses and doctors. Similarly, potential clients want to know that their attorney has actual experience under the supervision of an attorney and/or a judge before putting their lives and livelihoods in their hands.

Getting hands-on experience at law clinics

Through *clinical programs*, law schools offer free legal advice with students supervised by faculty attorneys. Clinics have become more popular as law schools realize that pure theory doesn't resonate with every student. Many students want more of a hands-on experience in practical lawyering that's similar to the kind of schooling that medical students receive in their clinics.

Your law school may have anywhere from zero to several clinics, all specializing in a wide variety of subject matters such as (but not limited to) immigration law, intellectual property, military and veterans services, prisoner civil rights, entertainment law, and education and disability law. Clinics are often located at the law school or on the university campus. Other times, they're out in the community and in this instance are usually called *external clinics.*

REMEMBER

You work on real cases and serve real clients as a student attorney in a clinic. You interview clients, manage intake files, write briefs and memos, and even represent clients in court (under a professor's supervision, of course). In fact, you're supervised every step of the way. Many students say that working in a law clinic is one of the more satisfying achievements of their law school careers because it's one of the few times they actually get to apply what they've learned.

Most schools require a course in conjunction with the clinic in which you find out how to interview clients, take depositions, practice your oral arguments, and discuss issues that come up in the course of your clinical work with the other students.

TIP

You sign up for clinics and receive academic credit for them the same way you do for any other course. Clinics usually carry the same amount of credit as regular courses. Because of the supervision requirements, however, many clinics have space limitations — often for only ten students or fewer — so check well in advance to find out what you need to do to secure a spot. Remember that law clinics generally are open only to upperclass students.

Taking externships for credit

Another opportunity that many schools offer is work at a public-interest organization, courthouse, or governmental organization for credit but no pay. You can often take these independent clinic courses or *externship courses* during the summer and during the school year.

Like clinics, externships are excellent for getting hands-on experience in a new legal environment. You're around many other attorneys and judges, so you can gain valuable information about a particular area of the law. The only downside is that unlike a clinic, you may not have as much client contact. Instead, you'll likely be doing plenty of desk work, such as legal research and memo and brief writing.

Generally, you arrange for an externship on your own and secure a faculty advisor in the relevant subject area. But your school's career services office may be able to help you with identifying potential placements. (See Chapter 20 for more information on how career services can help with general job searching.) Because you're providing free labor, not too much arm-twisting is necessary to convince an organization to take you on. However, you need to figure out transportation, which can become expensive.

REMEMBER

Depending on how many credits you want out of your experience, you can attend your externship from one day a week to all five, depending on your school's guidelines. Your student handbook outlines the minimum and maximum number of credits you can register for. Externships are often graded pass/fail. Many require you to keep log your work, hours, and activities and may involve some type of final project as well.

My judicial externship with a magistrate judge in my 2L spring semester was fantastic. The judge was covering both criminal and civil cases during the time I externed with him. He also had an excellent clerk who was very skilled, patient, and up for collaborating with all of the judicial externs to ensure we submitted memos and briefs that were well researched, thorough, and helpful to the judge. I was able to sit in court while the judge presided over cases as well as in chambers with him, his clerk, and the attorneys. Overall, I'm forever grateful for the opportunity to have worked so closely with a judge and learn the inner workings of the court, the appellate process, and the prestige of adding this experience to your résumé.

TAKING COURSES OUTSIDE THE LAW SCHOOL

Many law schools provide you with the option of taking a few classes outside the law school for course credit. Doing so can be a great change of pace. For example, taking a course about women in art can help refresh your spirit during a semester filled with antitrust, bankruptcy, and real estate finance law. An outside course also can help you gain a new perspective on the law — from a sociological, psychological, or anthropological perspective, to name a few.

Many schools limit this option to one course per semester or a maximum of two or three total outside courses. You want to check your school's policy about whether the courses must be strictly graduate-level classes and whether some departments or schools are excluded.

One of the more popular places for law students to take outside classes for credit is within the business school, especially for students planning to go into corporate law or solo practice. Taking a few courses at the business school, such as accounting, finance, or tax, can complement your legal skills well. Other popular schools or departments include social work, political science, education, social work, women's studies, sociology, creative writing, and foreign languages.

Of course, you can always audit a course outside the law school for fun (see Chapter 10), regardless of whether it's at the graduate or undergraduate level. Because law school may likely be your last foray into academia, I suggest you live it up and sample something entirely new.

Getting a Global Perspective from Study Abroad

As the legal profession becomes more global, understanding other legal systems and their approaches to legal problems grows ever more important. In response to this increasing need for global legal understanding, many law schools offer an array of study-abroad courses.

When you're interested in international law, for example, studying abroad can be an especially great opportunity to experience other legal systems firsthand. Many study-abroad programs include an *internship component*, which is an unparalleled opportunity to gain experience by working in a foreign court, non-profit, or governmental organization.

Some schools set limits on when you can study abroad; they may permit summer study abroad but forbid it during the academic year. Full-year study-abroad programs are rare in law schools; spending a semester or summer abroad is much more common. Additionally, some law schools have their own overseas programs, which feature their own professors. Other schools participate in programs formed by agreements they've reached with other schools that meet their academic standards and direct enrollment from agreements they've reached with foreign law schools. Still other schools offer only a few options. Check with your law school's academic affairs office, the course catalog, and/or its website to determine your options.

TIP

If you have your eye on a particular program that isn't affiliated with your school, don't hesitate to petition your dean for permission to enroll in it.

REMEMBER

Make sure studying abroad doesn't affect your graduating on time, because you still need to meet your school's graduation requirements. However, studying abroad during the summer may give you additional credits that may enable you to graduate early, if that's an option at your school.

Highlighting the benefits

If you didn't study abroad in college, you're in for a real treat. The main benefit of studying abroad is gaining an understanding of a new culture, whether it's Thailand, South Africa, China, or England. You're immersed in an entirely new culture and environment, which can do wonders for reawakening long-dormant law school enthusiasm. Likewise, you grow in ways you didn't think imaginable while traveling on your own, discovering your way around a new city (or country), and interacting with the locals.

Although you learn plenty academically because you take a course load similar to a normal law school semester back home, some students let schoolwork take a back seat to experiential learning. That's because you may soon forget some of the semester's worth of international communications law that you've taken overseas, but you won't forget about taking the train cross-country by yourself, climbing to the top of Mount Kilimanjaro, or haggling with merchants in their native tongue.

Choosing a program that fits your budget

The cost of studying abroad obviously is prohibitive for some students; on top of paying tuition, you may be required to pay special program fees that can run into the thousands of dollars. Add to that the amount of money you need to take with you for housing, food, and entertainment, and you can see that expenses can quickly get out of hand, especially in Europe or Japan. That's why when you're planning to study abroad, you need to plan early and responsibly.

Taking out extra loans in anticipation of these added costs is an option for some people. Other students, however, know in advance that they'll be studying abroad and save up money from their summer jobs or work part-time to accumulate enough cash during the school year. One hassle when you study abroad during the school year is finding someone to sublet your apartment. Some study-abroad students arrange to live with a friend for the remaining semester.

Although studying abroad takes some advance effort for smooth planning, it's by far worth it, especially after you acclimate to your host country and begin having the time of your life.

Chapter 19

Getting Involved in Law School

You'd be hard-pressed to find a law student whose mantra is "Law school is all work and no play." Getting involved in extracurricular activities provides a refreshing break from your academic work, a great way to beef up your résumé, and an opportunity to develop your interest in a particular area of practice. For example, you can captivate an audience as a moot court competitor, impress your professor as a diligent research assistant, or join the world of legal scholarship by working on a journal.

With so many options available, you may be wondering how you can best become involved. That's exactly what this chapter is for. I examine why law review is one the most coveted of all law school activities and show you how to land your spot. I cover the ins and outs of the moot court competition and discuss other ways to make your mark in law school through clubs, part-time jobs, and research and teaching assistant positions.

Note: At many schools, law review, law journal, and moot court are called *cocurriculars* because they're viewed as an academic complement to the curriculum, not as extra, more recreational activities. But other activities, such as clubs or writing contests, still fall under the extracurricular heading.

REMEMBER

You don't have to make the extracurricular activities I discuss here happen all at once. In fact, you're better able to fully devote your energy when you limit yourself to two or three per year. You have three (or four) years of law school, and that's plenty of time to sample all the activities you can fit into your free time.

Benefiting from Extracurriculars

When you think about law school, you probably think about studying for endless hours per week and dragging around those huge casebooks (see Chapter 8). However, law school is more than keeping your nose buried in books; it has a wealth of activities for you to explore. Getting involved in extracurricular activities provides numerous benefits that help you feel more in touch with your law school experience. Participating helps you:

>> Meet people you wouldn't ordinarily mingle with and interact with different groups of students, which is especially crucial when you're a first-year (1L) student

>> Build your leadership skills by taking an active role in deciding the mission and purpose of the organization with which you're involved

>> Enhance your professional competence and knowledge by improving your legal-research, client-interview, and brief and memo-writing skills (depending on the club or activity)

>> Find out more about what you want from the legal profession

>> Discover opportunities to get out into the community, regardless of whether you're volunteering at a domestic violence shelter, interviewing clients, or supporting small businesses

The most satisfied students say law school is an experience that can educate you in many ways inside and outside the classroom. It can also provide you with leadership and professional skills that enhance your personality and commitment to your community or a cause.

WARNING

As a first-year student, you're probably bound and determined to try out as many new extracurriculars as possible. Take it from me, however, that going overboard before finding out what you're capable of handling time-wise just isn't a good idea. After you've successfully conquered your first semester, you'll be better suited to determine how much time you can productively spend on outside activities.

Besides, when you're a 1L, some of the activities in this chapter probably aren't open to you, such as law journals and law review, (sometimes) moot court, and (usually) working part time outside the law school. However, finding out about these extracurriculars now puts you in a better position for deciding whether they're right for you when it comes time to apply.

Introducing you to various areas of practice

Clubs such as the Environmental Law Society, the International Law Association, or the Business and Law Society focus on areas of legal practice. Joining clubs like these provides you with the following:

>> Access to practitioners within the particular field the club represents (through speakers and presentations at the law school).

>> Information about the area of practice represented.

>> Experiences that are relevant to the particular area of practice you prefer, such as drafting a will for an elderly community member or performing environmental research for a nonprofit organization.

Another fabulous benefit of getting involved is finding out early on whether you're well suited for a particular kind of practice. (See Chapter 22 for more on practice areas.) For example, if you think employment law would be fun, join the Employment Law Society and offer to provide research for a project during the school year. Without spending the summer at an employment law job, your extracurricular involvement can quickly tell you whether the work fits with your personality.

Making connections

Extracurriculars are your opportunity to make new connections and create a great first impression with your peers, faculty and student organization advisors, student affairs staff, and other law school or university departments.

Volunteer to invite the featured speaker or firm, to be the point of contact for the day of the event, to create the program, or to read the speaker's biography. Doing so allows you to interact with the speaker or their executive assistant closely, which means more face time for potential connections and further engagement.

TIP

With this face time, take advantage of the opportunities to showcase your creativity, organizational skills, and budgeting skills.

Strengthening your résumé

Extracurriculars can give your résumé something beyond your GPA and internship experience. Although beefing up your CV shouldn't be your sole motivating force for becoming involved with anything, I'd be irresponsible if I didn't point out that employers love seeing résumés that show students who can balance their academic obligations with extracurriculars.

If you were on the other side of the table, which would you rather see: a student with nothing but coursework, or one who joined two or three activities, held leadership positions, and gained useful legal skills in the process? The latter, without question, of course. Employers are only human. They want multi-dimensional students who have something more to contribute to the firm or organization.

Understanding Law Reviews and Law Journals

Of all extracurricular activities in law school, working on the law review is by far the most prestigious, followed closely by working on a law journal. What's so unique about these kinds of publications compared to other student publications around the world is that they're entirely student operated and managed. They may have faculty advisors, but their roles are minimal.

Distinguishing between reviews and journals

REMEMBER

Law reviews and law journals are often generically and collectively referred to simply as *journals.* However, remembering that they're two different species is extremely important.

>> **Law reviews** are scholarly publications aimed at a readership of practicing attorneys, judges, and legal scholars. They're primarily *generalist,* meaning they cover wide ranges of legal topics, from employment to family law and everything in between. Inside, you find heavily footnoted articles, *notes* (student-written articles), and *case comments* (analyses of court rulings). Almost every law school has one law review, which usually is known as the *[Name of the College or University] Law Review.* Law reviews typically are published between three and six times per year.

>> **Law journals,** on the other hand, are specialist publications that are read mostly by practitioners and scholars interested in the particular subject areas or fields they're focused on. Their topics span diverse ranges — from the University of Arkansas's *Journal of Food Law & Policy* to the *Harvard Environmental Law Review* to Chapman University's *Journal of Computer Science Integration,* and on and on. Individual law schools may not sponsor any journals, or they may have many. The number of issues per year varies by journal.

Most practitioners aspire to be published in law reviews. Not that your school's regular journals are less important or less work, but landing a membership on a law review generally is more difficult than getting on a regular journal. Law reviews not only have higher standards but also usually see more people competing for positions.

Deciding whether journals are worth the massive time commitment

Law reviews and law journals are hands-down the single most time-consuming law school extracurricular activities you can do. If you thought studying a few hours a night was rough, try spending between 10 and 25 hours on a single cite-checking assignment (and then remember you'll probably be assigned between three and six of these tedious tasks as a 2L journal staff member).

As an editor, your time commitment skyrockets even more; however, many schools provide academic credit to editorial staff members. If you're an editor-in-chief, well, you can forget about your social life. Students in that position regularly spend between 30 and 40 hours per week on their journal duties — the equivalent of a full-time job!

REMEMBER

Becoming a member of a journal isn't for everyone. If you aren't going to enjoy it and reap the career-enhancing benefits, it isn't worth doing. You have plenty of ways to distinguishing yourself as a law student, and journals aren't the be all and end all of options. In other words, journal membership isn't the only key to law school success or happiness. When you don't make it, or don't want to join, you still can become a great lawyer.

Landing a spot on a journal

You need to follow your school's particular procedures to land a position on either type of journal. In general, however, here's how it works:

1. The whole process begins during the spring semester of your first year, when all the journals schedule an information session. The editors-in-chief describe the mission and content of their respective journals and their specific requirements.

2. At that point, you may receive a *preference sheet,* on which you rank which of the journals you're most interested in on a numerical scale (depending on how many journals your school has). At many schools, after you fill out this form, you can't change your mind. So if you're offered admission to your first choice journal, either you must accept the offer to join that journal or you won't be on any journal.

3. You then return the completed preference sheet to the journals, which alerts them to how many people are entering their competitions. After that, you bide your time until after spring exams, when the fun of the writing competition I cover in the following section begins!

Grading-on versus writing-on

In the past, some law schools appointed students to a journal based solely on their 1L grades. Today, however, many law schools take a more democratic approach where grades are only part of the selection process if any.

Most schools hold a *writing-on competition* in addition to considering grades for membership. That's where 1Ls receive a packet of cases, statutes, and law review articles at the end of spring semester exams and must write a journal article (within a certain time frame) based on those materials and the particular topic they're assigned. Students usually favor writing-on competitions because they see them as fairer to people who may be excellent writers and editors but not *magna cum laude* students.

Some schools also make an editing component part of the writing-on competition, meaning that students also get an article full of typos to mark up. The students who are more successful editors are awarded high scores. Although rare, a few schools are known to conduct personal interviews in addition to or instead of the editing competition. All in all, you may have a week or two to complete the assignment.

Acing the writing-on competition

When you're staring down a huge packet full of scholarly materials for your article, knowing where to begin is hard. You not only have to come up with a cohesive argument but also must add in case law to support your argument, refer to statutes as necessary, and supplement the discussion with references from law journal articles. Although everything you need is conveniently included in the packet, the work nevertheless seems awfully daunting. That's why I advocate the start-out-strong (take-the-break-first) approach.

TIP

Expect to spend anywhere between 10 and 30 hours on your writing competition piece. Sure, articles have been written the night before they're due, but with such an important position at stake, do you really want to leave it up to chance like that?

After you finish writing your article, don't forget to put the footnotes in proper *Bluebook* form, because the editors are also looking to see how good you are at citation. *The Bluebook: A Uniform System of Citation* (The Harvard Law Review Association) is one of the most universally used citing systems in the legal profession. You find out about *Bluebook* form as a 1L in your legal research class, so putting those skills to the test shouldn't be too much work (and a good review).

When you're done with your writing competition entry, submit in the format outlined in the instructions on your information sheet. When it reaches its destination, the 3L editors start to work. When you're off having fun in the sun or at the daily grind at your summer job, they sift through a large volume of entries, reading through them all and deciding which contestants are worthy of issuing invitations to.

You'll probably hear the results of the competition in late July, when students selected for journal membership are notified by email. This invitation tells you what you need to do to accept and when to show up for orientation, which is usually the week before school starts.

Working on Law Reviews and Law Journals

What you do when working for a law journal depends on your year in school. First-year students aren't allowed to participate, so 2Ls are the lowest on the totem pole. They serve as cite-checkers and proofreaders. Second-year students' other main activity is writing a *student note* (or student-written scholarly article) on a topic of their choosing. If the note is good enough, it's published in the journal. Some journals make note-writing mandatory; with others, it's optional.

As a 3L and 4L, you move up in the world, no longer relegated to cite-checking and proofreading grunt work. Instead, you serve mainly in editorial capacities, such as managing editor, executive editor, or editor-in-chief.

Most 3Ls and 4Ls elect to apply for *editorial board positions*, which are pretty much the same across all journals. These titles include managing editor, notes editor, and executive editor, among others. For students whose talents lie in areas besides editing, website editor and senior business manager positions also are available. (Note that specific job titles may differ from journal to journal.)

For many law schools, you can apply for one or more of these positions around February or March of your second year. That gives departing 3L or 4L staff plenty of time to interview candidates.

Arguing for Fun and Profit: Moot Court

Moot court is basically an *appellate* (after a decision has been made in a lower court and is appealed) *court simulation*. In other words, you go through the motions but no *real* cases are being decided.

Participating in moot court has a lot of upside:

>> **It's an especially valuable tool for students who want to become persuasive litigators (trial lawyers).** That's because of the great opportunities it provides you for working on your oral argument and advocacy skills. Part of being an advocate is knowing how to be persuasive. After all, you're trying to persuade members of the panel that your side should win.

>> **It gives you another chance to work on your overall legal writing skills.** Aside from their legal research and writing classes, many law students don't get another chance in law school to work on brief-writing, which, if you plan to be a litigator, is one of the main activities you'll be doing.

>> **It helps you improve your ability to maintain your poise while answering pointed, rapid-fire questions from your panel.** If you're not too swift at thinking on your feet, moot court may be a good opportunity to change that.

REMEMBER

One reason moot court is especially fun: The panel of judges for the competition often is made up of attorneys and judges from the community. Thus, you present your arguments in a somewhat realistic setting.

Moot court competition is waged on many levels both within your law school (intramural) and on the national level.

Competing on the national level

Many different schools participate in national competitions, which are sponsored at law schools around the country. You can participate on the national level in several ways.

» One common way is to join your school's mock trial team (if one's available), which competes in moot court competitions — usually once a year — in a variety of subject areas, such as intellectual property, health, and international law. Competing on a mock trial team usually requires a tryout, which typically takes place at the beginning of the school year.

» Another way you can participate in national moot court competitions is through extracurricular clubs (and some journals) at your school, which often send some of their members to national competitions relating to their fields of interest. All you need to do to be considered is be a member of the particular club (or journal) and show an interest in and dedication to preparing for the particular moot court competition.

» Alternatively, some law schools have specialized moot court teams dedicated to a particular subject area, such as the international law moot court team, which sends its team members to the corresponding annual national moot court competition. Sometimes members of these moot court teams are chosen from the most outstanding students of the previous year's school intramural competition.

REMEMBER

Regardless of how you end up participating in a national competition, you need to know that most teams consist of only a few people — usually three to eight. That's so they can intimately work together and be coached by fellow students, alumni, and/or faculty in the extensive preparation required to succeed at these competitions.

Competing on the intramural level

Members of the moot court board (or moot court honor society), who are students with stellar moot court credentials from the previous year, are invited to organize and coordinate the intramural competition within your school. The board chooses one topic *(scenario)* in any area of the law for the competition to be based on. At some law schools, you don't need to try out for moot court at the intramural level; there may be opportunities that are available to students that do not grade on or make it on the team by competing.

At some law schools, 1Ls participate in moot court as part of their legal research and writing course requirement. At other schools, moot court is only open to 2Ls or 3Ls. Check with your school's moot court board or its students activities website for guidelines.

Intramural moot court essentially involves teaming up with a partner of your choice and getting a packet of cases, law review articles, and statutes based on the assigned problem, which involves two issues. Each team member writes about one of the two issues (their choice). Each team of two students is assigned to take the same side — either plaintiff or defendant — and then argues against another team of two assigned the opposite side during each round.

Next, each team writes a combined appellate brief consisting of both of their assigned issues. After the brief is written, you and your partner practice oral arguments with each other for several weeks, asking each other difficult questions and playing devil's advocate. You help each other hone your arguments and counterarguments. You normally have about a month or six weeks between receiving the assigned materials and the first round of arguments.

Then the real fun begins. Moot court competitions generally are conducted in rounds that open with all competitors and then whittle away the field during the coming weeks until only two competitors remain and are declared moot court champions. During the first of (usually) three preliminary rounds, each team argues their respective issues against one other team. During the second round, they argue the opposite side of the same issue (so if they were plaintiffs in the first round they become defendants). During the third round, they're notified shortly before the competition begins which of the two sides (plaintiff or defendant) they'll be arguing. But they keep their same issues during all three rounds.

After the preliminary rounds, the moot court board tallies up the contestants' scores on their briefs and oral arguments, and the best teams advance on to later rounds. Besides the two champions, winners also are declared for the best brief and best oral argument.

Moot court is considered something of an entertainment event for the entire law school. As the championship rounds draw near, more and more spectators gather to watch the (often suspenseful) proceedings. The semifinal and final rounds in particular are typically well attended by law students and faculty. Auditoriums or courtrooms can be packed, especially when the two remaining moot court champions are about to be chosen.

Considering Clubs

When the two most visible law school activities, law journals and moot court, don't tickle your fancy (or even if they do), try joining a club or organization. Every law school has a wide variety of interesting clubs, from the Health Law Society to the Evening Students' Association and the Jewish Law Students Organization. You can even find clubs focusing on older students, volunteer-minded students, or even students with significant others!

TIP

Most law schools stage an organizations fair at the beginning of the school year to enable 1Ls, 2Ls, 3Ls, and 4Ls alike to find out what clubs their school offers. Sign up for as many clubs as you can. Attend their introductory meetings so you can find out what they're all about before deciding which ones you want to focus on. Throughout my law school career, I participated actively in several clubs and found them to be a fun way to meet new friends, score outlines from upper-division mentors, learn more about different specialty areas, and network with practitioners in a field.

With so many clubs to choose from, knowing where to start is tough. You may want to try a different club each year of law school or choose one to participate actively in for your entire school tenure. The following list describes some of the types of clubs available to you.

>> **Advocacy clubs:** Your law school is likely to have several clubs that focus on advocacy, such as the Street Law Society, Innocence Project, Legal Aid Society, Pro Bono Club, Prisoner Rights, American Constitution Society, and the Bill of Rights Institute. These clubs are an excellent way to become involved in a cause that you're passionate about. They're also useful for gaining relevant experience in preparation for summer or permanent work at nonprofit organizations. Nonprofits are notorious for requiring evidence of strong commitment to their causes, so if this is an area you're looking toward, getting a foot in the door through an advocacy club may be a good approach.

>> **Student government:** Just like in high school and college, each law school has its own form of student government. At many schools, the government is called the Student Bar Association (SBA) or Student Law Association (SLA). When your school has a Barrister's Ball, student organizational fairs, a Halloween party, and other social events and parties, chances are that your friendly SBA planned it. The representatives on the SBA generally select students to serve on various committees (such as educational and special activities) that organize these types of events.

- >> **Special-interest organizations:** The Women in Law, the Federalist Society, LGBTQIA+ organizations, Muslim law student association, and Christian Legal Society are among several examples of clubs that serve the interests of their members. You may also be interested in joining clubs for older students (often titled OWLS — Older and Wiser Law Students), for law students who are parents, and for law students who are married/have significant others.

- >> **Activity clubs:** Some law school clubs are quasi-involved with law, such as the drama club, which puts on plays with legal themes, or a club where you teach legal concepts in middle and high schools. If you're looking for a fun environment where you can meet new people and work on new skills, these clubs may pique your interest.

REMEMBER

Bear in mind that student organizations vary greatly in their usefulness from year to year depending on the leadership and membership. Some clubs put on a variety of events one year and don't offer much the next, depending on the effectiveness and enthusiasm of their leaders. That's why joining a club and getting elected to a leadership role is a great experience; *you* get to be in charge of that club's future.

HOW MANY IS TOO MANY?

You have so many opportunities available to you that you can easily overdo it. You have to prioritize what matters the most and what has the most impact on your career options. You still need to maintain your grades, outline, prepare for class, revisit your notes, go to office hours, update your résumé — you see where this is going. Getting excited about planning a fundraiser for the Constitutional Law Society speaker series or the Public Interest summer program stipends doesn't mean much if you've flunked out of law school and can't take advantage of these opportunities.

Take stock of where you stand academically, how you're feeling physically, and what you can handle. Pick one or two organizations/activities that you can fully commit to.

You don't want to be known as the student who takes on too many things and isn't reliable to your peers and the administration. Explaining to an employer that your grades dropped because you overextended yourself by getting involved in too many activities is difficult.

Jumping on the Research Assistant Bandwagon

Being a *research assistant* is exactly what it sounds like: You work one-on-one with professors on their research. Your duties depend on the particular professor, but most often they include the following:

>> Performing legal research online and/or in the library

>> Proofreading articles or book chapters

>> Giving feedback on writing projects

The opportunity can be invaluable in terms of gaining more legal research and proofreading experiences while also getting the chance to learn more about your favorite specialty area.

Finding an opening

Finding a research assistantship isn't difficult. Professors usually advertise openings during class or through the electronic message boards, the career services job portal, or the law school newsletter. They may ask for a résumé, an informal transcript, and references to help vet you (and any other applicants). At other times, they may even ask you directly, if you've done well in their classes or are a particularly vocal participant.

TIP

Choosing a professor in your specialty area of interest is usually the best way to go, but you can also try other popular approaches:

>> **Find out about your school's heavyweights by perusing the faculty section on your law school's website for various professors' credentials.** If you find someone whose courses and research interests match yours, then you can send them an email or visit them during their office hours.

>> **Do a Lexis or Westlaw database search for the names of faculty members at your school.** Review that information and decide whether working for that professor can help you in your career plans.

>> **Ask around.** Find out from upperclass students which professors worked at what firms and which professors clerked for which judges after law school. Find out who has ties to the organizations, courts, nonprofits, or firms you want to work for. Then follow up frequently!

When you're absolutely champing at the bit to work for a particular professor who hasn't advertised with career services or in the newsletter, approach them directly and ask whether they need any help. You never know when the professor may say something like, "Come to think of it, I could use somebody right now." And you'll be first in line!

Earning the benefits of an assistantship

One big advantage of being a research assistant is that such positions are considered prestigious because the professors handpick you to work closely with them on their research. You may even get an acknowledgment in their book or article for all your efforts, and you add this information to your résumé.

The following list details some of the other important benefits you gain from an assistantship:

>> **You get hands-on experience doing legal research and writing in your chosen field.** It's a prime opportunity to figure out whether the field is indeed for you.

>> **You have access to an expert in the field.** What better way to get all your nitty-gritty questions about health or corporate law answered?

>> **By working so closely with your professor, you're likely to get a personalized, stellar reference from a well-known authority in the field.** This benefit can give you an "in" in ways you can't begin to imagine, whether you're interviewing with a firm, for a clerkship, or for a law school teaching position, especially when your professor worked or clerked at the firm or court you're considering.

The cool thing about the job is that you're the first to know about your professor's new scholarly pursuits, and you can offer your advice and input, which can make you feel like an integral part of their projects.

REMEMBER

Because research assistantships are usually paid positions, you may see some financial benefit as well. The pay is generally low (often between $15 and $25 per hour), but your hours are usually flexible, and you often can do much of the work at home. Be sure to set up your paperwork with the law school's payroll department.

Getting Involved Outside the Law School

Getting involved with real practitioners outside your law school is something that many law students don't think about because it isn't often touted as an alternative to — or in addition to — the usual law school extracurriculars I cover earlier in the chapter. One of the best parts about this kind of involvement is that you don't necessarily need to be an upper-division student to take advantage of these opportunities (except for part-time jobs). Getting involved right away ensures that you get a head start on exploring your career path.

Joining your city, state, or national bar association as a student member

If learning more about your desired areas of practice, mingling with attorneys in your city of choice, and attending continuing legal education seminars isn't fun, then I don't know what is. Becoming a member of your city, state, or national bar association as a law student is a much-overlooked opportunity. And many organizations offer student discounts!

TIP

If you're really serious about networking and learning more about a field, joining the association in your hometown, or the town where you hope to work, is one of the best investments you can make, especially when you want to practice in a city other than where your law school is located. You can join another city's bar association and just attend functions whenever you're in town. Many bar associations offer virtual opportunities that you can take advantage of. Student members have no set requirements for the number of functions they must attend, which is one of the great benefits of joining. Simply do as much or as little as you want. This fact is particularly relevant to part-time and evening law students, who may have time to attend these functions only on weekends or during school breaks.

Using academic writing contests to garner fame and fortune (well, almost)

Okay, admit it: You have a writing genius inside you that just wasn't satisfied by your journal note or moot court brief. When you're hankering to crank out another 20-to-35-page paper, look no farther than the myriad writing contests open to law students of all years and areas of interest.

The best way to find out about contests is from flyers that are usually posted on bulletin boards around the law school's campus and in its e-newsletter. Some contests that pertain to subject matter of particular interest to journal members are also posted inside the respective journal offices.

RECYCLING YOUR WORK

So you've put hours' worth of blood, sweat, and tears into your journal note, only to have it denied publication. Or maybe you wrote one heck of a seminar paper and want to put your crowning glory to another use. Sound familiar? Check out the writing contests, because one is bound to be a match made in heaven for your paper. Believe me, the best part about this kind of recycling is that you've already done the hard work. You just need to tweak your submission a bit or adapt it to the specific subject matter, mail it off, and voilà — your paper can be on its way to stardom.

Sure, writing a submission takes plenty of time and effort — unless, of course, you happen to use something you've already worked on, which, in most cases, is already in the format of a law review article (approximately 25 to 50 pages long). In any case, putting forth the effort is worth it when you're truly interested in the topic and eager to have another writing sample that you can show potential employers. Besides, some of the contest awards are pretty hefty. They can range anywhere from a hundred to thousands of dollars! What do you have to lose?

TIP

If you're serious about winning some cash, try pursuing the more obscure contests, the ones where you think fewer people will show an interest in submitting. You never know which contest will be the one in which yours is the only submission!

Working part time during the school year

Many full-time law students opt to work part time, either to gain skills in a practice setting or make some extra cash to get through law school, take out less in loans, and begin saving for bar prep. Some 2Ls and 3Ls are able to arrange their schedules so they're taking classes at the law school only three days a week, meaning they can work the other two. Or some students choose only morning classes so they can work during the afternoons, or vice versa.

In essence, you have time for a part-time job if you choose to. After all, you're in the classroom for only about 15 hours a week, tops. That leaves plenty of time for studying and a part-time job after you've successfully completed your first year of law school.

Part-time and evening students, of course, don't have time for additional work *on top* of their full-time jobs. But full-time law students with spouses or children may have time for a part-time position that requires only a few hours a week.

Some of the most common part-time school-year legal jobs include working at private law firms, clerking for judges, or working at nonprofit or governmental organizations. Contact the firm, court, or organization you want to work for and explain your family responsibilities and how much time you're able to devote to part-time work. You'll likely be able to work something out, particularly in big cities where the opportunities are numerous and varied. Your career development/ services office may also have some suggestions for you.

Many law schools have created opportunities for their part-time/evening students to get legal experience in light of the ABA requirement for experiential learning (which I discuss in Chapter 18). These options may include working with a non-profit, clinic, or firm on the weekend. Some part-time or evening law students bank their vacation and sick time to take off for several Mondays or Fridays to get their time in to meet this requirement.

REMEMBER

The American Bar Association used to have a rule prohibiting 1Ls from working at all. Now, individual law schools have their own guidelines about whether full-time students can work during their 1L year. Many still mandate these students work no more than 20 hours a week in any semester in which they're taking more than 12 credit hours.

Employers within the legal field are less likely to hire 1Ls anyway because they generally aren't considered quite as efficient as upperclass students (with good reason — 1Ls still are heavily involved in the learning process at that point).

Your expected pay for these jobs typically depends on:

>> The size of the city you're in (larger ones pay more than smaller ones)

>> Your year in school

>> The type of organization you're working for (firms tend to pay the most and nonprofits the least, if at all)

You generally find the most opportunities at firms because they're especially plentiful in big and small cities, and many of them are interested in having part-time law students do legal research (read: cheap labor). Besides legal research, you'll also likely write memos and help file cases and other documents. Don't be surprised, however, when you're given nonlegal tasks to do, such as answering phones, making copies, stuffing envelopes, and writing nonlegal materials.

REMEMBER

Especially if your grades are mediocre, working at a court, nonprofit, government agency, or firm part-time during the school year is the perfect opportunity to show your employers what you can really do in a summer or permanent position. (See Chapters 20 and 21 for more on landing summer and permanent jobs.) When they see how indispensable you are, they may start to think about making you a summer or permanent postgraduation offer. Furthermore, when you work with these judges, attorneys, and their clerks during most or all of your second and third years, your employers definitely get a good sense of your attitude, work ethic, and competency, which can really make the difference when you're just a face in the crowd on paper.

5

Preparing for Your Future

Find a summer job that best suits you.

Investigate career options.

Consider an area of practice.

Explore alternative legal careers.

Chapter **20**

Landing Your Perfect Summer Job

When you're looking for your ideal summer jobs following your first, second, and possibly (for part-time students) third years of law school, remember that the job you choose can significantly impact your future professional growth. That's because your summer jobs in the legal field help you narrow down your interests to specific areas of practice (see Chapter 22), gain valuable hands-on legal experience, and determine what type of practice settings (see Chapter 21) most interest you.

REMEMBER

Whether you volunteer or find paid legal work during your law school summers doesn't matter; the *quality* of your summer job experiences is most important. Starting your summer job search early and having a strong grasp of the type of work you're interested in gives you a leg up in finding the best summer job fit. A great job is waiting for you, I promise. You just need a game plan to find it.

In this chapter, I walk you through exactly what you need to know about summer jobs, including the most popular types of jobs, such as clerking for a judge or at a firm, taking summer associateships, and working at nonprofits or governmental organizations. I also cover how to handle initial (on-campus) and call-back interviews. With perseverance and motivation, you'll not only land your ideal summer job but also gain a meaningful and instructive experience from it.

Major Factors That Impact Summer Job Options

Law school differs from college in that summer jobs are no longer simply a way to earn money. Instead, they're viewed as an important part of your legal education. Because much of what you discover in the classroom is theory-based, your summer jobs during law school are an opportunity to apply what you've learned in a hands-on legal setting.

Many rising second-, third-, and fourth-year students (2Ls, 3Ls, and 4Ls) find paid work or volunteer at a variety of workplaces, including nonprofits, governmental organizations, law firms, and courts. The goal of your summer job doesn't need to be making the most money possible or working in the most prestigious setting. (Although the money doesn't hurt!) Instead, if you concentrate on finding work that fits in with your personality, your interests in an area of practice, and your career goals, you'll come out head-and-shoulders above peers who are more shortsighted in their summer job outlooks. If your career services or career development office (CSO or CDO) or upperclass students haven't already filled you in, the summer job picture changes dramatically according to these three factors, which I cover in the following sections:

>> Your year in school

>> Whether you're a part-time/evening law student

>> Your academic record

Your year in school

The goal of your 1L summer job search is finding a job — not necessarily exactly what you want to do after graduation, but something vaguely in line with your interests. If your goal is to work as an environmental attorney after you graduate but all you manage to find during your first summer is a job clerking at a personal-injury law firm, it's no big deal. Finding your dream job, particularly paid work (which is a necessity for many students), as a rising 2L is difficult. My advice is that when you can't find your ideal job, you should just take whatever you can get as long as it has a legal bent. Trust me, the employers you interview with as a rising 3L next summer will be bowled over that you took the initiative to get your feet wet in *any* area of the law.

As a second-year student, your summer job search becomes much more important in the sense that you must press harder to find a job that's in line with your eventual career goals, because many students parlay their 2L summer jobs into permanent offers. If you like your 2L summer job and actually receive an offer, you're relieved of the pressure of hustling to find a permanent job during your third year. Likewise, when you interview for permanent jobs during your third year, know that employers prefer seeing a connection between your career interests and your second-year summer job if at all possible. That way, when they ask you why you took that particular summer job in estate planning, your answer appears more focused and less undecided when that's actually the practice area you want to pursue.

Whether you go to school part time/in the evenings

If you're a part-time or evening law student, devoting three months to a traditional legal summer job may not seem feasible. Given the fact that you're probably working (and depending on the steady income from) a full-time job, you may not be able to take a leave of absence for the summer to work as a clerk, summer associate, or volunteer.

Many CSOs recommend that evening and part-time law students do one of the following to gain summer legal experience or the equivalent during the year:

>> Leave their regular jobs to take permanent full-time jobs as law clerks year-round.

>> Hold a series of temporary full-time jobs through law school to make summer legal jobs easier to arrange.

>> Keep their current jobs but arrange their schedules so they can clerk or volunteer one half-day a week year-round. One way to adjust your schedule is arriving an hour early or staying an hour later at your regular full-time job every day so you make accommodations for taking a half-day off each week.

In this arrangement, you still get the same type of exposure to the real legal world that a full-time law student receives during the summer, only in a less-concentrated way.

Your academic record

The summer job picture changes based on your academic record. The sad truth is that your GPA matters somewhat in landing a plum summer job — especially when you're aiming for a summer associate position with a large law firm (aka Big Law). That's because summer associate positions for rising 3Ls and 4Ls often lead to permanent offers. As a result, those firms choose their summer associates judiciously. You often need to be in the top 10 percent of your class just to get an initial interview with a large firm; however, this requirement may be more lenient for students attending the top law schools.

Of course, your legal work experience and extracurriculars also figure in the equation, but firms are more eager to grant interviews when you have a strong academic record. That said, most law students with any GPA can find volunteer work with nonprofits, courts, and governmental organizations and clerking jobs in more out-of-the-way cities and towns.

The Early Bird Gets the Job

REMEMBER

Because you have many factors to consider when searching for your dream summer job, I recommend you start early. The time frame has changed over the years; your CSO team can guide you on when you need to be getting your application materials together. In some cases, that may be as soon as August, and in other cases, it may be October. It may seem early, but employers (particularly large firms) dictate much of this timing.

Any 1Ls not interested in a large firm job need to do the brunt of their summer job search activities for all other employers in January and February. Small and medium-sized firms, however, usually don't know their clerking needs very far in advance (see Chapter 21), so you need to keep after them throughout the spring.

Second-year students who want to apply for summer associateships at big firms must start sending résumés and cover letters in August before their 2L year starts. The hiring timetable for 2L summer associateships has changed drastically over the years. In some instances, you may receive an offer for your 2L summer as a fall semester 1L; other times, the schedule is late summer to early fall, with decisions generally made from Thanksgiving through Christmas. As for 2Ls who are looking for summer jobs with all other employers, they also need to focus the majority of their efforts in January and February, unless the particular employer they're considering has earlier or later posted deadlines.

REMEMBER

The time frame is a bit different for nonprofits, some government positions, and public interest agencies.

Letting your passions fuel your career choices

Figuring out what you're interested in summer job-wise may be hard when you're a first-year student who hasn't yet had the opportunity to choose any electives. Although you can choose from a plethora of areas of practice for your first legal summer job, knowing exactly what these practice areas entail is difficult, especially when you've only taken standard 1L courses like torts and civil procedures and have no other pre–law school exposure to law. That's why visiting your CSO as soon as you have an opportunity is a good idea.

Getting help from your CSO

Your law school's career services office is your best friend throughout your job search. Face it: At what other times in your life will you have access to around-the-clock, *free* career advice? Probably never, so take advantage of it now!

If you have no idea where the office is in the law school, ask an upperclass student or your dean for directions. CSOs are usually located right in your law school building, often near other administrative offices like the dean of students. Stop by and ask for a tour of the facilities. Get acquainted with all the resources there that can help you, such as summer and permanent job postings, books about areas of practice, and alumni career directories. You can also make an appointment with your career services dean to find out how individualized the assistance can be.

REMEMBER

Your CSO can help you in more ways than you can imagine. Most career services counselors say that many students mistakenly think that CSOs are in place only to help the top third of the class find jobs. (That's probably because the CSO usually is busy with on-campus interviews — one of its major activities — all fall.) But your CSO is there to help everyone find jobs. Just keep in mind that the CSO isn't a headhunter. CSO staff members can't hand you a job, but they can give you all the guidance you need to find one.

Appraising Your Summer Job Options

The good news about your summer job search is that everyone in your law school class can find a job. As long as you're willing to be flexible and potentially work for free, you'll be able to find *something* in the legal field (hey, everyone welcomes free labor).

When you're a 1L, the not-so-good news is that the paid jobs aren't as plentiful, though they do exist. Depending on the firm or organization, you may need to rank in the top of class to secure an interview. I did manage to find a paying job after my first year, despite the fact that I wasn't in the top third of my class. It didn't pay much, but it was at least above minimum wage, and it enabled me to see a field that I rarely would've encountered in traditional legal practice — alternative dispute resolution — and provided me with a valuable experience working at a dynamic nonprofit.

TIP

As a 2L, you have a much greater chance of nabbing a paying job; however, many 2Ls still end up volunteering because in doing so they have a wider range of options. One reason why landing a paying job is easier as an upperclass student is that 2Ls are more in demand. Most summer employers prefer hiring them because they have an extra year's experience under their belts and are more adept at research.

Getting a foot in the door by working for free

The main types of abundant nonpaying jobs include these:

>> Working at nonprofits like the American Civil Liberties Union (ACLU) or the Natural Resources Defense Council

>> Working at government agencies such as the Environmental Protection Agency (EPA) or Department of Justice

>> Working at a public defender's or prosecutor's office

>> Clerking for a state or federal judge

REMEMBER

You can do unpaid work in almost every specialty of law from environmental to wills and trusts to family law. The areas of law in which you're most likely to find unpaid work include criminal, poverty, environmental, civil rights, disability, and employment law.

Even if you dislike the idea of working for free, your job is still a great means of gaining new skills and finding out more about a field that interests you. Many students who need a steady flow of cash during the summer volunteer during the day and work at service jobs in the evenings. On the bright side, if you volunteer, at least you have more freedom to structure your hours and plan around your summer vacations. As a bonus, most employers for whom you volunteer your services are more understanding about accommodating part-time after-work job schedules. And some students even choose to work without pay in an externship arrangement (see Chapter 18) where they work for law school credit. That way, you can shave off a class and lighten your load for one semester — without any homework or an exam.

Making the grade when looking to get paid

If you're looking only for paid employment, your biggest obstacle in the job search will likely be your grades. Your chances of landing a paid job largely depend on what practice setting (see Chapter 21) you're aiming for and what your grades are. Large law firms, especially in big, glamorous cities like Chicago, Los Angeles, New York, and Boston, are the most stringent about grades. They look for students in the top 10 percent of their classes or who meet their class rank criteria. Most of these firms have pretty rigid cutoffs for grades, so even impressive extracurricular or personal achievements may be brushed aside in favor of your raw GPA. Not fair, you say? It sure isn't. These large firms pass over hundreds of bright, talented future lawyers who happened not to have a good exam day (or several).

If that's off-putting to you, keep in mind that not all employers are so grade-conscious. It's really only the large law firms with summer-associate programs that concentrate so heavily on grades. The rest — the small and medium-sized firms, judges, governmental, and nonprofit organizations — are more accepting of a diverse range of GPAs, but you still need to fight tooth and nail against many other students for any paid summer positions.

REMEMBER

If working at a traditional legal job (as a clerk, volunteer, or associate) doesn't get you excited, consider an alternative summer job, such as in legal publishing or law school administration. (See Chapter 23 for info about alternative permanent job options.)

Picking through an Assortment of Summer Jobs

Just like a kid in a candy store, your head will be spinning after you find out about all the possibilities for summer jobs. The summer job prospects include clerking for a law firm, nonprofit, government organization, or a judge. Whichever one you choose, you'll likely be doing plenty of legal writing and research.

In fact, you'll do legal research until you're blue in the face — everything from researching case law for briefs to writing pages and pages of memos. You'll spend hours rereading a single statute for nuances of meaning and days hunting down one elusive case for your supervising attorney's motion to dismiss. You'll become so familiar with the folks on the other end of the Lexis and Westlaw student research help lines that they'll know you by name before the summer's over. (Those people are lifesavers!)

The appeal of a clerkship

The term *clerking* simply means a law student working for a lawyer or judge (even if it's for free). You can clerk at a law firm, for a judge, or at a nonprofit or governmental organization. Clerking at a law firm (or other paid practice setting) means you're a temporary employee (paid or unpaid) who helps with legal research and writing.

Occasionally, clerking jobs can lead to permanent employment, depending on what the court's or firm's needs are and how well you wow them. Some summer clerking jobs can last into the school year; others are only for the summer. Regardless of how long you'll be clerking, be sure to do your job as well as you can so that you receive stellar recommendations that you can use in future job searches or even to score a permanent offer.

When you clerk at a *nonprofit* (meaning a business not conducted for the purpose of making a profit, including organizations such as Lawyers for the Creative Arts, Legal Aid DC, Institute for Justice, Federalist Society, or the Republican National Lawyers Association), you're likely doing the same kinds of things that you would at a law firm, only you usually aren't being paid. Many students like the more laid-back atmosphere of many nonprofits, especially when they've already sampled law firm life. See Chapter 21 for more about working at nonprofits.

Judicial clerkships involve plenty of legal research and writing for one particular judge in a sort of mentorship arrangement. Check out Chapter 21 for an in-depth look at what clerking for judges entails. The field for judicial clerkships (summer and otherwise) often is competitive, especially at the federal level. To land one of these positions in either the state or federal court system, you need outstanding legal research and writing skills and recommendations from your professors, especially when your grades are borderline.

TIP

Many professors clerked for judges, so ask around to see whether professors at your school have any ties to judges with whom you may be interested in working.

The lure of a summer associateship

When you work for a large law firm, you're not considered a clerk. Instead, you're usually considered a *summer associate,* even though you do the same tasks as a clerk. (Note that large law firms may have hundreds to just over a thousand or so lawyers. Big law firms generally have hundreds or thousands of attorneys in multiple offices in a variety of cities, states, and perhaps countries.) They're called summer associateships because large firms commonly use the term *associate* to describe the more junior attorneys at large firms.

In other words, in a summer associateship, you do the same work as a summer clerk, only you're paid at a flat rate — and that rate can run, on average, anywhere from $1,500 to $4,000 a *week*.

REMEMBER

In general, large law firms are the only ones that can afford to offer summer-associate programs. You won't find a ten-person law firm paying its clerks $2,400 a week!

One option that you may want to pursue as a summer associate is asking whether you can split your summer. *Splitting your summer* means spending the first six weeks (or so) at one firm and the other six weeks at another. You may even be able to split your summer across different cities if you want, although housing can become an issue unless you have friends or family with whom you can stay. Some firms strongly discourage this practice because it means you have less time to get to know their staff and operations, and vice versa. Others don't seem to care. You can find information about splitting the summer on the firm's entry in the *NALP Directory of Legal Employers* (free online at www.nalpdirectory.com or at your CSO).

TIP

Some summer associates are treated like first-year lawyers at large firms. Others are barely spoken to and are left to sink or swim on their own; it all depends on the firm. Talk to upperclass students about their experiences as associates at various firms and inquire at your CSO, which often maintains a file of students' perspectives on their summer employment that's categorized by firm. Finding out as much as you can about the firm before you start helps you know what to expect.

WARNING

Depending on the particular year, the economy, and other factors, some firms have poor summer associate-to-offer ratios. In other words, a firm may hire 40 summer associates but only plan to offer 10 of them positions. Or it may hire five associates but make no offers. That means many disappointed students have to hustle with the rest of the class as 3Ls and 4Ls out looking for permanent jobs. Besides looking at the firm's past history of offer and acceptance ratios (which you can find in the *NALP Directory of Legal Employers*) and speaking with your CSO, you can't do much else to predict how this summer will turn out.

Readying Résumés and Cover Letters

Before ever starting interviews, you need to make sure your résumé and cover letter are in tip-top shape. Because some of the most popular employers receive 100 or more résumés a week, you need to be professional and meticulous in your presentation. Your CSO can help you develop your résumé and cover letter, and I highly recommend stopping by and going over these materials line by line with your counselor. However, don't stop there: As the old law school adage about cover letters recommends, "Show it to at least three people." The following sections include some main points to keep in mind as you begin crafting your résumé and cover letter.

TIP

While you're working on your résumé and cover letter, don't forget to update your LinkedIn profile. Many employers visit your profile to verify information on your submitted materials, and others seek out potential clerks, interns, and so on by reaching out on LinkedIn.

Crafting a successful legal résumé

Think of a good résumé as your ticket to an interview. If you don't have the right ticket, you don't get in. After all, many CSOs have something called a *résumé drop* for summer employers, which means they collect résumés from all interested students, and the employer then determines whom to offer interviews. That's why your résumé needs to impress from the moment the interviewer starts reading the first line.

REMEMBER

A legal résumé is a little different from the one you used as an undergraduate because you want to:

>> **Make the law school section as meaty as you can:** You do so by including any extracurricular activities, leadership positions, and research assistantships you participated in or academic honors you received. This section goes first on your résumé, so you want to make it as memorable as you can.

>> **Leave off any undergraduate or postcollege jobs that involved flipping burgers at fast-food restaurants or less serious positions you've held.**

>> **Write a brief but detailed description about what you did at each legal job you held:** Unlike your undergraduate résumé, your previous legal experience (summer jobs, part-time school-year jobs, and research assistantships) is one of the main reasons an employer is going to hire you.

Tailor the descriptions of what you did at each legal job to the needs of your future employer. The main benefit of preparing your résumé with your target employer in mind is that it tells the employer that you're sensitive to its needs and that you're thinking about what the employer can gain from you (and not vice versa). For instance, suppose you want to work at an environmental law firm this summer. Instead of crafting your résumé solely from the viewpoint of what *you* gained from your previous legal experience, like "learned about federal environmental statutes," you need to put yourself in the shoes of your prospective employer and write more about what your employer will gain from what you've discovered through your experiences.

Therefore, you'd rewrite this example as something like "researched and wrote memoranda on federal environmental statutes with little supervision." This more specific, employer needs–based second approach turns more heads than the vague, student-centered first approach. The latter shows exactly what you did (rather than what you learned) and demonstrates that you're a self-starter.

TIP

The following are the ten most important elements of a legal résumé.

» **Perspective:** As I mentioned, write the résumé from the perspective of what you can do for the employer, not what you got out of each of your activities and jobs.

» **Action words:** Use action words (in the past tense) whenever possible. *Prepared, wrote,* and *collected* are all examples of evocative action words.

» **Page limit:** Limit your résumé to one page unless you're a more seasoned student with an extensive prior career history. In that case, two pages are perfectly acceptable (unless the employer says otherwise).

» **Section headings:** Make them powerful and specific. "Education," "Legal Experience," and "Publications" are good ways to begin a new section. Don't forget to list your law school, college, and any graduate school names under "Education." If you're a 1L applying for your first summer job and you have no legal experience, listing your past work history under the general heading of "Professional Experience" is perfectly acceptable.

» **Personal interests:** Adding them gives a human dimension to your résumé, but you'd usually only include them when you don't have much else to put on your résumé. For instance, if you're a rising 2L who has only one summer legal job and an extracurricular activity or two to put on your résumé, adding a section at the very end titled "Personal Interests" keeps your résumé from looking too bare-bones. Plus, you never know when a recruiter will pick up your résumé as a fellow Pilates or true crime enthusiast and offer you an interview based on your mutual passion. But use common sense when listing your interests — painting, traveling, tennis, and chess are safe.

» **GPA and class rank:** The general guideline is if your GPA is higher than 3.0, list it. If not, keep it off and wait until an employer asks you for it. Schools vary in how they report class rank, so talk with your CSO team to find out the best way to list it on your résumé.

- » **Extracurriculars:** List all your legal extracurriculars under your law school name in the "Education" section.

- » **Paper:** If you're submitting your materials during an interview or in person, choose lightweight bond paper rather than plain printer paper. Slightly textured, off-white stationery paper looks best, but avoid any colors other than off-white, pale tan, white, or gray. Make sure the envelopes match.

- » **Printer:** Use a laser printer whenever possible because it provides the crispest look to your résumé (and cover letters).

- » **Proofreading:** Proofread your résumé many times to make sure all information is factual and that no embarrassing spelling mistakes are evident. Don't rely on AI programs or the computer's spelling checker alone. You don't want to be applying to a law "farm" or have researched federal "statues."

Having two or three versions of your résumé is a smart way to go. The résumé you send seeking a job clerking for a judge isn't the exact same as the one you'd send to an intellectual property firm or family law nonprofit. All employers stress different qualifications and characteristics in their potential hires.

Creating credible cover letters

Your cover letter often is the first piece of information that employers read about you, so make it special! The best way to make yours stand out is to research the employer before writing the cover letter. Pack your cover letter with specifics about why you think the employer and you are a good fit: its clients, a lawyer or partner whose career you admire, its mission, recent or current cases it's handled, and tidbits you've read about it in the news. Then link what the employer does with your interests.

Making your cover letter memorable is always key to getting an interview. If you had to read hundreds of them a week, which is what many law firm recruiters must do, you're more likely to remember cover letters that are well researched and thought out than the ones that are blatantly mass-mailed and generic (in other words, no "Dear Sirs"). Make your cover letter top notch, and employers will take notice!

Researching employers

Researching employers is essential when you want your cover letter to stand out from the letters of all the other applicants applying for a summer position. The Internet makes researching employers easy. Spend half an hour per employer online and see what you can dig up from its website and from Internet searches. Talking briefly by email, video conference, text, or phone to alums who currently work for the employer is another excellent way of digging up the dirt for your cover letter. Prefacing your chat with "I'm very interested in applying for a summer job with your employer, and I was wondering whether you can spend a few minutes telling me what you think I need to know about it" is a good start.

REMEMBER

Now, you may think, "Why should I spend the half an hour or more researching this one employer just to write a cover letter? Can't I use my time in a better way, given that my letter may just be tossed in the trash?" But when you consider the thousands of dollars that an employer can spend interviewing, training, and potentially paying you, spending a mere half an hour researching each of the employers you contact doesn't seem so out of line. You can't expect employers to make an investment in you if you won't make a minimal investment in them.

Composing the letter

The traditional four-paragraph format works best for the body of a cover letter.

» The first paragraph serves as an introduction, revealing who you are and how you found out about the employer (through a job posting at your CSO, online, or through a direct referral).

» The next paragraph describes why you and the firm are a good match based on your interests and what the firm handles.

» The third paragraph discusses your qualifications for the position (be sure to mention information that's most relevant to that particular employer first, such as research and writing experience for clerking with a judge).

» The last paragraph directly requests what type of action you want to occur and informs the employer of your availability (such as "I will contact you next week to discuss summer intern opportunities. I will be returning to Chicago frequently throughout the spring and am available to meet with you at any convenient time for an interview.").

You may also want to mention any attachments that you're sending, such as a résumé and reference list.

Interviewing On-Campus

During *on-campus interview* (OCI) season, employers visit your campus and conduct interviews with students they usually preselect from a résumé/cover letter drop. *Note:* In the past, many schools offered OCIs during the fall only. Traditional OCI season still happens in the fall, but opportunities for OCIs now occur throughout the academic year.

A résumé/cover letter drop is the time and place that your CSO designates for all students interested in a particular employer to drop off their application materials (usually just a résumé and/or cover letter). Then, that employer reviews the stack of résumés and cover letters and contacts the students it wants to interview. Your CSO may also request that you do your résumé drops online through its portal. If that's the case, the CSO sends out notices to all students about how to log onto this service and upload your documents.

The number of firms or other organizations that conduct OCIs at particular law schools varies significantly according to many factors. These factors vary from year to year depending on such things as the state of the economy, but your school's (perceived) prestige, its ranking, and its size (see Chapter 3) can be a huge factor.

Large firms and some governmental organizations are mainly the ones that conduct interviews on campus. The smallest firms and nonprofits simply don't have enough people on their staffs to send lawyers out for the day to interview. You need to use a different strategy (other than OCI) when contacting these employers. Your initial interviews with these employers may occur over the phone, on video conference, or in person at their offices; the choice varies from employer to employer. (When you volunteer, you're more likely to get an expense-free telephone initial interview instead of trekking out to their office.)

WARNING

OCIs often are big sources of stress. Seeing your classmates come to school in suits triggers inferiority complexes in many law students because who got the interview that day and who didn't becomes clear (unless, of course, your school is the type where students regularly come to class in suits). Because on-campus interviewing is so visible, many students fear that if they aren't selected for OCIs, they'll never get summer jobs. Many CSOs, however, routinely indicate that at many schools, only 25 to 30 percent of students in a particular class secure jobs through OCIs. The National Association for Law Placement (NALP) notes that the majority of offers for positions for the summer of 2025 (56 percent) were secured through direct applications, job postings, alumni connections, résumé collections, and referrals. This shift shows a decreased reliance on OCIs.

Posting your résumé

The first step to getting an interview through an OCI is finding out your CSO's policy on how to submit résumés. Some career centers ask for paper copies. Others want students to post them online through a service like 12Twenty, VMock, or Symplicity, where employers who subscribe to the service review résumés online and notify you online about interviews.

Whichever approach your CSO takes, make sure your résumé is polished and proofread so you can make the best impression. You can read more on résumés in the earlier section "Readying Résumés and Cover Letters."

Dressing for success

REMEMBER

First impressions matter a lot, and appearance makes an impression, especially when candidates have similar qualifications.

Make sure you have a professional-looking suit. Navy, charcoal gray, and black are the safest colors. Conservative skirt or pantsuits often make the best impression on conservative interviewers, and you should avoid loud/busy ties. Additionally, keep jewelry and makeup to a minimum.

Don't be nervous if you have no idea how to dress for an interview. Ask your mentors, CSO team, and alums about the firm culture. You may also be able to get an idea by looking at the firm's website.

Honing your writing sample

Every lawyer has to write; it's in the job description. And to prove that you have a command of the English language, you may need to bring a writing sample to your on-campus interviews (or any initial interview, regardless of where it takes place) for each employer that you plan to meet with. Although some on-campus interviewers don't even ask for a writing sample, many do, and having one ready makes you look thoroughly prepared.

You don't have to be an SAT-vocabulary spewing prodigy, but your writing sample needs to make sense and read well. And just any old piece of writing won't do. That means no short stories, papers you wrote in college, or submissions to the law school newspaper. Most first-year students use a sample (three to five double-spaced pages maximum) of the brief or memorandum they wrote for their first-year legal writing class (after making corrections or changes that their writing instructor suggested, of course). Most upper-division students use a piece of the same length that they wrote during their summer jobs or a piece from that same legal writing class (if they don't have anything more recent).

TIP

Here are a couple of additional suggestions:

>> **Make sure it doesn't violate attorney-client privilege.** When you use a piece of writing from your summer job, checking with your supervisor first is extremely important for determining whether you need to *redact* (cross out with an opaque black marker) the names of parties or other identifying facts. Otherwise, you may risk a breach of attorney-client privilege, and that can land you in serious hot water with the employer and your law school.

>> **Know the contents of your writing sample inside and out.** You may be asked to explain in great detail the circumstances surrounding the writing sample.

WARNING

Whatever type of writing you decide to use, make sure that it uses impeccable grammar and is typo-free. Although the number of interviewers who actually read the writing sample is open to debate, if your interviewer does decide to read it, you want to present the most favorable picture you can. A sloppy writing sample covered in correction fluid isn't going to do that.

Asking (and answering) tough questions

When you get to the actual interview, which probably will last about 20 to 30 minutes, make sure you have a list of questions to ask the interviewer either written down or committed to memory. If you don't have any questions, an interviewer may think you're not interested in the employer and may end up passing you over for a call-back in favor of more enthusiastic applicants as a result. Having thoughtful questions always signals that you've gone the extra mile to find out about a particular employer.

TIP

The best questions are tailored to the particular employer, but asking general questions is okay, too. Here's a good guideline: If it's a really basic question, like how many offices the firm has or how many lawyers work there, skip it. Otherwise you look like you just decided to interview with that firm on a whim. Use basic facts about the firm as a foundation for questions that probe a little deeper. For instance, you can ask, "Do you anticipate expanding beyond your current six offices?" A great place to find such fodder for your questions is the firm's website or promotional materials.

Whenever possible, finding out beforehand who your interviewers are is also an excellent idea because you can then learn some things about them ahead of time. Your CSO often can tell you who the interviewers are, and you can surf the employer's website and read their bios, if they're available. Otherwise, you can check LinkedIn, Google Scholar, or Bloomberg Law for each of the interviewers' names and read whatever comes up. Of course, you don't need to go to heroic lengths just to find out this information, but anything you can find out can only help your chances of succeeding in the interview.

When the subject of grades comes up . . .

During an interview, the interviewer probably will ask you about your grades. This question is a big problem for some students whose grades are mediocre or poor. Students who fall into this category usually wait for the interviewer to mention their grades first, without volunteering the information themselves. That way, if the interviewer doesn't bring it up, they assume that their grades just aren't a problem.

However, that isn't necessarily the right way to approach grades you'd rather not showcase. Instead, always mention your grades (even when they're poor) by offering a short, concise statement about them at the beginning of the interview — and preferably not something like, "I don't do well on essay, multiple-choice, or short-answer exams." For instance, you may say something like "I know my grades aren't the highest, but I believe my work on the law journal and my job as a research assistant for Professor X speak more to my abilities." When you don't say anything at all about your grades, the interviewer is left to come up with their own explanations, like that you're a slacker or you just can't handle law school–level work. Because that isn't the impression you want to present, take the time now to compose a solid explanation.

Additionally, you never want to make the mistake of pretending that your grades don't exist or hoping the interviewer forgets to ask about them. That's the kiss of death. Neither do you want to avoid explaining any inconsistent grades. The interviewer usually has your entire transcript anyway, which makes scanning first for inconsistent grades or semesters easy. For example, if you're usually an A− student but you received a C+ in your property class, the interviewer will likely ask, "What happened in property?" Or if you have a consistent B average but one semester you received a straight 4.0, your interviewer will likely be interested in why that happened.

Most students normally have some idea of why they bombed a particular class or semester — "I hated civ pro" or "I partied too much that semester." (For what it's worth, I actually loved civ pro!) However, sometimes your grades are a total mystery. That's what happened to me. The class I'd study hard for was my lowest grade, and the ones I was less diligent in were often my highest. It made my transcript into something of a conundrum. If you're unsure why your performance is all over the map, make an appointment with your academic support/success and CSO teams. They may be able to point out patterns you can't see. For example, they may discover that you do better on closed-book exams than on open-book ones. Then you gain some insight into your performance and can offer interviewers an explanation much more coherent than "I dunno."

Other points of discussion to remember

In your interview, don't forget to talk about your work experiences, extracurriculars, and volunteer work. Don't ever assume that your interviewer actually has read your résumé and knows all about what you've accomplished in law school thus far. Many times, your interview is the first time an interviewer has ever laid eyes on your résumé (if they even bother to look it over at all).

Keep in mind that one of the more crucial interview questions you're likely to be asked is why you want to be a part of the firm, agency, court, or nonprofit. Retention is a huge issue, especially with law firms, and that's why you need to have a carefully thought-out answer, especially when you can't show any tangible reasons for making a commitment to the firm.

Managing the Call-Back Interview

Many employers require a call-back interview to complete the interview process. The *call-back* interview is when you travel (at either your own or the employer's expense) to the employer's offices for a final round of interviews. These generally last half to three-quarters of a day, including one meal (usually lunch). Many firms require call-backs, but nonprofits and governmental organizations tend not to. The general guideline is that if you're volunteering your services, you won't have a call-back.

REMEMBER

The call-back is an opportunity for the employer to conduct more interviews with you, generally with several to many lawyers at the firm or organization. At half an hour per lawyer, that's a good half to three-quarters of a day of interviewing. However, while they're interviewing you, you also need to be interviewing them and deciding whether this particular employer is where you can see yourself working.

Many students find call-back interviews to be stressful. When you're interviewing with a large firm, you may be traveling to another city, sleeping in a hotel for the night, enduring four to eight interviews in a short time frame, and having a meal with your interviewers. After such a high-intensity day, you may be exhausted and ready to unwind.

When interviewing for a job at a small or medium-size firm, nonprofit, or government organization, you'll have a similar day of interviews, probably without the meal, but you'll often be expected to pay for everything yourself (travel and hotel). For all interviews, you'll be expected to be on your best behavior, have interesting questions to ask, and maintain the highest level of etiquette.

Reviewing your etiquette

The call or email that you receive from an employer explains that you're invited to interview with the firm (at its expense or not) at the firm's office in the city you're interested in. If they're picking up the tab, the firm either pays you outright or reimburses you later for your travel, meals, lodging, and ground transportation. That doesn't mean, of course, they'll cover the cost of the new suit you buy for the occasion or a dinner for you and your buddies at the most expensive restaurant in town.

If they're picking up the tab, the firm or its travel agent usually arranges your flight and lodging for you; all you have to do is show up. If you need to cancel, make sure you do so well in advance. I've heard horror stories about students at other law schools not showing up for call-back interviews and the firms they jilted deciding not to recruit at their schools ever again. Law firms, like elephants, have long memories.

REMEMBER

Regardless of the size or type of the employer, make sure that you've done your homework on the firm and the lawyers who will be interviewing you before you leave campus. Look up your interviewers' bios on the firm's website or search law blogs or www.martindale.com. Make sure to note whether any of them went to your college or law school and whether they practice in areas that interest you. Find out what kinds of awards they've won, whether they worked on a journal, and what cities they're from. This material becomes invaluable when you face a lull in the conversation. Plus, it shows your enthusiasm. What interviewer wouldn't be wowed by a student who goes that extra mile?

Getting ready

When you're in your hotel room the night before your interview, make sure that:

>> You go over your notes about the firm and lawyer bios

>> Your suit is pressed and presentable

>> You have your *portfolio* (leather or faux leather case in which you keep copies of your résumé, transcript, and writing samples) with you and many copies (at least one for each interviewer) of your résumés, writing samples, and transcripts

>> You get a good night's sleep to be at your best the next day

In the morning, be sure to allow ample time for getting to your call-back interview. Leave at least 20 minutes more than you think you'll need, especially if you're not staying near the firm or if it's raining or snowing. If you're really worried, leave an extra half-hour. If you find that you have some extra time when you arrive at the employer, take some time for yourself in the building's lobby before going up to the firm. After all, you don't want to look too eager by arriving 20 minutes early and just sitting in the waiting area. Instead, park yourself on a couch in the building's lobby, take a moment to relax, and review your lawyer bios and questions.

REMEMBER

The call-back interview usually has two parts: the in-office interviews with attorneys and the lunch (or, less frequently, dinner) component. If you're interviewing with a large firm, lunch or dinner is always included, but it may not be with a small firm, medium-sized firm, or governmental organization.

Here's a quick rundown of how the in-office interview (usually) goes:

>> **When you arrive at the firm's office, you greet the executive assistant or receptionist pleasantly.** By all means, don't be brash or curt. These folks often have more influence on hiring decisions than you think, so if you're rude to the executive assistant, they may alert the hiring partner about it.

>> **Next, you're directed to the interview space, where you chat for a while (small talk) and then receive a folder with your schedule for the day.** But don't let your guard down at this or any point during your call-back interview; for all practical purposes, every conversation you have, no matter how big or small, is an interview. Your schedule lists attorneys with whom you'll be interviewing and the length of time you'll meet. The lunch portion of the interview is also listed on the schedule and so are the attorneys with whom you'll be dining.

>> **Your interviews with the lawyers usually last a half-hour each.** Keep in mind that each lawyer you meet with may already have a copy of your transcript, résumé, and writing samples (which are either requested by the firm prior to the call-back or the ones you or had already provided to the initial interviewer). Although the lawyers ask some questions, the biggest part of those interviews features *you* asking questions. So come prepared with a huge list of them. Make your questions meaningful; they need to be even more thought-provoking than the ones you asked during the initial interview.

Munching through the Lunch Interview

The lunch portion of the interview often makes students the most nervous; most students are puzzled by whether they're officially being interviewed during the meal. On the one hand, your interviewers aren't asking you typical interview questions, so the lunch has a more relaxed feel. On the other hand, remember that these people aren't like your friends, so you don't want to become too comfortable with them.

The best answer to whether you're being interviewed at lunch is always a resounding "Yes." No matter how friendly your interviewers may seem, they're still evaluating every move you make, from whether you order inappropriately to whether you're rude to the waitstaff. Treat the meal component the same as you would the other parts of the interview: formal, but not stiff.

WARNING

You must follow many elements of good etiquette during an interview meal. Making a major faux pas here can greatly hinder your chances of receiving an offer. When you're at home, eating a meal seems like second nature. But in an interview situation, you need to think about strategy. Instead of reaching across someone's chest for the rolls, you need to ask someone to pass them to you. The main things to keep in mind are to be friendly to the servers, always say please and thank you, and generally mind your manners.

Observing ordering protocol

One area where many law students make their first big mistakes is when ordering. At first glance, ordering seems pretty straightforward; when the server asks what you want, you just choose something. But it involves more strategy than that. When ordering, you need to follow the interviewer's lead whenever possible. It sounds old-fashioned, but it's the way things need to be done in the interviewing world.

TIP

If the server asks what you want first, politely say that you haven't yet made up your mind or that you need a few more minutes to make a decision. That way, you can see what your interviewers order. The reason you want to wait? Your job is to order something in line with what the rest of the group orders — nothing too expensive or inexpensive. Sure, you may feel like this silly rule stifles your sense of self-expression, and that if you want to order the peanut butter and jelly sandwich then you should go ahead and do so. But when you're in a high-stakes interview scenario, playing it conservatively and following your interviewer's lead often is best.

In addition, make sure you steer clear of ribs, spaghetti bolognese, or anything else that's too messy. So stick with something that's easy to eat, easy to cut, and not drowning in buckets of sauce.

Taking on table talk

One important lunch-interview technique is keeping up your end of the conversation by asking questions and showing initiative. You don't want to sit there like a bump on a log. The point of the lunch interview is to see how you interact in a quasi-social setting (like when you'd be interacting with clients). You need to be alert, engaging, and inquisitive. Don't spend all your time eating or listening; break it up by throwing out some conversation starters. Ask the same sorts of questions you'd ask in a regular interview. But, for variety, tossing in questions about where everyone grew up and in what neighborhoods yields intriguing responses. Just remember that certain topics like relationships or salaries are inappropriate for this lunchtime conversation.

TIP

Brushing up on your current events by reading a local newspaper (online or on paper) before your interview starts always is a good idea. That way, when the interviewers are talking about what the mayor said yesterday or the new downtown building, you may have something to contribute.

(Not) picking up the tab

If the server happens to place the check in front of you, just wait until your interviewer picks it up. Paying the bill is never your responsibility, but picking it up yourself and placing it in front of the interviewer is bad form. And never check the bill to make sure it adds up correctly; it won't go over well with your interviewers, no matter how helpful you want to appear. After the bill is paid, be sure to thank everyone individually and make sure you know how you're getting back to your hotel or the firm and whether you'll be escorted.

Writing thank-you notes/emails

Thank-you notes are the order of the day with call-backs (and for any interviews, really). Everyone likes to feel appreciated, and many students omit this crucial bit of etiquette to their detriment.

REMEMBER

You need to type thank-you notes in business letter format — no handwritten notecards — and address them to each of your interviewers individually. Email is never a good option. Send thank-you notes as soon as possible after your interview; if you receive their decision prior to mailing them out, it's your call whether to go ahead and send it. (If it's a yes, definitely do it; if it's a no, you may not feel like wasting a stamp.)

Chapter **21**

Getting the Lowdown on Careers

Whether you're a rising second-year student (2L) who wants to get a head start or a second-semester 3L who's just getting around to it, the job search can be overwhelming at times. With everything that you must do to find a decent job, from regularly sending résumés and cover letters to networking with alums, maintaining a successful job search can take on the same time commitment as a five-credit law school class.

But nothing is more exciting than searching for your first real lawyer job! What makes it such an exhilarating process is that you never know where a lead may take you. One minute you're set on a judicial clerkship, and the next you've happened on a different dream job as a bankruptcy court clerk, perhaps. Whatever your current career plans (or lack thereof), the sky's the limit with your juris doctor (JD) degree.

I know how intimidating the job search can seem at first, so in this chapter, I help you break down the process. First, I examine the most common lawyerly job opportunities and how you need to approach each one. Next, I take you step-by-step through mapping out your job-search goals and provide you with insider information about employer hiring practices.

Exploring Practice Setting Possibilities

Finding a job can seem like the most important part of your law school career, and for jobless second-semester 3Ls or 4Ls, it seems like life-or-death. Remember, however, that you've already won half the battle: Armed with a law degree (and eventually a passed bar exam), you have a ton of options for your first job within the legal field. Sure, most of your classmates will probably end up working in private practice at law firms or in government, but you don't have to follow that path. Branch out and discover that your options are nearly limitless: Imagine clerking for a judge, trying life-and-death cases as a prosecutor, or calling all the shots as a solo practitioner. And of course, you have dozens of areas of practice to choose from (Chapter 22 has a complete discussion of these options).

If, out of this limitless sea of choices, you still can't find anything that tickles your fancy, consider an alternative career, such as legal publishing, law school administration, or law librarianship. See Chapter 23 for all you ever wanted to know about JD advantage and nontraditional legal jobs.

WARNING

Sadly, many law students and new graduates never explore many of the diverse career options because they're too caught up in what everyone else seems to be doing. And much of the time, what everyone else seems to be doing is interviewing for positions with government agencies or big firms. True, large firms are attractive workplaces, with their huge starting salaries and luxury offices, but they sometimes come with golden handcuffs, as I explain in the upcoming section "Large firms."

Before getting caught up in the big-firm frenzy, take a peek at all your other options. You may be pleasantly surprised: Working with a nonprofit or small or medium-size firm may be a more satisfying fit.

REMEMBER

Although you want to gain experience, make connections, and build your network throughout law school, you really don't need to start thinking about your future until the summer before your final year. Any later than that, however, and you're setting yourself up for a major meltdown. During this specific summer is when you need to conduct all your self-assessment (talking to your career services office [CSO], reading career self-help books, and thinking about what you really need in your career), job shadow, talk to alumni and your mentors, and pin down a few areas of practice that truly excite you.

Taking the private practice route

Private practice simply means that you work in the for-profit business sector rather than the governmental or nonprofit sectors. Private practice, like any other job, has its benefits and drawbacks. Most lawyers enjoy higher salaries overall in private practice than they do in the public sector. Lawyers like working in private practice for several other reasons, too. Here are some of them:

>> **They're able to engage in *client development*, which means recruiting new business and nurturing clients they already have.** This activity is virtually nonexistent in the public sector.

>> **A greater variety and number of positions are generally available in private practice.** Plus, *upward mobility* — meaning job advancement (the ability to make partner) and/or salary increases corresponding to experience — is generally faster than in the public sector.

>> **You have greater flexibility to *specialize* (choose a practice area that interests you) in private practice.** In the public sector, you tend to have a more definitive job description.

On the other hand, higher salaries often mean a correspondingly lengthy workweek. Another common complaint about private practice is that most lawyers are required to keep track of their *billable hours,* the number of hours a firm is able to bill a client in exchange for a lawyer's work. Billable hours aren't an issue in the public sector because the client isn't paying the organization or agency.

Most firms quote their billable hour requirements in terms of how many hours per year you must bill. Generally, firm billable hour requirements are within the 1,700 to 2,300 hour range. Of course, the larger the firm, the more likely you'll have to bill more hours (because you're getting paid more). As you can probably imagine, keeping track of your time with a billable hour system (which usually breaks down into keeping track of your time in six-minute increments) can be highly annoying.

WARNING

Though many people pursue private practice, it isn't necessarily the road to happiness. The 2025 Law360 Pulse Lawyer Satisfaction Survey reported that overall job satisfaction had dropped to its lowest level in the five-year history of the survey, with just 61 percent of lawyers indicating they were satisfied or very satisfied with their jobs — a five-point drop from 2024. Satisfaction with billable hours, advancement opportunities, and *collegiality* (relationships with coworkers) also hit record lows.

Large firms

If obscenely high starting salaries, a posh working environment, general prestige, and a support staff working for you around the clock sounds like your cup of tea, consider tossing your hat into the ring for a job at a large law firm. *Large firms* are generally defined as having more than 100 lawyers. They usually boast dozens of practice areas; many of them are highly specialized. At a large firm, you generally have two ways to hook up with a particular area of practice: You either choose to specialize in a specific field (such as labor law) right away or rotate through different practice areas until you make up your mind.

Expect plenty of competition in applying for a large firm job. Large firms have the luxury of choosing from the cream of the crop, so keep in mind that your odds of making it are generally slim unless you're in the top 5 or 10 percent of your class at a law school that firm traditionally recruits from. These are the employers to whom grades matter the most; if it's really your dream job, make sure you earn the best grades you can throughout law school so that you'll be a competitive candidate come application time.

New lawyers with large firms often are known as *associates*; when you start, you're usually placed in an *associate class.* Yes, it smacks of your elementary school days, but that's the lingo. Throughout your years at the firm, you're referred to by your class year (for example, "a seventh-year associate").

Big firms are sometimes known for having poor attrition rates for one primary reason: *burnout,* also called the *golden handcuffs dilemma.* When you have $150,000 to $200,000 in loans breathing down your neck, who wouldn't love a sweet $150,000 or higher starting salary? But this huge paycheck comes with a price. After their first few weeks, associates at large firms don't blink an eye at 80-to-100-hour workweeks, and putting in *face-time* (showing up just so partners and other lawyers know you came in) on the weekends is usually expected. If your family situation or personal interests don't allow such a massive time commitment to your work, you probably won't last long at a large firm.

Applying for jobs with most large firms is easy because they generally have predictable hiring seasons that typically begin during the late summer or early fall (though this timeline is becoming earlier each year). Many third-year law students start submitting résumés and cover letters beginning in August, and initial interviews usually take place from September through early November. You can find the deadlines for applying with large firms on their respective websites, through your career development/services office (CDO or CSO) portal and announcements, or in the NALP Directory of Legal Employers, which you can find in your CDO/CSO or search free online at www.nalpdirectory.com.

But keep in mind that most large firm jobs are procured from offers by the firm during your 2L/3L summer associateship (see Chapter 20). In other words, if you're not hired on as a summer associate during your 2L or 3L summer, odds are against your finding a large firm job during the fall application and interview season (though all hope isn't necessarily lost). That's because many firms aren't seeking additional new associates at that point; they've already filled their associate class from the summer associates who accept their offers.

THE TRAITS OF SUCCESSFUL BIG LAW ASSOCIATES

The following advice comes from Lauren Jackson, Esq., Assistant Dean, Career & Professional Development, Howard University School of Law.

In my experience working directly with law firm partners and supporting students entering the Big Law space, the students who thrive share a consistent set of traits. They demonstrate intellectual success but pair it with a clear vision of their trajectory in the environment and a willingness to continuously learn. They take ownership of their work, communicate proactively, and manage their time with discipline and intention. Strong Big Law associates are dependable under pressure, adaptable in fast-moving environments, and responsive to feedback without taking it personally. Perhaps most importantly, they show emotional intelligence: the ability to read a room, collaborate across differences, and build trust with both partners and clients. There is also a surety about themselves that allows them to withstand the ever-changing pressures of the space by both internal or external factors. They don't allow those pressures to cause them to question who they are nor their value.

Small and medium-sized firms

When you consider that only a small percentage of all lawyers in private practice in the United States are at the big firms, you may be wondering where the heck the rest of them are. The answer: Most work at small and medium-sized firms. According to the ABA Profile of Legal Education (2024), almost 80 percent of all attorneys in private practice are employed by small firms (including solos). *Small firms* often employ 2 to 20 attorneys. *Medium-sized* firms are generally defined as having between 21 Small and medium-sized firms have many things going for them.

>> **Because they're not quite so large, you don't feel like you're just another face in the crowd.** In other words, you get to know your fellow associates better and may form more long-lasting and personal relationships with them.

>> **Their clients are typically individuals and small businesses.** That's compared with largely corporate clients that large firms service, so you get to know who you're representing more intimately.

>> **They appeal to many law students and new graduates because some offer a more balanced lifestyle.** You'll need to ferret out those that do, however, if that's important to you. Keep in mind that many small and midsize firms work you just as much as the big ones do but may not have the prestige or the fat paycheck of the large firms.

>> **Their lawyers tend to take on significant responsibility earlier, including representing clients and taking on their own cases much sooner than at large firms.** Generally, the smaller the firm, the quicker you gain responsibility, so don't be surprised when you're going to court by yourself your very first day at a four-person firm.

The upside of life at small and medium-sized firms can also be its downside, however: Being part of a closer-knit group can make having confrontations with your colleagues difficult. In other words, being part of the family can make conversations with the higher-ups about a raise or a problem colleague at the firm more difficult. Another often-cited downside of small and medium-sized firms: They provide fewer resources than larger firms. For example, you probably won't have as extensive a network of support staff at a small firm, so you may find yourself doing all your own research, filing, and mailing. That's one reason small and medium-sized firms pride themselves on finding people who are willing to roll up their sleeves and get the job done.

REMEMBER

Having fewer working lawyers means small and medium-sized firms can't afford to pay their new associates $100,000 starting salaries. Their starting salaries are in the range of $40,000 to $85,000. Typically, the larger the firm, the higher the salary, but the size of the city factors in, too. A firm in Chicago pays more than one in Biloxi, Mississippi.

TIP

Self-motivated people fit in best at small firms. Because smaller firms often don't have the resources to provide extensive training, working at one means that you must be a self-starter because you can't rely on as much supervision from the higher-ups. Medium-sized firms also value quick studies, but they may offer more in terms of mentoring than very small firms. Either way, you need to be comfortable with the concept of business development because small and medium-sized firms sometimes expect their associates to recruit new clients early on. At a large firm, this activity is largely left to the partners.

WARNING

You may be thinking that small and medium-sized firms sound like a great fit and that you want to start off your job search as if you're looking for a job at a large firm. Using that tactic won't get you far. Small and medium-sized firms require a different approach for two reasons:

>> **They can't always anticipate their needs far in advance.** They don't always know their hiring needs very far ahead of time and don't have specific hiring schedules. For instance, most of them don't hire a certain number of new lawyers each year; they tend to hire as someone leaves or they get an onslaught of new business. As a result, you need to keep querying them until you get a bite.

>> **They're often less visible than large firms.** You probably won't find many of them around for on-campus interviews (OCI). They simply don't have the time or the money to send a lawyer to your school for a day or two of OCI. Instead, finding them is up to you, and you do that through research. (You can read more about OCI in Chapter 20.)

Here are the job-search methods you need to undertake in finding a job at a small or medium-sized firm.

>> **Putting your research skills to good use:** Small and medium-sized firms don't always have robust websites or deep online presences. And they're not usually in the news the way large firms often are, so you'll need to put your research skills into action to sleuth out their contact information.

Start by browsing www.martindale.com as a directory and a source of professional ratings. You can search by firm size, location, and area of practice. You can also check your CSO for resources, such as any local or state directories of small and medium-sized firms. Or simply speak with your professors, mentors, and alumni for suggestions.

>> **Writing a carefully tailored cover letter:** You want to distinguish yourself — and catch the hiring lawyer's eye — by giving the clear impression that you didn't just pull the firm's name from the Internet (even when that's what you really did). Show that you've done your homework in your cover letter by mentioning that newsworthy case the firm just won, a practice area it has that interests you, or a particular lawyer at the firm whom you admire. These firms are interested in finding lawyers who make a good fit, so don't forget to mention any ties you have with the city or town (such as having grown up there). Flip to the later section "Targeting your résumés and cover letters" for details on putting together these documents.

>> **Including your résumé but making sure it explicitly emphasizes your practical experience:** Similar to your cover letter, you want to tailor your résumé so that it highlights all the practical experience you've gained, such as working in law clinics, at summer jobs, and as a research assistant. Small and medium-sized firms are looking for lawyers who can handle significant responsibility early on, so they're particularly wowed by extensive on-the-job legal experience. Furthermore, they don't have the resources to spend much time on mentoring, so they expect you to be a quick study. Doing a good job at your past workplaces is evidence of that ability.

>> **Turning up the schmooze:** Networking is hugely important when approaching small and medium-sized firms, because jobs aren't usually advertised the way they are for large firms (on firm websites, through LinkedIn, or at on-campus interviewing at your school). Attending local and state bar events, going to law school alumni mixers, and spreading the word to everyone you meet are great ways of building a network of contacts.

Solo practice: A shingle of one's own

Not everyone wants to work with other people; many intrepid souls eventually choose the solo route. Emphasis on "eventually": Percentage-wise, only about 1 percent of lawyers start their own practice right out of law school, according to the ABA as of March 2025.

Going solo certainly has its rewards: You call all the shots, you don't have to share the profits, and no one says you can't come to work in your pajamas or take a five-hour lunch break. Solo lawyers need to actively recruit business, so you'll be out and about and talking with potential clients a good portion of the time.

On the other hand, very few people go *right* into solo practice as new graduates for a very good reason: You have your work cut out for you. To put it bluntly, as a new graduate, you don't know what in the world you're doing. It's the rare person (unless you have plenty of pre–law school experiences working at a firm) who can make it in a solo practice right out of law school. That's why most new grads interested in this path find a job and a mentor for at least two or three years before setting off on their own. But I mention it as a career option so you can get a head start thinking about it and researching it. The ABA's 2025 Solo Attorney Well-Being Trends Report found that 74 percent of solo practitioners were either satisfied or very satisfied with their professional lives, so it's worth considering.

You're the only person to whom you'll be applying for a job; several things you can do now to knock your own socks off later include the following:

>> **Taking relevant courses:** Forgo some of the theory courses in exchange for things like accounting for lawyers, negotiations, law school clinic courses, externships for credit, tax law, and any other practical or skills courses. You may find out later that doing so helps you out immensely when you're figuring out how to keep track of the firm's finances or need to negotiate with a difficult client.

>> **Learning about business management and the mechanics of running a law office however you can:** Talk to current solo practitioners, job shadow them whenever you can, and focus your summer jobs on working in small or solo law firms. Soak up all you can about the ins and outs of actually being an entrepreneur.

>> **Taking a course or two at the business school, particularly those related to entrepreneurship or financial management:** Knowing how to write a solid business plan can be a key to obtaining the kind of start-up capital you need during your first few years out on your own. And knowing how to manage your finances will make you less dependent on outside help for this type of essential business ownership work.

Working in a boutique firm

Boutique firms are law firms that specialize in one particular area, such as intellectual property, employment, tax, or environmental law. Boutiques are usually small and medium-sized firms. Working for a boutique is appealing when you have a burning interest in a particular area of practice and want to fully immerse yourself in it. You can find boutique firms the same way you'd look for a regular small or medium-sized firm job. Joining your local or state bar association and then joining specialized bar association committees is a wonderful way of networking with potential boutique jobs leads.

Becoming in-house counsel for a corporation

Working as *in-house counsel* means that you're a lawyer for a corporation. You have one client and one client only: that organization. Think of big corporations like Disney, General Mills, Simon & Schuster, and Boeing. All probably have several to many in-house lawyers staffing their legal departments.

TIP

I'm including in-house counsel in this book, even though it's rare for new graduates to find these jobs, just to give you a jump-start in thinking about the possibilities. Most in-house positions generally require at least three to five years of experience (and some as many as nine years). But it's certainly something to think about, and if you know you want to work for a particular type of corporation (like a media company or health-care organization), you can start gaining experience in relevant practice areas now.

Most in-house counselors will attest to the numerous benefits of working in-house. The first is that these positions tend to offer a better quality of life than firm jobs because the workweeks aren't as long and hectic and client development isn't really an issue (you already have your one client). Thus, lawyers can focus all their energies on solving the corporation's legal problems. On the flip side, you usually don't make as high a salary as in a firm, but at some corporations, stock options can be very rewarding.

Working in the public sector

Law students who explore working in the public sector are often amazed by the variety of available choices. Many attorney job titles are available in government, and you can find even more in administrative agencies and public-interest organizations.

Working for the government

You can find legal-related jobs at every level of government, from the city attorney's office to the U.S. Department of Justice. And don't think that you're limited to particular areas of the law when you work for the government. You'll find everything from civil rights to environmental law to tax to torts. Working for the government nets you a salary somewhere in between public-interest and private practice jobs. The National Association for Law Placement (NALP) reports that for the candidates with a law degree as of July 2025, the GS-11 step 1 base salary is $63,163, but in Washington, DC, the locality pay rate is $84,602. (For those that work in government positions, this language is familiar to you. For those of us that have not held government roles, the classifications relate to the status of the position and the rate of pay.)

Many government jobs become available in predictable hiring seasons, so check the websites for departments in which you're interested. These job applications typically require tons of paperwork, so apply well before the deadlines. Another good way to find government jobs is to meet lawyers (particularly receptive alums) who work in the public sector, can keep you informed of job openings before they happen, and can help get your name out. Informational interviewing (see Chapter 22) is a great way to go about doing this.

Working at a nonprofit

Public-interest and *nonprofit organizations* are essentially the same thing; they're organizations often devoted to a particular cause on whose behalf you represent people who can't otherwise afford legal services. Nonprofit lawyers are some of the happiest around because working at public-interest organizations is one of the most satisfying ways to change the world.

Nonprofit lawyers are advocates for economic justice, criminal justice reform, the elderly, LGBTQIA+ rights, animal rights, and human rights, just to name a few. You may work for an arts organization representing low-income artists and writers, a legal aid office helping people with such issues as landlord-tenant disputes, or an educational advocacy organization helping people with disabilities overcome discrimination in K–12 schools.

The pros of nonprofit work are many. You get,

>> Extreme job satisfaction — you're helping those who need it most

>> A more relaxed working environment (no billable hours, client development, or partnership track concerns)

>> Tons of client interaction and counseling

>> Dedicated folks on staff

The cons to public-interest work include some of the lowest salaries around (starting salaries generally range from $55,000 to $128,000 depending on the geographic location and employer), which may seem low when you've got back-breaking loans to pay off. In fact, NALP reports that for the graduating class of 2024, the median starting salary at a public-interest job was $72,000. That's the main reason that many new graduates who'd otherwise love a public-interest job just can't afford to take one.

Finding a public-interest position as a new grad is challenging (but not impossible). Here's why:

>> Few positions are available.

>> These organizations don't have much money to hire many new lawyers.

>> Entry-level positions are hard to find because these organizations don't have the money to extensively train new lawyers.

>> Nonprofits want to see a high level of commitment, demonstrated through past public-interest work experience.

Set yourself apart from the crowd by garnering plenty of impressive public-interest experience as a law student. Try working as a summer intern or volunteering at the organizations you want to work for throughout the academic year. If you show the staff lawyers what you can do, you'll be looked upon more favorably come hiring time.

Clerking for a judge

When you think of the term *clerk*, you may imagine someone who works in a retail store. But a *judicial clerkship*, despite its funny name, is simply a mentorship arrangement with a judge — one where law school grads are hired to do legal research and writing for one particular judge.

Law students highly covet judicial clerkships for two key reasons:

>> **Prestige:** The entire legal profession considers clerking for a judge an honor by (especially firms seeking new lawyers). For one thing, you're working for one highly influential person. Plus, all you do is legal research and writing, so when you finish the clerkship, you're assumed to be a highly competent researcher and writer. And that spells instant credibility.

>> **Flexibility:** You can't beat a clerkship's flexibility in terms of job duration and your quality of life. Most judges hire clerks for a period of one to two years, depending on the particular judge's policies. Many clerks view their jobs as

good career bridges between law school and practicing law. Because these jobs are short-term, many new graduates enjoy the opportunity to experience a new city, take some time to think about what they want to do after the clerkship, and focus on networking in their geographic locations.

New graduates love clerkships because they're known to offer unparalleled practical experience. Depending on your judge's personality, you'll provide research for many different opinions, report the findings of your research (suggest the outcome) to the judge, and perhaps even outline or completely write the judge's opinions. Think of the power in that. You're the one writing the opinions and deciding which side should win! Of course, the judge has the final say in the matter, but you're doing quite a bit of the work.

Besides getting firsthand experience in potentially shaping the law, you also discover how to navigate in a wide variety of areas of the law. Regardless of whether you later work at a firm, nonprofit, or governmental agency, clerks often say that you'll never be exposed to such a broad variety of law again (unless you later become a judge!).

WARNING

Those who probably wouldn't enjoy the experience include people who:

>> **Crave recognition:** Your name doesn't go on the opinions; only you and the judge recognize your good work.

>> **Need a sky-high salary:** Pay for clerks can be $60,000 to $85,000 depending on the level of the court and the geographic location.

>> **Dislike legal research and writing:** Because the main task of judicial clerks is engaging in legal research and writing, you'd better like it, because you'll do it 24/7. That's what your job description is, in a nutshell. Some view clerkships as the equivalent of writing a lengthy paper every few days.

>> **Need constant social stimulation:** The work is usually just you, the law library, and your computer screen.

>> **Aren't self-motivated:** You need to be a self-starter to meet tight deadlines and get your research and writing started.

You need to really flex those research muscles to get a clerkship, because although tons of judges are out there, few clerkship openings are ever advertised. So after you decide to explore a clerkship, narrow down where in the country you want to be. Then decide at what level court you want to clerk; your options include:

>> The state systems, with their district, appellate, and supreme courts

>> The federal system, with its federal district courts, federal courts of appeals (circuit courts), or the Supreme Court of the United States

Another clerking option is specialized courts within the federal system, which are often called *courts of limited jurisdiction.* They include courts that deal with bankruptcies, taxes, and intellectual property areas, among others. Of course, the higher you go in the court system, the more competitive landing a clerking spot is. For example, getting a clerkship with the state supreme court is usually harder than snagging one with a state district court.

When you aren't limited by geographic location and want to clerk, start sending out résumés in the federal or state systems. Some clerking opportunities are publicized in CSOs, but most times individual students discover them on their own and/or and with the help of their professors. You can find judges' names and contact information by going to state or federal websites.

When you're working on your cover letter, try working in a tidbit about what you know about the judge. If you're an admirer of their opinions, say so. If you're impressed by something they wrote, mention it.

Figuring Out What Legal Employers Really Want

Welcome to the wide, wonderful world of hiring practices! I know from personal experience that as a law student, you often feel in the dark about what goes on behind the hiring committee's closed doors. And yes, many times hiring decisions seem extremely subjective, but that's why you need to arm yourself with as much information as you can about what legal employers want.

The true weight of grades

Although you may think every employer ideally wants to see the top third of the class, the law review, and top-notch work experience, that really isn't the case. Yes, the cold, hard truth is that you're unlikely to be hired at a *large* firm unless you're in the top 10 percent of your class or attend a top law school. But after all, if only the top 10 percent ever got jobs, where would the other 90 percent of the class end up?

Every workplace has its own ideas about how grades and everything else fit into the picture. Many judges looking for clerks prefer that their applicants have stellar research and writing skills; some don't give a hoot about all those B-minuses on your transcripts. And small and medium-sized firms tend to place more emphasis on your extracurricular and work experiences, along with being a good fit, over grades.

The reason these types of employers aren't overly concerned about your grades is that they're selecting potential employees largely from the middle of the class, after large firms have snapped up the top people. Because distinguishing a B average from a B+ without more information is difficult to do, they want to see evidence of your legal competence outside the classroom. Solid work experience during summer jobs, work in a law school clinic, participation on a law journal/law review and moot court, and leadership experience in a law school club all can catch their eyes.

The importance of attachments

As you can probably guess from any jobs you've ever held, your résumé and cover letter are important. These show your accomplishments and that you know something about the employer. But your attachments — your writing sample(s) and any references (either in list or letter form) — are equally, if not more, important, for some employers.

Some employers specify on their website or employment information how many writing samples and/or references they want. Others don't specify, but you still need to send some anyway. If the employer doesn't indicate how many it wants, the general guideline is to include one writing sample that's about five double-spaced pages long and one page containing the names of three to five references. Law school professors and legal employers are your best reference bets. Your CDO team will guide you if you're unsure.

Pay particular attention to your writing sample, because you can be sure the hiring attorney will go over it with a discriminating eye. Judges in particular scrutinize your sample for analytical skills and the strength of your arguments.

Preparing for an initial interview

TIP

You want to convey a certain message to all types of legal employers in your interviews: "I'm interested, I know all about you, and I have what it takes to be a great addition to your staff." Beyond exuding this message in the three *P*'s — preparation, presentation, and personal grooming — you can impress employers in some other key ways:

>> **Before the interview, find out who your interviewers are and do some advance research on them.** You don't need to go digging up their FBI files, but you can look up their bios on the employer's website and LinkedIn or type their names into www.martindale.com to find out where they went to school and any published law review/journal articles they have.

>> **Do your research into what types of law the employer practices.** Review the firm's website and ask your CSO for any information about the firm and the attorneys (especially any alums) that work there.

>> **Chat with an alum who works (or used to work) where you're planning to interview.** One of the best ways to get the inside scoop for an initial interview is talking to someone who can provide you with the kind of insider information that makes it look like *you* did all the work! By talking to an alum, you can get the kind of details that can impress your interviewers with what you know!

Chapter 20 features detailed information on what goes on in the initial interview.

Acing the call-back interview

In contrast with an initial interview, the call-back interview is something only some legal employers do. A *call-back interview* is where the employer invites you to its offices for a second (and last) round of interviews. These interviews aren't so much interviews in the traditional sense as they are a mutual chance for both parties to check each other out one more time.

REMEMBER

Call-back interviews give you an opportunity to get a feel for the employer, so don't just sit there like a bump on a log, obediently answering questions. Instead, take the time to really look — don't be shy — at your surroundings. One question needs to run through your mind: Can I imagine working here?

You're generally expected to pay your own way to a call-back interview (for all but the largest firms). Head to Chapter 20 for detailed information on how to handle the call-back interview for summer employment, which is exactly the same for permanent employment.

Handling a Job Offer Properly and Dealing with Rejection

A hearty congratulations! You've done everything right, and you have a plum offer in hand. Before you call everyone you know, whooping it up that you got a job, you need to seal the deal with style.

Responding to an offer with enthusiasm

Think about how you'd feel if you were an employer handing out an offer only to be met with a casual "Hmm, let me think about that for a couple of days." You'd be pretty annoyed, right? Don't treat your offers with such casualness, particularly in rough economic times. If you're ready right then and there to accept, then respond with an automatic "Yes! That's wonderful! I can't wait to start!" Clearly, you'll start off on better terms with your employer.

If you're not quite ready to commit, make sure to convey your needs with a positive attitude — not one that says this employer is the last link in your job-search food chain. If you're not enthusiastic, the potential employer may feel that it's made a bad decision and feel negatively toward you before you've even started! That's the last thing you want.

Finding out what's negotiable

After you receive an offer, you need to start being realistic about the salary. Specifically, you need to find out exactly how much money you'll be paid, what the benefit setup is, how many hours you're expected to bill, what kind of clients you'll be dealing with, how much vacation time you'll get, and any other deal-making or deal-breaking stipulations you may encounter. If you're unsure about what exactly to ask for, talk with your CSO a few weeks before you expect to receive your offer. You want to write all these items down because sometimes they're hard to remember when you're so excited about your offer.

REMEMBER

As everybody knows, salaries can be touchy topics, and as a new lawyer, you may have little leverage. But negotiating is certainly worth a shot, particularly when you bring something highly desirable to the table (such as extensive work experience, fabulous grades, or a published journal article). Be thoughtful but ask for what you need now because you may not have a chance to change things after you start.

Accepting rejection or waitlisting

Alas, the worst has happened. You've been rejected — either as a summer clerk immediately applying for a permanent job at the firm or as an independent applicant. It happens to everyone at one time or another. The key to handling rejections with grace is to always act positively. I know that's easier said than done, especially if all you want to do is sob under the covers or wring your former prospect's neck. However, you don't want to burn any of your bridges lest you want to work for this employer in the future, so just grin and bear it, and save your outrage for a punching bag.

If you're not accepted or rejected outright by your potential employer, you may be put on some kind of waiting list, similar to ones colleges and law schools use. You may feel you can do little to propel yourself off the dreaded waiting list and onto the acceptance list. But that isn't true!

TIP

If you present yourself as an enthusiastic, grateful candidate and make sure the employer knows it's your first choice, you'll be perceived better than the person who immediately gives up and withdraws or presents a negative attitude. Likewise, you want to show the employer that you're the right person for the job by asking whether you can do or submit anything else to bolster your case. These tasks can include providing an updated reference list or additional writing samples, or perhaps returning for an additional interview.

Chapter **22**

Narrowing Your Focus: Choosing an Area of Practice

D eciding on an *area of practice* (or specialty) is one of the most exciting aspects of the entire job-search process. For students merely beginning their job searches, focusing on an area of practice can entail a great deal more time and work than you ever thought possible. That's why you need to start considering practice areas as soon as you're ready to explore your career options by thinking about your personal strengths and skills, talking to practitioners in fields that interest you, and working summer jobs or finding part-time school-year jobs (see Chapter 19) in particular areas of the law.

To start you off right, in this chapter I examine why focusing on a few specialty areas in law school may benefit your job search later. Most law students just want to accept the first bona fide job that comes their way, regardless of specialty. But I show you why doing so is a bad idea and how to ferret out your particular area of practice based on your law school experiences. Finally, I list the 18 most popular areas of practice.

Focusing on Some Key Areas of Practice during Law School

Take the time during law school to gather as much information as possible about the areas of practice that interest you. Although you don't need to select a single specialty area, narrowing the field to only a couple helps focus your job search. (Chapter 21 has details about the job-search process.)

REMEMBER

The majority of law students don't have a clue what their area of practice will be until they've gone through at least a semester of law school. Some people fall into an area of practice by chance; usually, it's whatever area they happen to get into with their first post-graduation jobs. Others have a more personal reason for their choices. For example, they take a civil rights class and positively fall in love with the subject matter, or they've known from birth that they'd become estate planning lawyers because of their fondness for counseling people about financial issues. More realistically, though, you won't really know what you enjoy until halfway through law school, after you've had the chance to sample a few electives.

Making the major decision of choosing a practice area

Many law schools don't have anything like college majors; the ones that do have something called *certificate* or *emphasis programs*. But some are known for their specialization and expertise in particular areas, such as Vermont Law School's link with environmental law or Santa Clara's connection with intellectual property. In other words, when you graduate, your law school diploma normally doesn't say "JD in Internet law," nor is your area of practice denoted on your transcript (unless you're participating in a certificate program).

Some prelaw students choose their law schools because they've heard or seen that the school excels in a particular area, such as corporate or entertainment law. These schools typically offer plenty of courses in the specialty areas, well-known professors in their respective fields, and sometimes even semiformal concentrations, or *tracks*, in them. Many students, however, decide to take matters into their own hands and informally specialize in an area of practice while attending law school. Of course, some students prefer the liberal arts approach to law school, taking as diverse a schedule as they can without focusing on any one area. I cover a variety of approaches to course selection in Chapter 18; whichever path you take is completely up to you.

Understanding how employers view specialty applicants

Most employers don't expect you to choose an area of practice while you're still a 1L or 2L in school. But when they come across students who have — and who've also demonstrated their commitment by excelling in the relevant classes, choosing summer jobs in the field, and holding leadership roles in relevant clubs — they may be impressed by your commitment to a specific area of law. In other words, showing this sort of focus can set you apart during the hiring process.

In fact, some employers highly value applicants who show initiative in a particular area. They think that because you're this focused already, you're probably a better employee than someone who hasn't yet taken the time to figure out what they want to do. Regardless of whether that's really the case, having an employer view you as more focused and committed never hurts. Keep in mind that boutique firms — the ones that concentrate in a particular practice area only — may be more receptive to students with a strong grasp of their practice area interests.

TIP

One of the best ways to sample a practice area in-depth as a rising 2L is to land a summer job (paid or unpaid) in that area (see Chapter 20). Don't be afraid to explore an area of law you hadn't considered or an organization that you didn't know much about before speaking with your mentor or professor. You may find that you're really good at tax, evidence, or corporate law.

TIP

Narrowing your focus will likely lead to more success in your job search. You'll be better able to articulate your "why" — the reasons you're interested in the specialty area — in your cover letters and explain why you and that organization, firm, or company are a good fit for each other. The benefit of being focused also translates into the search for permanent jobs (which you can read more about in Chapter 21).

Putting on Your Career Counselor Cap

Because law schools (generally) don't have the equivalent of majors, you're more or less on your own to figure out which areas of practice interest you. Law schools don't offer advisors in the different practice areas the way colleges do. However, you *can* form an informal advising relationship with a professor who teaches in your area of interest and can serve as a valuable resource.

No one expects you to be completely in the know about areas of practice right off the bat. I didn't even know that such a thing as areas of practice existed until after my first semester of law school, for heaven's sake! So don't beat yourself up whenever you don't have the slightest clue about what different practice areas entail. When you start doing research, particularly informational interviews, you get the idea soon enough.

REMEMBER

You can take matters into your own hands by figuring out exactly what the specialty of your dreams is. All it takes is a little self-assessment and self-reflection, as the following sections explain. Keep in mind that starting your self-assessment journey by analyzing all areas of legal practice is fine, as long as you're able to cross off the areas that don't interest you. Otherwise, your job search may grow too far out of control to be helpful.

Deciding what courses you liked best

TIP

The key to finding the best area of practice for you is being able to figure out what courses really get you excited every time you think about them. Did you ever read ahead in any courses because you were so interested in the subject matter that you just couldn't wait to get to it? Have you done outside reading on your own initiative, such as law review or journal articles, based on topics you learned about in a particular class? Whenever you go the extra mile to find out more about what you've covered in class, that's a sure sign that class is an excellent candidate for being a legal specialty.

Identifying your favorite classes sounds like a no-brainer, but you'd be surprised how difficult making these determinations actually is for many students. Some law students love everything; they can't decide among the choices of family, real estate, immigration, or health law. A few, on the other hand, make it through law school without ever finding their true legal passions. (To find out what to do when that happens, flip to Chapter 25.)

If that's the case for you, try very hard to narrow down the courses you've taken to at least one or two that weren't quite as bad as — or maybe were a little better than — the others. (I know, sometimes that's hard to do.) If you find that you can't even do that, then check out Chapter 23 for some honest advice about alternative careers in the legal field that may be more what you're (consciously or subconsciously) looking for.

TIP

When you're still stumped, try focusing on whether you enjoy litigation or transactional matters more. Briefly, *litigation* involves adversarial work, such as preparing for and going to trial, while *transactional* work involves making deals, negotiating contracts, and often using counseling skills. Identifying which of the two camps you fall into can make recognizing the classes you enjoyed much easier. For instance, when you prefer litigation, estate planning and wills and trusts probably weren't among your favorite subjects, but trial advocacy and criminal law probably were.

Recalling impressions of your summer employment

Summer and part-time school-year jobs are useful for giving you an inside look at particular areas of practice. You gain up-close-and-personal experiences with the kind of work you'd be doing, with practitioners who are involved, and perhaps even with the types of clients you'd encounter.

Similarly, these jobs in particular help you find out the truth about an area of practice. For example, as a 2L, I loved my classes in anything related to criminal law — evidence and criminal procedure — and thought it'd be a great practice area for me. I thought I wanted to be public defender, but several professors and two student mentors suggested I try interning at the DA's office. I loved it. I used my social work and counseling skills quite a bit and ended up participating in two different internships there in the domestic violence unit and general crimes and misdemeanors. But then I ended up in an externship with a federal magistrate judge and loved that, too. He was overseeing some criminal cases but mostly covering civil cases, and I used my love of civil procedure.

To sum it all up, explore a variety of opportunities! You may start law school with a clear idea about what area of law you want to pursue, but keep an open mind. What you are most passionate about during your 1L first semester may end up being an area of law that you ultimately despise. And you may find yourself in an internship or clerkship that changes your life.

Determining what practice areas fit best with your desired location

You can find the more common areas of practice — corporate, criminal, securities, real estate, and wills and trusts — in virtually all locations. Other areas, however, are more location-specific. For example, when you want to be an *admiralty* (navigation and shipping) lawyer, you probably won't find many opportunities in land-locked Omaha, Nebraska. Instead, you want to make a run for the East or West Coasts, focusing your job search in cities like Seattle, Boston, or Miami. Or, if entertainment law is your bag, you probably won't have as much luck in Tuscaloosa or Phoenix as you would focusing your job search on New York, Atlanta, Nashville, Los Angeles, or Chicago.

TIP

The best way to find out what cities are prime prospects for which specialties is by checking with people in your career services office (CSO), alums, and other practitioners. Search for the firms or organizations that focus on the areas of law you're interested in and see where they're located. Remember, though, that also means you have to be open-minded about potentially moving to a new city or state!

Informational interviewing with practitioners

Conducting informational interviews is one of the most successful approaches to figuring out what you want to do. Essentially, an *informational interview* is when you make an appointment (usually lasting 30 to 45 minutes) with a practitioner to get information and advice about a particular field. In an informational interview, you're not soliciting for a job; you're just asking questions and finding out more about the practitioner's field.

Unlike formal interviews (see Chapter 20), informational interviews have a laid-back and relaxed feel to them: No one is judging or scrutinizing you. However, you should still be prepared. How you prepare depends on whether the interview is in person, by phone, or via video call (Zoom, Teams, and so on).

>> **For in-person interviews,** you still need to bring along a portfolio with your résumé, a transcript, and a writing sample just in case your interviewer asks for them (but don't provide these materials unless you're first asked to do so). You never know when your informational interviewer will remember that a colleague at another firm is looking for a new summer clerk or permanent associate and wants to pass on your résumé.

>> **For a phone interview,** be sure you are in a quiet location. Have your notes and questions prepared and in front of you. Be sure to have the company, firm, and/or organization's website up on your tablet or laptop in case you need to quickly learn more about the people interviewing you.

>> **For a video call interview,** check your internet connection beforehand. Check your lighting. Ensure the area around you is clutter-free. Have your notes, note pad, or other tablet off to the side. Be sure to dress professionally. This is still a formal interview, and appearance matters.

TIP

The key to conducting a useful informational interview is asking probing questions such as the following:

>> How did you choose this area of practice over all the others?

>> What courses do you recommend I take to best prepare myself for your field?

>> If you were hiring for your position, what skills, courses, and clinics would you want the candidate to showcase on their résumé?

Finding people to interview is easy: Just ask your career services dean or director to point you to alums or review the firms or organizations in the CSO portal (or whatever tool your law school uses). Internet searching also works. *Note:* Finding the right people to interview is easier after you narrow your choices for an area of practice to three to five contenders as I discuss in the preceding sections.

Previewing Popular Areas of Practice

The range of practice areas you can enter today is diverse and ever-changing. In fact, as areas of practice merge and overlap, dozens more are bound to become available in years to come. In this section, I give you a quick peek at the most popular areas of legal practice right now. This listing by no means represents *every* practice area (because that would fill another entire *For Dummies* book). If you want to delve further into any of these areas, talk with your CSO and conduct some informational interviews. You can also check out a helpful book, *The Official Guide to Legal Specialties: An Insider's Guide to Every Major Practice Area*, by Lisa L. Abrams (Harcourt Legal & Professional).

REMEMBER

Unlike doctors and medical specialties, lawyers and legal specialties tend not to have different salary rates based on how technical or prestigious they are. Instead, differences in lawyers' salaries are linked more to sizes and types of practice settings and number of years in practice. The only exception to this rule is the intellectual property field, where patent lawyers are often paid more than any other lawyers, mainly because they're required to take a separate bar exam, the *patent bar*, and usually required to have a bachelor's or advanced degree in a science, such as chemistry, engineering, or computer science. (See Chapter 4 for more about how science-related majors can aid you in law school.)

The following list comes from Google, the Law School Admission Council (LSAC), the American Bar Association (ABA), and the National Association for Law Placement (NALP):

>> **Administrative:** Administrative law lawyers deal with rule-making, enforcement and *adjudication* (final determination or resolution), government agencies, and compliance.

>> **Corporate:** Corporate lawyers are often involved in transactional work that involves negotiations and drafting contracts. You may help companies with the initial stages of selecting how they want to operate their businesses, with tax planning, and with mergers and acquisitions. Many corporate lawyers work in large law firms.

>> **Criminal:** The two types of criminal lawyers are prosecutors and defense lawyers. *Prosecutors* hold government jobs; defense lawyers work either in law firms or for the public interest (for the government), often in public defender's offices. As a prosecutor, you take the position represented by federal or

state laws, prosecuting people charged with crimes. As a defense attorney, you defend people charged with federal or state offenses, including crimes that involve drugs, embezzlement, sex/pornography, various forms of misconduct, and homicide, with penalties ranging from a slap on the wrist to the death penalty.

>> **Data privacy and cybersecurity:** These lawyers deal with the protection of personal data, data breaches, corporate data, cyberattacks, privacy regulations, and so forth.

>> **Elder:** Elder law lawyers may help with guardianship, estate planning, retirement planning, *advance directives* (such as living wills), health-care, and long-term care issues.

>> **Employment (labor):** Employment lawyers handle work permits, matters dealing with employee restructuring, hiring, termination, safety, and welfare. You may also deal with equal employment practices, sexual harassment, confidentiality agreements, and noncompete clauses.

>> **Environmental and energy:** As an environmental lawyer, you cover issues addressing land use, regulatory compliance, toxic substances, and potential environmental liabilities. You work heavily with federal environmental statutes and may be involved in policy work. Energy lawyers deal with energy production and distribution.

>> **Estate planning:** Estate planning lawyers assist with wills, trusts, and the management of assets to help with the transfer of property after death.

>> **Family:** Family law deals with divorce, adoption, prenuptial agreements, alimony, and child custody. You can also represent the interests of children in family court, protecting them from abusive or neglectful parents.

>> **Health/health-care:** Health-care lawyers deal with medical malpractice suits filed against doctors and hospitals, Medicare and Medicaid disputes, and interpretations of the Americans with Disabilities Act. You may work with pharmaceutical companies, hospitals, educational institutions, health maintenance organizations (HMOs), and industry associations.

>> **Immigration:** Immigration lawyers focus on visas, deportation hearings, compliance for businesses and their employees, and citizenship.

>> **Intellectual property:** Intellectual property (IP) lawyers are involved with the enforcement of trademarks, patents, copyrights, and other forms of intellectual property rights. You can work on the transactional or litigation side in IP. You may also work in the areas of trade secrets, unfair competition, entertainment, and computer law.

>> **Litigation (civil):** Civil litigation lawyers focus on torts claims, property disputes, contract disputes, financial recovery because of loss or damages, and so on.

>> **Personal injury:** Personal injury lawyers deal mainly with automobile and other catastrophic accidents, product liability, and medical malpractice. They're exclusively litigators who frequently are in court.

>> **Real estate:** Real estate lawyers represent clients needing assistance with real estate finance, acquisition, closings, development, and ownership. They're also experts on regulatory issues that affect real estate activities.

>> **Regulatory and compliance law:** These attorneys work with businesses to ensure compliance with local, state, and federal law.

>> **Tax:** Tax lawyers help clients (companies, nonprofits, and individuals) navigate their tax returns, deal with tax problems, tax exemptions, and tax disclosure issues.

>> **Technology and AI law:** Tech and AI lawyers address issues related to AI, liability, digital platforms, cutting-edge tech, and emerging issues in the field. Additionally, these lawyers may deal with computer software licensing, development agreements, and distribution agreements.

Chapter **23**

Considering Alternative Legal Careers

H ave you ever wondered whether using your JD in an alternative way suits you better than a traditional legal job or what working in legal publishing, in law school administration, as a law professor, or in mediation is like? If you have, you're in good company. Every year, hundreds of law school graduates forgo practicing law with firms, the government, or nonprofits in favor of a non-practicing or alternative career. Such careers can offer you benefits that many traditional ones can't, including flexibility, creativity, and variety.

In this chapter, I explain why some people choose alternative careers and point out the benefits and drawbacks of this option. I take you step by step through the process of determining whether you need to try something outside the box. I also take a closer look at a handful of the more popular alternative legal careers.

Bucking Traditional Legal Careers

Even if you went to law school bound and determined to practice law, no rule says that you can't suddenly change your mind. Many students do. According to data from the American Bar Association (ABA) for the class of 2023, approximately

14.4 percent of law school graduates pursued an alternative or *JD Advantage* career as opposed to a traditional legal practice. This figure is part of the larger employment outcome data reported about 10 months after graduation. Will you be one of those 14.4 percent? Although getting out of the mentality that law school equals practicing lawyer isn't easy, knowing that a traditional legal career isn't your only destiny can be comforting.

TIP

If you don't intend to practice law, you can use your JD in two alternative ways:

>> **By entering a career related to the legal field that uses the skills you learned in law school (or where your law degree comes into play) as an important credential:** Teaching law, legal publishing, and working in law school administration are a few examples. This option often requires a JD, prefers one, or makes having one a major selling point for getting hired. Be sure to make connections with the administration and faculty while you're a student so they know you're interested.

>> **By entering a career that's completely unrelated to the law, where you'll probably never use your law degree again (and be proud of it!):** This career can be pretty much anything, such as marine biology, teaching high school math, or investment banking. In fact, this second option is a bit tougher to pinpoint because your options are endless, and including a discussion of the entire world of jobs that you can find is beyond the scope of this book. (Check out *Careers For Dummies* by Marty Nemko [Wiley] as a good starting point.) But your JD probably won't help you out much in these completely unrelated careers, and in some instances it can even prove to be a hindrance (when you have to keep explaining your JD away to suspicious employers). But when you're intent on pursuing a career completely apart from the legal field, go for it!

As you can imagine, most JDs who decide to go outside the box choose a job that's related to the legal field. They do so for several reasons:

>> **After enduring three (or four) years of law school, knowing that your degree is being put to good use is nice, even when you're not actively practicing law.** In other words, you can be content knowing that you're capitalizing on your JD but that being a practicing lawyer won't be part of your identity.

>> **Your starting salary for a job that prefers or requires a JD is likely to be higher than the nonlegal, entry-level positions you may find.**

>> **People who go to law school are usually already interested in the law in some fashion, so they tend to pursue careers where they have some contact with the profession or practicing lawyers.**

TIP

The best way (besides reading this book) to find out about the breadth of available alternative careers is talking with people, particularly alums. Your career services office (CSO) is probably able to put you in touch with some alums who are doing interesting and unique things with their JD degrees. Hearing their stories helps you reinforce in your mind that anything is possible when you're willing to think outside the box. Also check out the wide variety of books that specifically address alternative careers, such as:

>> *What Can You Do with a Law Degree? A Lawyer's Guide to Career Alternatives Inside, Outside & Around the Law* by Deborah Arron (Lawyer Avenue Press)

>> *Leaving Law: How Others Did It and How You Can Too* by Adele Barlow (CreateSpace Independent Publishing Platform)

>> *Life After Law* by Liz Brown (Routledge)

Recognizing that practicing law isn't an absolute necessity

No one says that you must practice law, especially if you don't like it or don't *think* you'd like it. But when you go straight into a career that's unrelated to the legal field after graduation, many people (including mentors, professors, and family members) may harass you with the proverbial "Why don't you at least give law a chance?" speech. The problem: Giving it a chance has its own set of problems down the road, such as getting trapped by a high-paying position or feeling like you're too caught up with clients and business to leave, even when you really want to.

People considering alternative careers generally fall into two camps:

>> Those who knew before law school, or shortly thereafter, that that's the route they want to pursue

>> Those who went all the way through law school without a clue as to how they'd eventually use their degrees

When you fall into the first camp, you may have decided to go to law school just to get a legal education or to use your JD in an alternative career where it's required or preferred. That's wonderful; I applaud everyone who fits this description. You can head over to the section "Sampling JD Advantage or Nontraditional Legal Jobs" later in the chapter because you've probably engaged in all the self-assessment you need to do to reach a decision about your preferred career path.

On the other hand, when your situation is more in line with the second camp, trust your gut instincts. If you're having serious doubts about your future as a practicing lawyer, it's probably because you never found a true legal calling, no matter how much you wanted to. If an alternative career is what feels right, then go for it, no matter what your friends, parents, dean, or CSO advisor may tell you.

Understanding why nonlegal employers value JDs

As everybody knows, getting into law school isn't easy. You need to do well in college, take and nail the LSAT (see Chapter 4), and have a few personal or extra-curricular achievements to round out your application, among other things. Because only a small percentage of the American population has a graduate degree of any sort, you've already distinguished yourself by showing motivation, the smarts to succeed, and the desire to continue your education.

Getting into law school is impressive, but making it *through* law school is another feat entirely. Just getting through those three (or four) years of blood, sweat, and tears signals that you have outstanding research abilities, can write pretty well, and are capable of quickly learning large quantities of information, all of which are attributes many employers outside the legal field cherish.

Proceeding toward an Ideal Alternative Career

If you're considering an alternative career, you know you have much to think about. You can't just say, "I don't want to be a practicing lawyer," and expect that your new job search will simply fall into place. So many options are available in the alternative arena that you're going to have to do the same kinds of self-assessment and soul-searching that finding a traditional legal job requires. (See Chapters 21 and 22 for more about finding traditional legal jobs.) Additionally, you must consider the many trade-offs and compromises that result from deciding not to use your JD to practice law. For instance, you need to:

>> **Think about whether you need or want to take the bar exam:** If you don't plan to maintain an active license, you may want to forgo the bar exam altogether. (See Chapter 24 for suggestions about when skip the bar exam.) If you're going into a career that's completely unrelated to law, think deeply about whether the costs of the exam and prep courses, extensive studying involved, annual bar dues, and requirements for maintaining continuing legal education (CLE) credits after passing the bar are worth the benefits of taking the exam.

>> **Consider what you're getting and giving up:** Sure, an alternative career is likely to offer you increased flexibility, better working hours, and more creativity in your work, but you must give up some things, too, such as a (usually) better salary, the prestige of being a lawyer, and the ability to enter the practice of law with ease after you've been out for a while. If you decide to enter business, an avenue that many JDs pursue, keep in mind that although you may make more money than a practicing lawyer, your hours are likely to be as long or longer, corresponding with your sky-high salary (especially in investment banking or management consulting). Politics may offer better working hours (overall) and more creativity in your work but may require large amounts of personal (and other) capital to fund your campaign(s).

Pinpointing why you don't want to practice law

The first component of a good alternative job search is figuring out why you decided against practicing law. You want to avoid duplicating what you don't like about practicing law in your alternative career. If you don't figure out now what you like and dislike about practicing law, you won't have much luck determining what *exactly* it is that you want in your new career.

Although it may seem like a no-brainer because you're shelling out the big bucks to go to law school, at some point you probably entertained the notion of practicing law. If you decided before law school that you wanted to go into an alternative career, you've already covered this base, but I highly recommend that everyone else give this question some serious thought.

For example, here are some of the most common reasons law students cite for deciding not to practice law:

>> I hated law school and didn't find anything about the experience that attracted me to becoming a lawyer.

>> I didn't like any of my legal summer jobs and couldn't see myself performing the tasks of a lawyer day in and day out.

>> I thought that an alternative career would better enable me to make a difference in society.

>> I don't like what lawyers do; I find legal research, writing memos and briefs, and interacting with clients boring or distasteful.

>> I went to law school because I didn't know what else to do with myself, but I still haven't found a passion in the law.

>> I decided that I want to move up to a leadership position at my previous (or another) company.

>> Through my discussions with lawyers, I became disenchanted with the legal profession and decided that being a lawyer just isn't for me.

>> I thought the legal profession would accommodate my creative spirit, but I was wrong.

>> The income potential in another career is greater than what I can make as a lawyer.

>> I need/want to work a normal 40-hour workweek or work part time.

>> The legal market is so bad right now that I can't get the type of legal job that I want or be in the city that I want to be in.

WARNING

If you're judging the entire legal profession on what you observed or discovered in your legal summer jobs, clinical experiences, and/or internships, make sure your experience was representative enough for you to honestly make such an important judgment. In other words, if the reason you don't want to practice law is because you hated both your summer jobs in labor law, the solution may be in finding an area of practice that better suits you rather than abandoning the thought of becoming a practicing lawyer altogether. Be sure you consider your overall experience, including law school, legal jobs, and your conversations with practicing lawyers, when evaluating your feelings about the law as a career.

Pondering your personal likes and dislikes

You need to think about your personality type and what sort of career is the best fit for you. Are you someone who can't stand sitting still (so a legal job behind a desk would drive you crazy)? Do you think you wouldn't like law because it lacks creativity? Do you need constant and varied stimulation, which repetitive legal research often lacks?

Here are some important questions that you need to ask yourself to clarify specifically what you like and dislike about the law:

>> **In what situations have I performed supervised lawyerly tasks?** Think about the legal summer jobs you've worked, your work in law school clinics, or your job as a professor's research assistant. What have you liked and disliked about these experiences? Are those factors things like writing memos and briefs, which you probably won't find in an alternative career? Or are they things like writing in general, which you probably will find in many nonlegal careers?

>> **Do you want to be associated with or interact with people in the legal profession?** Do you enjoy being around lawyers? Or would you prefer a career that's more or less disassociated with lawyers and the legal profession?

>> **When you think of yourself as a practicing lawyer, what feelings come to mind?** Pride? Prestige? Or irritation and disenchantment? Think about how your identity in an alternative career may differ from your present feelings toward lawyers.

Of course, if you discover through this self-assessment that you really are interested in a traditional legal career, be sure to check out Chapter 21, which provides everything you need to know about finding a fulfilling traditional legal job.

Sampling JD Advantage or Nontraditional Legal Jobs

As someone seeking an alternative job, many different options are open to you — everything from compliance roles to risk management positions to legislative or policy analysts. The following sections cover some of the most popular opportunities open to (mostly) new graduates who don't plan on practicing law. Bear in mind that this list isn't an exhaustive list; for more possibilities, talk to your career services/development office (CSO or CDO), alums in JD Advantage or nonlawyer positions.

TIP

The National Association for Legal Placement (NALP) has a great JD Advantage career guide, along with other JD Advantage resources, on its website at www. nalp.org/jd_advantage.

Legal publishing

When you enjoy writing and reading and like to work on other people's written work, legal publishing may be a good fit for you. Legal publishing is a wonderful career for *bibliophiles* (book lovers) and people who want to work in a congenial, flexible environment with optimum lifestyle considerations (most jobs are 9 to 5). It's also a good fit for people who like working with legal issues but don't necessarily want to be practicing law.

You have two main options here: legal book or periodical (including directory and other legal resources such as loose-leaf service) publishing. Legal publishing may also involve positions in electronic media, where you find innovative formats that help others learn about the law. General trade book publishers may also have legal sections that you may want to look into, and commercial book publishers sometimes publish legal how-to books for the public.

Positions in book publishing may include *acquisitions editor* (someone who acquires new book projects), *project editor* (one who oversees general editing and coordinates all facets of the writing process), and *managing editor.*

Additionally, people in book publishing may work directly with authors of casebooks and hornbooks or focus more on the product development side of the business. Periodical publishing positions include *periodical editors* (who edit magazine, encyclopedia, or journal text), *researchers,* and *newsletter or magazine article* writers.

REMEMBER

No single set way exists for finding out more information about the legal publishing field. One option is taking a look at your commercial study aids, law casebooks, or the law section of a bookstore to find out who publishes those materials. Then you can do an online search for those companies and check out their application policies or job openings. Alternatively, you can find out from your CSO whether any alums are in the field and contact them for informational interviewing (see Chapter 21) to find out more about how to land a job in the field. Faculty members may be able to introduce you to someone they work with at their textbook's publisher, especially if you were their TA or research assistant.

Law school administration

If you enjoy the university environment and want to work with students, consider a career in law school administration. Some of the positions open to new graduates who haven't practiced law include working in the admissions office, the CSO, or the alumni affairs office or as an assistant dean of students or dean of international programs. Some deans' positions require a few years in legal practice so that the person brings real-world experience to the job when counseling students. I have colleagues who have become general counsel for universities, vice presidents, provosts, and so on.

TIP

Some law schools may encourage you to at least try a lawyer-type role first. This is just to ensure you're making the best decision in the short term and long term and that you have no regrets.

Having a fairly regular workweek (usually close to 40 hours) is one of the best parts about jobs in law school administration. You also work with talented, interesting students in a noncompetitive working environment and enjoying a more relaxed pace than in legal practice. In addition, many of these positions require or prefer a JD, so you'll feel positive that you're bringing many of your law school skills into play on the job.

TIP

A good way to find out about law school administration jobs is through the individual law school websites, the ABA website, LinkedIn, the *Chronicle of Higher Education* (www.chronicle.com), NALP, and the American Association of Law Schools (AALS, www.aals.org).

Teaching law

All you need to be a law professor is a JD; no formal preparation is required of anyone who teaches at a law school. However, landing a teaching job at a law school isn't as easy as it sounds. Teaching law is an extremely competitive career, one in which you pretty much need a sterling law school transcript. In the past, you had to have a degree from one of the top five to ten law schools in the country to be able to choose from the best selection of positions. Nevertheless, it's a popular ambition for many new graduates.

Besides an amazing academic record, people interviewing for teaching positions also need stellar academic references (from their law school professors). Academic references don't have nearly the weight in other careers that they do in teaching law. If this career is something you're considering, start making the appropriate contacts before you graduate, particularly with highly revered and esteemed professors who taught your courses. You want to shine in your classes so these professors can later trumpet your abilities to faculty hiring committees.

Taking small seminars with research papers is particularly valuable so that your professor comes to know you more closely and can comment on your research and writing abilities more concretely.

If you aren't in the top echelons of your graduating class, aren't a member of the law review, or haven't done a prestigious clerkship, your prospects of getting a teaching job are doubtful but not altogether lost. If you didn't graduate from one of the top law schools, take comfort in the fact that law schools increasingly are looking for people who bring a special perspective to the study of law (translation: a PhD in a related discipline, such as economics or political science). Thus, getting a JD and a PhD can help give you an edge when your academic record can't. Sometimes, getting an LLM (master of laws) in the area in which you hope to teach also helps.

REMEMBER

Pure intellectual firepower also is valued in teaching the law; that's why only people from the cream of the crop generally are selected. As a law professor, you need to be able to think quickly on your feet in class, respond to students' questions and *interrogatories* (legalese for a list of questions one party in a case sends to the other and must be answered in writing by the other party under oath) with an immediate critique, and generate original ideas for scholarly research and publication purposes.

People love teaching law because it's a rare opportunity to read, think, and write about interesting things, work with smart people, and get paid for all that. In addition, the pace is relaxed because you're usually teaching only one or two courses a semester, and that gives you time to research and publish.

The best way to find out about teaching positions is through the ABA website, individual law school websites, the various mailing lists many law school faculty and administrators belong to, LinkedIn, HigherEdJobs (www.higheredjobs.com), the *Chronicle of Higher Education*, and the AALS.

Legal journalism

Imagine writing stories about cutting-edge cases or legal developments in your community for a local newspaper, or freelancing articles for a legal magazine or newspaper. Welcome to the world of legal affairs journalism. This field doesn't strictly require a JD, but having one serves as a huge benefit for most employers.

Legal journalists generally fall into two categories: those on staff at a particular organization/company/station, blogs, think tanks, or publication (legal or nonlegal but covering legal affairs) and those who freelance. When you work for a publication, such as a newspaper or magazine, you're usually assigned articles to go out and write. When you freelance, you pick and choose your own projects by sending *queries* (emails introducing you and the topic you want to write about) to news outlets, publications, etc. Some legal journalists do a mixture of both.

Because jobs in legal journalism are unlikely to be posted in your CSO, you need to find them on your own. One way to go about that task is sending résumés and cover letters to legal newspapers and magazines you want to work for, along with some *clips* (examples of your writing). You can find these publications by reviewing digital resources like these: Law360, *Scotus Blog*, *The National Law Journal*, Above the Law, Courthouse New Service, Brennan Center for Justice, Brookings Institute, ACLU, and JURIST.

You may have noticed the increase in lawyers on TV news shows. This arena is another opportunity to use your training and skill set by commenting on the Supreme Court docket, recent rulings, case law, and politics.

Law librarianship

Although traditional paper law libraries have dwindled, law students, attorneys, law clerks, and their judges still need assistance. Law librarians are now gaining an even more sought-after set of skills: knowing all about the latest technology. As a result, today's law librarians are savvy electronic gurus who can help streamline research time enormously with their vast knowledge of databases and other online resources. Because technology is ever changing, to be a law librarian, you need to enjoy learning about technology and be able to keep up with the newest developments.

Law librarian jobs are coveted because you're always:

>> Working in a pleasant and quiet location

>> Receiving immediate satisfaction from helping people dig up hard-to-find information

>> Developing a better reputation for knowledge in your subject area

>> Working hours that can't be beaten (usually 9 to 5)

In addition, teaching opportunities in law school libraries are common, because someone has to teach all the first-year (1L) legal and research library classes or advanced legal research classes to 2Ls, 3Ls, and 4Ls. Talking to law librarians at your school's library and other academic or law firm libraries is the best way to find out the range of duties law librarians perform.

REMEMBER

Law librarians aren't limited to working in only law school libraries: You also find them in law firms and government libraries. Law librarians in each workplace specialize in different things and different areas of the library. Some concentrate on government documents, while others focus on teaching law students or lawyers how to conduct legal research.

Many universities offer joint JD/MLS (master of library science) programs, which are generally four years long. Most library law jobs require at least a master's degree, and although you don't need the JD to get a good job with a law library, the two combined enhance your options.

When you're looking for a law librarian job, check out the website for the American Association of Law Libraries (AALL). Don't miss its extremely informative section on Education for a Career in Law Librarianship at `www.aallnet.org/careers/career-center`.

Modifying Your Job-Search Tactics

Your alternative job search isn't radically different from a traditional job search, but it may be slightly more difficult. This section takes a look at a few of the reasons.

Convincing leery employers of your interest

One unfortunate fact of life for someone with a JD who's seeking an alternative career is that employers sometimes are suspicious when they know you've gone to law school but aren't practicing law. They may think that you couldn't get a job in law and that you're just "making do" with them. As a result, you need to turn up the volume on your sales skills like never before.

Show an employer that its job *is* your first choice to allay those fears. Volunteering in a related capacity somewhere else — whether during law school, after you graduate, or even while you work another job — helps you accomplish that feat. Then you can add that experience to your résumé and submit it to the employer you really want to work for. Another way to help convince an employer of your sincerity is to learn all you can about that employer and its work through informational interviews (see Chapter 21). Armed with the knowledge you glean from your informational interview, you can wow any employer into realizing that you're serious about this career commitment.

Touching up your old law school résumé

REMEMBER

Your old law school résumé won't cut it without some editing when you're seeking an alternative career. You need to look at your résumé from the perspective of your potential alternative employer and specifically tailor it to your new alternative position.

For example, if a job as a legal affairs journalist is what you want, play down the moot court and chairing the Bankruptcy Law Association and play up your writing experience. In fact, you want to include a special section on your résumé, titled "Writing Experiences" or "Publications," where you list all the relevant activities you did in law school and college.

6

Wrapping Up Your Law School Career

Prepare for the bar exam.

Meet your graduation requirements and enjoy graduation day.

Chapter **24**

In a Class of Its Own: Preparing for the Bar Exam

The first thing you need to know about the bar exam is that it's completely *doable*. Sure, you've probably heard many horror stories about how hard it is and how much it takes out of you. The truth is that in spite of what people say, the majority of test-takers pass every year. And you can be one of them!

You've made it this far (either deciding to apply to law school or already succeeding in law school); don't let the bar exam be the one hurdle between you and your dreams of becoming a practicing attorney. To ensure that you don't, I introduce you to the four sections of the bar exam in this chapter. Then I explore in detail the features of bar review prep courses and explain how to decide whether they're the right tools for you. Finally, I discuss a few things to consider as the exam date draws near.

The bar exam has changed dramatically since the previous edition of the book and will continue to evolve. Keep in touch with the changes on the American Bar Association (ABA) website — www.americanbar.org — and through your law school's academic affairs and bar support offices.

Deciding Whether to Take the Bar Exam

Not every graduating law student takes the bar exam. If you decide against taking it, you're still a bona fide law school graduate (JD); you just can't call yourself a lawyer. Although some graduates like to have the bar exam under their belts as something to fall back on, paying the test fees, taking expensive prep courses, and using three-quarters of your summer preparing for it makes little sense when you're never planning to practice law.

If you don't pass the bar exam and aren't admitted to your state bar, you can't practice at all. But if you're entering a career where practicing law isn't a component, thinking deeply about the pros and cons involved in undertaking such a time-consuming and expensive endeavor is wise.

The main purpose of the bar exam is to ensure that all a given state's lawyers have the same minimal level of legal knowledge. Because they've all passed the bar, they have at least a passing knowledge of fundamental legal concepts, regardless of the quality of their respective law schools. And that's comforting for anyone seeking the advice of an attorney.

TAKING THE BAR EXAM IN ANOTHER STATE

If you're planning to take the bar in a state other than the one where your law school is located, work with your law school administrators, such as bar support, academic success, career services office (CSO), and/or student affairs. You need to know right away whether the bar examiners in the state you plan to practice in have any requirements you must handle as a first-year (1L) student. For example, in some states, including Alabama, California, Florida, Iowa, and Texas, you have to register for the bar as a 1L. Other states, including Louisiana, Mississippi, North Dakota, Ohio, and Oklahoma, require registration during your second year.

You may want to focus on taking certain courses that cover certain subjects covered by the bar exam in the state where you want to be licensed. For instance, the bar examiners in Louisiana function under civil law as opposed to common law. Nevada and North Dakota have state-specific exams.

The ABA Standard 509 report (see Chapter 3) has information for each ABA law school and the top five jurisdictions in which the school's graduates' bar exams rate.

Explaining the Bar Exam

The main point of taking the bar exam is to be formally admitted to the practice of law. After you're admitted to a state's bar, you're all set to hit the ground running in your new career.

REMEMBER

Familiarizing yourself early (such as in the first month of your final year of law school) with your state's bar exam application deadlines and registration procedures is important. States vary in how early you need to register with their bar offices so that you can take the bar exam. Some deadlines are so early that you need to start getting your application materials together many months before the actual exam. Although registering for a state's bar exam after the regular deadline has passed is possible (by registering before the late deadlines), *substantial* fees are often associated with doing so. In a similar vein, if you have accommodations (such as for a disability), make sure you check with your jurisdiction early on so you can find out what you need to do to receive those accommodations for the bar exam.

The bar exam used to be a three-day event, depending on your state, and that didn't include the professional responsibility exam given on other dates. These days, the bar exam is likely to be a two-day event. It happens twice a year, in late July and late February. Most people take it in July, right after graduation, but the small number of people graduating in December usually opt to take the February bar exam.

TIP

Although each *jurisdiction* (state, U.S. territory, or Washington, D.C.) gives its own bar exam, they're generally similar across the board. Because some particulars — requirements, fees, registration dates, and parts of the exam — differ between jurisdictions, you need to go to the website of your state bar to find out the specifics. For a comprehensive listing of state bar offices, check the National Conference of Bar Examiners (NCBE) website and click on "bar admission offices" for a complete listing (www.ncbex.org).

If you want to practice law in a state that's different from the one where you take the bar exam, you need to check with the other state to determine its policies regarding admittance.

The Uniform Bar Exam (UBE) has three components as of this writing, though these can vary by jurisdiction:

>> **Multistate Bar Examination (MBE):** This exam is a 200-question multiple-choice test that focuses on core legal subjects, such as civil procedure, contracts and sales, evidence, and torts, among others. You know, the stuff you learned — and have forgotten — from first year. This portion counts for 50 percent of your score.

>> **Multistate Essay Examination (MEE):** This exam has six 30-minute essay questions. It covers second- and third-year (2L and 3L) topics, such as business associations, constitutional law, family law, and property, to name a few. Only some jurisdictions require test-takers to take this particular test. It counts for 30 percent of your total UBE score. Otherwise, you will take a state-specific essay exam.

>> **Multistate Performance Test (MPT):** This exam contains two 90-minute tests that focus on practical lawyering skills. Besides answering questions about fact analysis and problem solving, expect to actually review a client file and answer questions about it. It counts for 20 percent of your total score.

REMEMBER

The NCBE is slowly phasing out the UBE and replacing it with the NextGen bar exam, which I cover in the following section. The final UBE administration is scheduled for February 2028.

The Multistate Professional Responsibility Examination (MPRE) isn't part of the UBE even though it's required in most jurisdictions. The MPRE is a two-hour, 50-question multiple-choice test given three times per year (not corresponding to the bar dates) in March, August, and November. It tests your knowledge of ethics and professional responsibility.

REMEMBER

Always keep in mind that exactly what you'll be tested on depends on your particular state. States differ in terms of how many of these parts they test, and how much time (for example, half a day versus a whole day) they allot to each part. To find out specifically what you do and don't need to take, contact the state where you're seeking admission.

Getting to know the Next-Generation bar exam (NextGen Bar)

The NextGen bar exam features four major differences from the UBE:

» It's computer-based.

» It focuses on practical skills along with legal knowledge.

» It offers an integrated format. The MBE, MEE, and MPT are incorporated into one exam. The test includes integrated question sets and performance tasks based on common scenarios.

» It tests fewer subjects (eight). These subjects include the following:

- Business associations
- Civil procedure
- Constitutional law
- Contract law
- Criminal law
- Evidence
- Real property
- Torts

Some jurisdictions are already transitioning to the NextGen bar. The timing of its implementation varies greatly, but here are some guidelines as of this writing:

» **July 2026:** Connecticut, Guam, Maryland, Missouri, Oregon, and Washington

» **2027:** Arizona, Iowa, Kentucky, Minnesota, Nebraska, Oklahoma, Tennessee, Vermont, and Wyoming

» **2028:** Alabama, Colorado, Florida, Illinois, Kansas, New Hampshire, New York, Pennsylvania, Texas, and Virginia

Check out www.ncbex.org for the latest on what will happen with other jurisdictions.

Multistate Professional Responsibility Exam

The MPRE stands out in that it isn't given at the same time as the three other parts. In fact, you can often take it while you're still in law school. Many people take it either in November or March of their final year, but it's also offered in August. The MPRE also is graded separately from the other parts of the bar exam, so your score on it doesn't affect your score on the other parts. Each jurisdiction also determines its own passing score.

Taking the MPRE while in law school has its benefits. For starters, taking it then gets it nicely out of the way. Plus, the exam tests you on standards regarding a lawyer's professional conduct, which is the kind of information you find out about in your professional responsibility and legal ethics course. Most people take that course during their upperclass years (see Chapter 18), so the information should be relatively fresh in your mind. Some jurisdictions require you to take a certain number of law school credits before sitting for this exam, however, so check with your state to see whether this timing can work for you.

REMEMBER

The MPRE is required for all U.S. jurisdictions except Wisconsin and Puerto Rico. Connecticut and New Jersey don't require the MPRE if you take and successfully complete a law school professional responsibility course.

Multistate Bar Exam

The MBE features questions specific to the fundamentals that all lawyers need to know and most of which you discover as a 1L. You're asked 200 multiple-choice questions in seven subjects: civil procedure, constitutional law, contracts, criminal law and procedure, evidence, property, and torts. In general each subject receives equal weight. (175 of the 200 questions are scored.)

This exam is six hours long, but at least it's divided into two three-hour periods with a hundred questions during each period. You're also allowed a lunch break between the two parts of the exam, which you definitely need to take. Make sure you:

>> Walk around a bit because you're likely to feel quite cramped after sitting through a tense, three-hour block of time

>> Don't overdo lunch and wind up sleeping through the second part

As for the nitty-gritty of how to answer the questions: Each question is followed by four potential answers from which you choose the dreaded best answer. I always hated those best-answer questions because my answer always seemed to be second best. Although you're not marked off for wrong answers, you receive credit only for correct ones.

Besides the immense amount of law the MBE covers, the tricky thing about the exam is that the questions aren't straightforward. Instead, they're written by professional test-makers who plot how to throw you for a major loop. Just knowing the law isn't good enough; you also need to know how to deal with how questions are written. That's why taking a bar review course is a good idea. (See the "Considering a Bar Review Course" section later in the chapter.) After you discover the fundamentals of interpreting the question, you can better determine how examiners want you to answer.

REMEMBER

If you're planning to practice in Louisiana or Puerto Rico, you're in luck because you don't have to take the MBE! Louisiana follows a different legal system (civil law). Both Louisiana and Puerto Rico have their own bar exams.

Multistate Essay Exam

The MEE tests the same skills that are tested in law school exams, such as identifying legal issues raised by a fact pattern and deciding what is and isn't relevant in that fact pattern, among other skills. (Check out Chapter 15 for more about fact patterns.)

The MEE is a three-hour exam made up of six questions about the following areas of law: agency and partnership, commercial paper, conflict of laws, corporations, decedents' estates, family law, federal civil procedure, sales, secured transactions, and trusts and future interests. Questions can test more than one topic, so jurisdictions can choose all or some of these topics to test in their six questions. Other jurisdictions come up with and administer their own additional essay questions, which can mean more or fewer than six essays to answer.

REMEMBER

The MEE is administered in 48 jurisdictions. At this time, only 15 jurisdictions required it. It isn't required in California, Delaware, Georgia, Florida, Louisiana, Puerto Rico, and Virginia.

Multistate Performance Test

The MPT is an interesting phenomenon; it's two 90-minute, three-question skills tests that ask you to perform the kinds of functions that a lawyer encounters on a daily basis. It doesn't test your knowledge of substantive law. Instead, it tests skills such as accurately interpreting documents in a client file and analyzing a fact situation from a hypothetical client problem. You're asked to produce an end product for each question, such as a memorandum, client letter, or brief, among others.

Many students often find this portion to be the least stressful of all bar exam components. Many students think it's easier to handle because tests how well you can work with different factors such as statutes, case law, and a client's facts and then engage in a lawyerly task rather than your knowledge of the law.

REMEMBER

As of March 2025, all 50 jurisdictions require this test.

Preparing for the Character and Fitness Review

When applying to take the bar exam, you go through a screening process (background investigation) to determine whether you're morally fit enough to become a member of the bar of a particular jurisdiction. In some jurisdictions, you have to submit your character and fitness application prior to sitting for the bar exam.

The process is extensive and can be a bit intrusive. You share information such as the following:

>> Educational background

>> Work history

>> Academic honor code violations

>> Criminal and civil lawsuits

>> Driving history

>> Whether you've ever filed for bankruptcy or been fired from a job

The examiners also review things like your law school applications, credit history, and criminal history (if you have one).

REMEMBER

The character and fitness application process usually isn't too hard for most law students to pass. But fully disclosing any past transgressions (such as an arrest or DUI) is important; not disclosing is often viewed worse than the transgression itself (because now you're lying on top of the transgression you committed in the past). In fact, the most common reason that applicants failing the character and fitness review is that they fail to disclose a transgression during the law school application and/or bar licensure process. Check with your particular jurisdiction to find out more about what issues, misdemeanors or felonies, charges, and convictions on your record may prevent you from being certified to become an attorney.

The best thing you can do is disclose everything and answer every question asked. Ask clarifying questions if you need to.

Considering a Bar Review Course

The purpose of commercial bar review courses is plain and simple: to get you to pass the bar. These courses are generally six to seven weeks long and are like an intensive boot camp at which you'll probably learn more actual *black letter law* (straightforward rules) than you did in law school. Bar reviews usually begin about two months before the start of the bar exam and end right before it.

Much like commercial SAT or LSAT test-prep courses, bar review courses market themselves heavily on the rates of their students that pass the bar exam. They don't teach you how to think like a lawyer the way law school does. Instead, they focus mainly on tricks and tips for conquering each question you may encounter. One of the benefits of taking a bar review course is that you don't have the stress of taking all the bar courses (see Chapter 18) in law school because you know you'll get all the information you need about the subjects tested on the exam during the review course.

Many students believe that taking a bar review course is a no-brainer. Much is riding on your passing the exam, and sticking to a hard-and-fast study schedule is nearly impossible without the structure of a review course. Although they can be expensive (around $200 or more), many students are able to take advantage of early registration discounts that some courses offer.

If you can't take time off to attend bar review classes during the day, you can take a home study program or combine home and away programs to get ready for the bar exam.

Bar exam courses have many benefits; I cover a couple in the following sections. They generally give you books of outlines for each subject area that's tested. These outlines are invaluable for getting the essence of the laws and concepts that are actually on the test.

>> **Making you stick to a schedule:** As everyone knows, tackling huge quantities of information is much easier when you have a schedule, and bar exam prep courses give you that kind of structure. They also provide you with an actual schedule so you can chart your studying and know exactly how much time you can afford to spend on each topic you need to study.

>> **Allowing you to take simulated practice exams:** One great thing about bar exam prep courses is that they make you take simulated practice exams. If left only to your own devices, can you really say that you'd sit down and take a six-hour test on your own time? Probably not. And taking these practice exams is one of the best ways to gain valuable experience answering the practice questions in a timed format. When you have experience doing multiple exams in a timed setting, you find out how well you can handle time-pressured questions, and that's key to doing well on the exam!

TIP

Many bar prep companies — and even law schools — offer a mock bar exam so you can truly assess your needs, control your stress and anxiety, manage your time, and be laser-focused during the bar itself.

BAR EXAM ADVICE FROM A RECENT LAW SCHOOL GRADUATE

The following advice comes from Lovia Ofori-Ampofo, McGeorge School of Law Class of 2023, who is now an associate attorney.

While studying for the bar exam, I learned that preparation must be treated like a full-time job. Commit to eight to ten hours of focused study each day, and structure your schedule to mirror the actual exam format. For example, during the day, start your morning session with essays and an afternoon session of multiple-choice questions. Rotate your practice days accordingly. So on one day, start with three hours of MBE questions in the morning and spend the afternoon on three hours of essays. The next day, begin with essays in the morning and complete MBE practice in the afternoon.

Make it a goal to work through every available bar exam question, even if you are only issue-spotting. Equally important, dedicate substantial time to reviewing the questions you answered incorrectly. Careful review is where the deepest learning happens; understanding your mistakes allows you to avoid repeating them.

Above all, protect your mental health throughout the process. Maintain a strong, resilient mindset and remind yourself that you will pass — even on the days when your confidence falters.

Tips and Tricks to Prepare for the Bar Exam

By far, the key to doing well on the bar exam is preparing well in advance. It's a far cry from law school finals, where you can cram the night before and pull off a decent grade. (Not that you *should* study for finals that way.) You need to prepare for the bar like the major academic challenge that it is. Although courses you took in law school, especially during the first year, help you to a certain extent, the exam features ways of testing you just won't be familiar with at all.

TIP

When your bar review course begins, you definitely want to follow its recommendations for how many hours a day you need to study. But in general, several hours a day is highly recommended for the first month; thereafter, most students kick into high gear and study between six and eight hours per day until the test. Don't wait until well into the review course to start studying.

Taking advantage of your law school's bar resources and discounts

Whatever bar prep tools, resources, or opportunities your law school offers, I encourage you to take advantage of all of them; don't leave anything on the table. Some law schools work with bar prep companies to create incentives for their students. These incentives often lead to discounts on the very expensive (but necessary) bar prep courses. If you can't find information on these opportunities, ask. If they don't exist, make the suggestion and see what happens.

Hiring a private tutor

Some graduates hire a private tutor to help them prep for the bar exam. This route can be quite expensive, but depending on your learning style and learning differences, it may be exactly what you need. For some, setting their own schedule and having one-on-one time with an expert is the key to success. Some people even take a commercial course in conjunction with bringing in a private tutor.

Get your bar support team's advice. You may find they can help you identify someone who's bright, patient, and an excellent tutor to help you.

Submitting your accommodations paperwork to the bar examiners

If you receive accommodations in law school and believe you need them for the bar exam, make sure you have copies of all your documentation. Review the bar examiner's information about accommodations, paying close attention to the deadlines and the type of documentation required.

TIP

Don't add to your stress and anxiety by missing the window for submitting your documentation and seeking approval for what you need as soon as possible. You worked hard for three or four years, and you want to ensure you give yourself everything you need to pass that bar exam.

Chapter **25**

Moving toward Graduation — And Beyond

H ave you ever noticed how enormous law school diplomas are? They make your college diploma look like an index card by comparison. Soon, that baby, complete with your new title ("Doctor of Jurisprudence"), will be in your hot little hands! That magical time you've waited for is almost here — the day you can finally call yourself a law school graduate. Your three (or four) years of hard work have paid off, and soon you'll start a new life and a new job, maybe even in a brand-new city. If that's not exciting — and even a little scary — I don't know what is.

Don't spend all your time daydreaming about your graduation day just yet though; you need to take care of some more mundane business first. In this chapter, I walk you through satisfying your final graduation requirements. I take a closer look at the feelings of insecurity and doubt (graduation jitters) that hit many law students during their final year and what you can do about them. I also discuss the all-too-common realities of postgraduation unemployment and give you some simple tips for landing your dream job.

Winding Up Your Law School Career

As scary as it may seem, your days as a student are numbered. Soon, you'll leave the protective shell of academia and head into the unknown abyss of the real world. If you're a *K-JD* student (one who went into law school straight after undergrad), you've been in school for 20 or 21 consecutive years; this realization can come as a real shock, and you may be nervous about what lies ahead. *Remember:* Taking things slowly and tying up loose ends in a methodical fashion is the best way to gradually cut the scholastic apron strings. The first thing you want to do is make sure you won't have any nasty surprises on graduation day (such as your name not being called — imagine the embarrassment). That means checking with the registrar and dean of students to confirm that everything is all set before the big day.

Fulfilling all your requirements

All law schools have graduation requirements. As a result, you need to make sure that you've satisfied all of them before you ever begin thinking about walking across the stage.

REMEMBER

Some graduation requirements are easy to forget about, such as an upper-division writing requirement or applying for graduation (see Chapter 18), so log in and scour your transcript to ensure you've covered them all. If you still need to fulfill one or two graduation requirements as a second-semester 3L, register early or alert your registrar so you don't get closed out of courses that fulfill these requirements. Meet with the dean of students or your academic dean as soon as possible to ensure you can adjust your schedule and stay on track.

Making sure you graduate on time

No awakening is ruder than realizing a few weeks into your 3L spring semester that you're one credit short. If that happens, you probably have few options besides making up that credit during the summer or next semester (unless you have an understanding registrar or dean of students).

TIP

Avoiding this problem at all costs means ensuring that everything is in order credit-wise long before your 3L spring semester starts. Here are some suggestions:

>> **Use whatever degree audit tools your law school has, but also keep track of your requirements separately.**

>> **Check where you stand at the start of each semester/term or during registration.**

>> **Don't hesitate to reach out to the registrar to make sure that what you're registering for in your final semester gives you enough credits to graduate on time.** At this meeting, don't forget to review any courses you've taken outside your law school to confirm that your credit or institutional credit residency requirements have also been met. You want to make sure you have taken the minimum number of credits at the law school you are graduating from.

Getting a Professional Graduation Photo

Strike a lawyerly pose and show those pearly whites, because your graduation photo's going to serve you well for a long time. Almost all schools offer a graduation photo opportunity, usually in the fall semester of your third year.

The main purpose of this photo shoot is often to provide the school with a picture for its *class composite*, which the school usually hangs in a special hallway (or room) with all the other class composites. You're adding to the legacy of your law school.

Remember that you get something out of smiling for the camera, too. Most of the time, you can purchase your own photos from the proofs the photography company sends you, which are fun graduation gifts to give to friends and family. Plus, having something tangible (besides your diploma) that you can look at and that commemorates your three (or four) years of hard work feels good. Compare it with your high school senior year photo, and you'll see how far you've come!

Taking a picture-perfect photo

When having this photo taken, you want to put your best headshot forward because you're unlikely to get a retake when you don't like the outcome. To ensure that no one mistakes yours for one of those bad passport photos, check out the following list for some picture-perfect tips:

>> **Wear a dark-colored suit.** Navy, dark gray, and black are good bets. Because your photo will be positioned in alphabetical order with the other members of your class in the composite photo, you'll stand out when you're the only one in the fuchsia suit. However, a brightly colored blouse or brightly patterned tie can be a stylish contrast against a dark suit.

>> **Bring a makeup, a brush and/or comb, a small mirror, and an extra tie/blouse with you.** Your photographer probably won't provide items like these

and probably won't notice whether you have a hair out of place or a big chunk of spinach in your teeth. A quick check in the mirror enables you to properly arrange yourself before the shoot.

Putting your photo to good use

If you're tempted not to order any copies of your photo for yourself, think twice. Even when you don't want to give them as gifts, you'll probably run into a few situations in your professional life when they come in handy. Think about updating your LinkedIn profile!

TIP

For example, your employer usually features a bio page on its website (or promotional materials) and may request a professional photo from you. Your law school photo is a great one to use for this purpose, because it's recent and shows you in a suit and in a professional pose. Order some wallet-sized prints and set aside several for this purpose. Besides, what else are you going to give them — a snapshot of you on vacation?

Looking Forward to Your Future Career

The final year for some law students is marked with nagging feelings of self-doubt and insecurity. For example:

» Some students wonder whether three (or four) years and $100,000 to $200,000 was really worth it for a degree that they may be ambivalent about.

» Second-career students who sacrificed a previous career or family obligations to attend law school may be stressed when they realize that a law degree doesn't always equal the job of their dreams.

» The lucky ones with job offers in hand may start to wonder whether they can hack it in the stressful, competitive legal world.

» Others doubt how much they've actually learned and wonder how good a lawyer they're really going to be.

If you still haven't found your legal passion — or you disliked your internships and/or summer jobs in the legal field — and still don't know what you want to do, you may feel like you're floundering. This situation can lead to anxiety and even panic as you realize that your grace period is about to come to an end. Hearing classmates talking with excitement about their recent job offers and the new lives they'll be starting after graduation is hard when your future still is uncertain.

Take your time in figuring things out. The end of the world hasn't come if you're still unemployed at the end of the summer or even six months down the road. In fact, taking some time off between law school and your new job is an empowering way to recharge your batteries and find yourself. After all, when will you get such an extensive break again after you're gainfully employed?

TIP

The following list details some productive methods for figuring out what you want to do in your final year, at your own pace:

>> **Continue (or start) doing informational interviews.** *Informational interviewing* is best described like this: You meet informally with a practitioner to get information, advice, and further contacts. You're not actually announcing that you're looking for a job, but you are making known the fact that you're looking for advice and networking opportunities, so your interviewer (and anyone else) thinks of you when any new job openings arise. Informational interviewing also is an excellent way to gain general information about a field. See Chapter 22 for more details about this topic.

>> **Job shadow as many people as you can.** *Job shadowing* is when you spend a half or whole day on the job with a job-shadow host, observing what they do during a typical day. In the process, you discover valuable information about how much time that person spends on paperwork or client contact. A day of job shadowing, although not conclusive, helps you determine whether you're well-suited to a particular career. Chapter 21 has more information about job shadowing.

>> **Research careers that are outside the norm or traditional law jobs.** Whenever you're unsure whether you really want to be a lawyer, start considering the myriad jobs out there where you're not practicing law but a JD is an asset. Ask your career services office (CSO) to put you in contact with alums from your school who are working in alternative careers and then arrange to job shadow and conduct informational interviews with them as much as you can. Check out Chapter 23 for more details about careers outside the box.

>> **Talk with as many people as possible regarding any doubts about the law.** If your career plans are uncertain in your final year because you're just not sure whether the law is for you, share your concerns with caring CSO staff, your dean of students, or alums. You'll soon find out that many people with JDs have (or had), doubts about whether law is really the right career for them. Keep in mind that you're far from alone when you didn't know from the first day of torts that the law was definitely for you.

>> **See a new career counselor.** Take matters into your own hands when, for whatever reason, your law school's CSO just isn't doing it for you. Perhaps it's time to seek out a different perspective from someone else — maybe a faculty

member that you connected with, another administrator you trust, your alumni mentor, or a former supervisor from your internship or externship. You can also consider a private career counselor. Of course, they don't work cheap, but if you're truly undecided in your career plans or professional path, discussing your situation with a career counselor is an investment you at least need to think about. Spending a few hundred dollars now on professional advice can save you thousands in heartache and job changes later.

>> **Read plenty of job-advice online and in books.** This tactic is a good (and cheap) substitute for hiring a live private career counselor. You can find these books in your local bookstore in either self-help or careers sections.

Treasuring the Magic of Your Graduation Day

The light at the end of the tunnel is finally here — your graduation day! If your school is like most, graduation takes place on a weekend, and you're scheduled to attend lunches or dinners and other festivities planned by the school, such as a mix-and-mingle cocktail party for friends and family.

REMEMBER

Make sure to purchase (if required/allowed) enough tickets to these events ahead of time; your favorite aunt won't be too pleased if she's left out.

On the day of the actual ceremony, make sure that you do the following. Although these may seem like fairly simple things to remember, you'd be surprised how many students are tripped up by the distractions of all the graduation activities and events.

>> Know where to be for any school-sponsored group photos and at what time

>> Note when and where you actually have to line up to march

>> Make sure you've brought your cap, gown, hood, and honors cords, which you usually pick up a few days before the ceremony

>> Find out how you need to shake hands with your presenter as you receive your diploma

REMEMBER

At many law schools, you don't receive your actual diploma on graduation day. Instead, you get a plain old piece of paper that says "Congratulations!" or the equivalent. Diplomas are then mailed in July or August after the spring semester exams are graded and overall credits are tallied. If you didn't pass your exams or satisfy all your graduation requirements, you won't receive a diploma at that time.

CAN YOU CALL YOURSELF A LAWYER NOW?

When you become a law school graduate, are you actually considered a lawyer yet? Although the term *lawyer* is thrown around casually, you technically shouldn't refer to yourself as a lawyer until you actually pass the bar exam and are admitted to the bar. Until that glorious day, you should refer to yourself only as a JD or law school graduate (no matter how frequently your parents brag about you as "my child, the lawyer"). That's because people who haven't passed the bar exam and aren't admitted also aren't permitted to perform lawyerly tasks (Chapter 24 has more details).

After you pass the bar exam and are admitted to the bar, you're a bona fide lawyer or attorney at law. With both titles, you can also add "Esquire" (or "Esq.") after your name. If you work in a nonlegal position after you pass the bar exam and are admitted, you can call yourself a lawyer but not a practicing lawyer (more specifically, you're a non-practicing member of the state bar). In other words, only when you're actively engaged in the practice of law are you a *practicing lawyer*. But no matter what you go on to do in life, you'll always be able to write "JD" after your name.

Dealing with the Prospect of Being Unemployed at Graduation

Being unemployed at graduation (or beyond) isn't the unheard of. As the economy changes, the job market changes. In fact, you'll probably find that many of your classmates are in the same predicament as you.

Looking through the employer portal of many law school CSOs, you're likely to find some sort of statistic showing what percentage of the school's students were employed within nine months after graduation. Interestingly enough, that statistic isn't broken down to say in what *types* of jobs those graduates were employed. That should comfort you because it means that even when the percentage is high, the likelihood that every single one of last year's graduates found legal positions right after graduation isn't that great. Some of them are probably working in nonlegal positions, JD advantage jobs, temp jobs, and legal temp roles.

Here are a few recommendations from a former Career Services staff member:

>> Focus on passing the bar exam the first time you take it. Many legal employers, particularly small and mid-sized firms, hire only licensed attorneys. Thus, passing the bar exam can be the key credential that helps you get hired.

>> Continue searching for a job throughout the summer by checking job postings through your CSO on a weekly basis, arranging informational interviews, and attending networking events.

After the bar exam is over, consider working for a legal temp agency to make use of your skills. Not only can temp positions turn into full-time positions, but the structure and routine of work keep you focused on your ultimate career goal of finding a full-time position, help build your résumé, and generate some income.

Despite trying to maintain an optimistic outlook, ignoring the fact that being unemployed at graduation doesn't feel all that great is tough. Being in that position can take some of the joy out of a festive occasion, especially when you realize that you're moving right back in with your parents after the ceremony or starting your new job as a restaurant server the next day. But as the next few sections explain, you can do many proactive things to improve your job prospects.

Spreading the news

If you're planning to stick around the city where your law school is located, use your last semester to make contacts in your field of interest. Find every single local alum and talk them into having coffee. Be as assertive as possible in making sure that your name is circulating, even when you feel like you're being a pest. Keeping in frequent touch with these alums or other contacts you come across may help them suddenly remember your name the moment a colleague mentions that they're looking for a new associate.

TIP

When you plan to move to a new city, you want to do the same types of things, but you'll rely more on email and the telephone while you're searching for a long-distance job during your last semester of law school. Again, find out the names of all your school's alums in your new city, email them, and set up meetings with them when you're in town. During your last semester's spring break is a prime time for doing this vital task, so be sure to schedule a week's worth of appointments in your target city whenever possible.

REMEMBER

When you let everyone in your circle know that you're looking for advice and information about a field in their city, opportunities start happening for you. After all, when people don't know that you're looking, they can't present you with the opportunities that do come around.

Moving to your desired city and getting involved

If you're still unemployed after graduation, you may want to move to your new city and take the bar exam (if you're planning to practice law) or start getting involved (for all jobs). If you're not busy studying for the bar, you can at least get a few months' head start.

As you settle in, you have many options (besides alumni networking) that you can use to improve your chances of landing your ideal job. These suggestions are also good even if you need a bit of a breather after law school (or the bar exam) and don't want to start work at your permanent job right away:

>> **Work as a legal temp.** Yep, that's right, they have temps in the legal field, too. Just sign on with a legal temping firm; many cities have them, but they tend to cluster in the larger cities. You do short-term projects for as long as you're available and get paid by the hour. If you've passed the bar exam, you get bigger and better projects, but you can still be a temp even without passing the bar exam at most temp agencies.

Although you don't receive any perks or benefits, your pay will surely net you more than if you worked in some other service type of job. The main benefit of temping is that you can sample a variety of workplaces and areas of practice, and if you impress an employer, that can be your back-door ticket to a full-time job!

>> **Volunteer to do the kind of work you really want to do.** When your new city has a nonprofit that's in your ideal area of practice, spend a few months helping out wherever you're needed. That way, when any of the organization's attorneys hear of openings, you'll be perched right under their noses and first on their minds. You can pursue volunteering while also working at a coffee shop, department store, or your local library to bring in some income if your savings are running out.

>> **Join your state or local bar association and start attending functions.** Mixing and mingling with lawyers (and potential employers) is another important way of getting your name and interest in a particular practice area out there. Sign up for a committee or two in your area of interest and attend continuing legal education seminars. Don't be shy — go right up and introduce yourself! You may want to get some inexpensive business cards made up to hand out on the spot.

>> **Get a random temporary job.** Working as a temp to make ends meet is okay, but during your free time be sure that you continue to send out cover letters and résumés, attend local bar association functions, and get your name out within the legal community.

7

The Part of Tens

Explore the best and worst things about law school.

Get some inside tips for success in law school.

Chapter **26**

Ten Best and Worst Things about Law School

After you're a bona fide law student, every new experience puts you in a better position for determining what you like and don't like about law school. Like all things in life, this educational feat certainly has its positive and negative aspects, and you need to take what you don't like in stride. This chapter looks at the good, the bad, and the ugly about law school and gives you tips about how to accentuate the positives and minimize the negatives. If you anticipate some of the potential negatives and plan your strategy to deal with them in advance, you can have a more satisfying law school experience.

Gaining Valuable Public Speaking Skills

One of the best parts about law school is that even if you enter it terrified of uttering a single word in class, by the end of the first month you'll be a public speaking pro. Unlike in college, where you can hide in the back row of a 700-seat lecture hall, the typical law school classroom has stadium-style seating, where the professor has an unobstructed view of every single student. Crouching low in your seat just doesn't cut it because you can't hide (but check out Chapter 8 for strategic seating arrangement tips to minimize being called on).

Becoming a Better Writer

Because students come to law school with a variety of writing skills and competency levels, one goal of your first-year legal research and writing course is getting everyone up to roughly the same speed. Achieving that goal may mean that former math majors have to work much harder than former English majors, but achieving a higher skill level in writing is something that all lawyers must do.

REMEMBER

Writing is to lawyers what science is to doctors; you use it on a regular basis to practice your craft. The majority of most lawyers' work is made up of writing briefs, memos, and letters, and writing is the way lawyers communicate with clients, other lawyers, and judges. That's one of the reasons many law schools have additional writing requirements for graduation, such as an advanced writing course in the second year and a research paper seminar course in the third.

Discovering How American Society Works

The nonlegal stuff you learn in your years of law school is kind of like majoring in political science, civics, and American history all rolled into one. By reading the assigned cases, you find out how the courts, political process, and justice system work. The cases also expose you to the seamier side of societal relations, such as bitter divorces, horrific surgical mishaps, and toxic waste dumping, which is an education in itself. Overall, the amount of knowledge you can gain about American society in general from law school makes you a more informed citizen.

Developing Legal Skills You Can Use Even If You Don't Become a Lawyer

Even if you decide not to take the bar exam and become an attorney, the practical legal skills and knowledge you gain in law school can benefit you throughout the rest of your life. For instance, before you came to law school, you probably signed contracts for credit cards and leases without thoroughly looking them over. As a law school graduate, however, you'll scrutinize every last word with a lawyer's trained eye. You'll also have at least a rudimentary understanding of which provisions in a contract are okay and which ones are suspect. And you'll have the research skills to look up what you need to know in a law library.

Learning How to Look at Both Sides of an Issue

One invaluable skill you discover in law school is being able to consider both sides of an issue, not just the one you're emotionally or initially drawn to. Even if you decide not to become a lawyer, this skill is useful to have, regardless of whether you're arguing with your parents or trying to empathize with a co-worker. Being thoughtful, logical, and able to quickly assess both sides of a discussion or situation can be invaluable in a variety of situations. When you want to hone this skill, make sure you participate in moot court in law school. Thinking quickly on your feet and writing the required brief help you find out how to argue and analyze both sides of virtually any issue.

Becoming More Disciplined

One of the worst things about law school is that it takes more than just intellect and desire to succeed. You need a strong dose of motivation, discipline, and excellent study skills, too. (Chapter 13 has tips about acquiring good study habits.) Although many qualified and talented people are admitted to law school, not everyone does as well as they want to because they don't recognize that the study habits, note-taking system, and so on that worked in their undergrad or grad program may not work in law school, and they struggle to adapt. In other words, you can arrive in law school from the top of your undergraduate class, but unless you put in the required hard work, you won't enjoy similar success in law school.

Although it sounds trite, the one key attribute that the most successful law students have is self-discipline. Discipline helps you not only in law school but also as you start your career as an attorney.

Being with the Same People 24/7

One fortunate or unfortunate fact about law school is that it's kind of like being in high school again. You're with the same people virtually all the time (particularly as a first year, or 1L). As a result, you may actually feel like you're regressing to the ninth grade. For older students, this type of high-school environment can really tax your nerves.

Being with the same people all the time has its good and bad points. Being surrounded by familiar faces is somewhat comforting when you're all going through the trauma and drama of the Socratic method for the first time. You also build up tolerance for know-it-alls, which comes in handy when you have to deal with rude clients as a lawyer.

The downside is that making new friends is hard when the only people you know are in your *section* (the one you're assigned to at the beginning of the year). Plus, when you see the same people nearly every waking hour, gossip runs rampant (as you can imagine). Having everyone know your business gets old fast. But you can't escape it, because you're stuck with the same section for the entire year.

Not Getting Enough of a Hands-On Education

Law school differs greatly from, say, medical school, in the sense that nearly all your class instruction is theoretical rather than clinical or practical. In other words, what you learn about in the classroom is theory, not what lawyers actually do. This emphasis on the theoretical is a major drawback for some law students who learn better by doing than they do by just sitting in class absorbing material.

The way you can gain hands-on experience while in law school is by signing up for clinics and skills-based courses, such as mediation and negotiation. (See Chapter 18 for information on both these topics.) Doing summer and school-year externships for credit and jobs also gives you more of a realistic sense of what lawyers do.

Facing Stiff Competition from Classmates

Law school is made far less pleasant by the fact that you're always competing directly against your classmates for grades and jobs. Because of the grading curves many law schools impose, how well you do depends on how everyone else in your class does on a particular exam. That's why you're bound to hear a plethora of stories (some of them true) about pages being ripped out in library books and people refusing to share notes. Some people's attitude is that too much is at stake when another person gets a leg up. This constant reminder that your fate rests on the performances of other people sometimes makes the law school environment feel adversarial and cutthroat.

REMEMBER

The best way to avoid being sucked into this kind of competitive environment (that is, if you don't want to be in it) is to maintain a healthy outlook on life. Chapter 10 has guidance on keeping everything in perspective.

Many law schools spend time during orientation discussing the importance of working with each other, fostering a positive reputation, and remembering that the legal community and profession aren't that big. Your reputation and word matter, because you never know who's going to be on the other end of a hiring panel or serve as the judge or opposing counsel in one of your cases. Being kind and respectful can go a long way.

Note: Part-time and evening law students tend to report that their classmates aren't nearly as competitive as those in the full-time programs. Perhaps that's because these programs attract more older students simultaneously working full-time jobs, who thus have less time for the immature, petty acts that sometimes characterize relations among full-time law students.

Realizing That the Law Is a "Jealous Mistress"

Everyone knows that being a student generally is easier than working a full-time job because you have much more free time during the day (and can sleep in when your schedule allows). However, all the studying that you need to do, particularly as a 1L, can really eat into your free time. Non–law student friends and families may become jealous of how much time your law school studies and activities are taking up. That's why a well-known quote attributed to Supreme Court justice Joseph Story that "The law is a jealous mistress . . ." is especially fitting.

Whenever you have a significant other or a family depending on you, you may especially need to prioritize your time. Reassuring them that you're still committed to them, but that you have to devote a lot of your time right now to law school because of its demands, may help ease their concerns. Remind them that it's only three or four years of your life.

TIP

Come up with ways to include your loved ones in your law school life, starting in the application process, and they'll start to understand the volume of work, intensity, and stress you may experience.

Although the law may be jealous, it doesn't need to become an out-of-control, green-eyed monster. Here are a few ways to demonstrate your continued commitment to the people in your life:

>> Be thoughtful.

>> Schedule time for family and friends.

>> Do your part around the house.

>> Don't forget birthdays, anniversaries, soccer games, and so on.

Chapter **27**

Ten Little-Known Law School Secrets

One of the best parts about writing this book is the opportunity I have to share tips about law school that I gleaned during my three years of studies. Some of these facts I discovered the hard way as a brand-new first-year (1L) student; others I realized only through hindsight. So what follows are ten especially important tips that can help you as you progress through law school.

Working Part-Time during the School Year Helps with Your Financial Aid

The American Bar Association (ABA) regulations no longer limit law students' ability to work as full-time students, but many law schools strongly discourage or even forbid their full-time law students from working at all during their 1L year. (The rule used to be that you were prohibited from working more than 20 hours per week of part-time employment while taking more than 12 credit hours in a semester.) However, within these parameters, you can easily make enough money from 2L and 3L school-year part-time work to at least offset some of your living expenses.

You can average a decent salary to pay for rent, shopping, or food, depending on your city (bigger ones tend to pay more) and what type of part-time work you do (working as a clerk pays more at a large firm than at a small one; Chapters 20 and 21 have more on workplace options). Just keep in mind that you'll be paid by the hour and won't have benefits. Although most students prefer finding jobs in the legal field, working in nonlegal settings, such as retail or food service, can also be profitable. And because you're offsetting your living expenses, you can take out fewer loans. The less you need to pay back later, the better!

Choosing Study Group Members Doesn't Have to Be Hard

As a 1L, initially you probably won't know anyone with whom to form a study group. If you don't make any connections during orientation or have any friends you can ask to join you early on in the first of your classes, focus on figuring out who the more competent members of your class are and corralling them into your group as early as you can. The best way to do so is to listen intently in class. Who seems to know what's going on? Who provides insightful and thoughtful comments? Consider approaching them after class or in an email and saying something like "I really appreciate your comments in class. Would you be interested in forming a study group with me and/or a few others to toss more ideas around?"

TIP

Even if your law school arranges study groups for you (and some do), you can still seek out other students that you may connect with. Sometimes working with different students with different skill sets and perspectives helps.

Using a Laptop in Class Saves Time Come Exams

Not every law school professor allows students to bring a laptop to class, so this tip may not help everybody. But if you do have the laptop option, the time you save when exams roll around is well worth lugging it to class because you don't have to put much effort into making an outline later. After all, all your class notes are already neatly typed and organized. Likewise, with a laptop, combining your reading or study-group notes with your class notes is easy, provided you keep it up and running during these meetings or while you read. When you have everything saved as different computer files, cutting and pasting into one outline document is a snap. Plus, typing everything out makes it much easier to insert headings or rearrange material.

Getting Commercial Study Aids Early Helps You throughout the Semester

As a 1L, falling behind in your classes right from the beginning is easy. Your best bet for avoiding that problem is taking a few weeks to get a feel for each of your classes, diagnosing your problem areas, and then talking to upper-division students and academic success professors about which commercial study aids work best for the courses you're taking (head to Chapter 14 for more on choosing commercial study aids). After you've done that, you can purchase the study aids within the first month. That way, you can follow along in your commercial outline all semester, which helps you clarify confusing concepts before they get out of hand.

TIP

Don't be shy! Ask your mentors or study group leaders if they have study aids you can borrow. Don't make the mistake of waiting until the middle of your 1L fall semester before purchasing any commercial outlines.

Having a Low Profile Keeps You More above the Gossip Fray

The fact that gossip spreads through a law school like wildfire comes as no surprise. Most law students don't enjoy being the target of such gossip, so they maintain a low profile at parties and other social events. Law students have long memories; don't forget that after graduation, your classmates become your colleagues. If that isn't a good reason for keeping your personal life under wraps from everyone except your closest friends, I don't know what is.

Second-career students who aren't as involved in the party/social scene usually have an easier time staying out of the law school rumor mill. They may not be as keen as younger students to jump on the gossip bandwagon and as a result are better able to separate their law school and outside lives. The maturity and boundaries they bring can help you stay focused on why you're in law school.

Getting Friendly with Professors Early Ensures Good References Later

Every law student needs references when applying for summer jobs, permanent jobs, scholarships, fellowships, or clerkships. Because most law classes are large and you don't really get to know your professors in class, you need to work at cultivating good relationships with them outside of class. Here are a few tips for getting started:

>> **Make yourself stand out in class in a good way.** Raise thoughtful questions; doing so impresses professors more than someone who's perpetually eager to answer their every question.

>> **Attend office hours frequently.** Because so few students ever take advantage of this opportunity, you not only stand out but also spend valuable one-on-one time with your professor.

>> **Try to land a research assistantship or TA position.** A *research assistantship* is the ultimate opportunity for cultivating meaningful relationships with your professors so they can comment on more than your achievement on one final exam or classroom participation. Check out Chapter 19 more about the value of a research assistantship.

Another option is working as a teaching assistant (TA). You have to do exceptionally well in the course because the professor will trust you to explain things you didn't understand in the way they want you to learn it. As a TA, you build a great working relationship with the professor, which can benefit you down the line in terms of both recommendations and general support and guidance.

Doing Externships for Credit Kills Two Birds with One Stone

Many schools offer opportunities to participate in externships for course credit. An *externship* (sometimes used interchangeably with *internship*) involves working at a public-interest organization, courthouse, or governmental organization for credit but no pay. It's a great way to inject variety into your course load while doing something new and different, getting more credits under your belt, and gaining more legal experience. You can often take externship courses during the summer and during the school year. You gain not only hands-on work experience but also a refreshing break from classroom-based theory. On top of that, you can cultivate another valuable reference from your supervising attorney or judge. Another plus about serving an externship in summer is that it can enable you to take a lighter course load one semester in the next year.

Joining a Club Gets You Access to Course Outlines

An added bonus of joining a law school club is the opportunity it offers for gaining access to a bevy of course outlines. (You can read more on clubs and all types of law school extracurriculars in Chapter 19.) Many club officers maintain an outline bank or a drive with outlines from past members and make them available to all current club members, as long as they pay their annual membership dues (which usually amount to only a nominal fee). With outlines, the more you have, the merrier, so don't overlook this fabulous opportunity to score some extras.

Graduating in December Sometimes Gives You a Leg Up

Only a handful of students elect to graduate in December at law schools that make doing so an option. Those who do often find more receptive job markets. Students who graduate in December, after 2½ years of law school, usually have taken summer school, studied abroad to gain extra credits (see Chapter 18), or started early, in the summer before their first full year at schools that offer summer starter programs.

Understanding why December graduates often have a leg up isn't hard. Competition for jobs is much less during winter months than in the late summer and fall. December grads may have a better shot at responding to postings in their schools' career services offices (CSOs) and want ads in the paper because fewer people are likely to be job-hunting at that time of year.

Making Use of Alums Boosts Your Job-Search

The majority of jobs — both traditional legal and JD advantage/alternative jobs — are found through connections, not through job postings at your career services office. Employers like to hire people who are personally recommended to them instead of taking a chance on some unknown entity whose résumé just happens to land on their desk. Having an alum pulling for you (either one who works there or who is known to the hiring staff member) can make all the difference between an offer and a rejection. This point is true regardless of whether you're looking for summer jobs after your first and second years or a permanent job.

TIP

The best way to find alumni connections is to sit down with your career services staff members and tell them what type of work you're interested in and in what geographical location. Using information from electronic alumni databases, LinkedIn, alums of the student organizations you're involved with, and so on, they can match you up with alums in your area of interest. Just compose a quick email requesting an informational interview (more on these in Chapter 22) to find out more about their work and gain advice on entering that field.

TIP

A bonus tip: Being a work-study student in the CSO doesn't hurt your job search. You get to see all the opportunities first!

Index

A

AALL. *See* American Association of Law Libraries

AALS. *See* American Association of Law Schools

ABA. *See* American Bar Association

Above the Law (digital resources), 317

Abrams, Lisa L. (*The Official Guide to Legal Specialties: An Insider's Guide to Every Major Practice Area*), 303

Academic Planner | School Agenda (Erin Condren), 138

academic support team, 208, 213

academic writing, contests, 251–252

accelerated programs, 44–45

acceptance
 contract, 117
 into law school, 38, 76

accommodations
 bar examiners and, 334
 deadlines for, 89
 ensuring exam, 200–201
 paperwork, 108
 for students with disabilities, 31–32

accreditation, 45, 231

ACLU (digital resources), 317

acquisitions editor, 314

action words, résumé, 267

active-duty military members, 34

adjudication, 303

administration, career in law school, 315

administrative law lawyers, 303

admiralty lawyers, 301

admissions committee, 60
 charting coursework and work history, 62
 ideal applicant traits, 61
 letters of recommendation, 56, 61, 63, 64, 73
 "major" problem, solving, 62–63
 prelaw advisors, 63
 "standing out" misconception, 60–61
 use of GPA, 58

admission to law school. *See also* application, law school
 acceptance, 76
 admissions committee, 60–63
 application process, 54–59
 challenging coursework, benefits of, 62
 commitment to multiple law schools, 77
 deciding between schools, 77
 deferments, 79–80
 extracurricular activities, 61, 74–75
 "major" problem, 62, 63
 prelaw advisors, utilizing, 63
 receiving law school decisions for, 76
 rejection, dealing with, 79
 using online tools for, 70
 waitlist, handling, 78–79

advance directives, 304

adverse possession, 118

advisors, 63

advocacy clubs, 247

age, student, 27–29. *See also* older students

alternative legal careers
 administration, law school, 315
 alumni as resource on, 309
 bar exam and, 311
 business, 311
 considerations involved in, 309–310
 frequency of choosing, 307–308
 informational interviews and, 318
 information resources, 309
 JD degree, value of, 309, 310
 job-search tactics, 318–319
 journalism, 316–317
 librarian, 317–318
 likes and dislikes, assessing, 313
 politics, 311
 publishing, 314
 reasons for pursuing, 308–309, 311–312
 resume for, 319
 teaching law, 315–316
 volunteering, 318

alumni, 309
 contacts, 340, 342
 databases of, 358
 informational interviews with, 302, 358

American Association of Collegiate Registrars and Admissions Officers (AACRAO), 58

American Association of Law Libraries (AALL), 318

American Association of Law Schools (AALS), 316
 website, 315

character and fitness
   exam, 330–331
checklist, 130–131, 173, 192
Chicago Kent, 46
choosing a school, 37
   ABA-approved vs non-ABA-
      approved, 45
   big fish/small fish dichotomy, 38
   city size and employment
      opportunities, 41
   cost, 41
   course selection and
      breadth, 47–48
   dual degree/joint degree
      opportunities, 45–46
   duration, 44–45
   employment of graduates, 50
   fellowships, 42
   financial aid packages, 42
   global study
      opportunities, 48–49
   interview, scheduling, 51
   library, quality of, 49
   local law schools, 43
   location, 43–44
   national law schools, 42
   private schools, 40
   public interest,
      commitment to, 48
   reach school, 38
   regional law schools, 43
   renewal terms, 42
   reputation, 42–43
   safety, campus, 43
   safety school, 38
   scholarship opportunities, 42
   size of school, 38
   specialization, 46
   state schools, 40
   student-to-faculty ratio, 41
   target school, 38
   teaching quality, 46–47
   tuition, 40, 41
   urban vs rural or suburban, 44
   using ABA 509 reports for, 40

   visits and, 50–52
   weather, 44
   work-study funds, 42
Christian Legal Society, 248
Chronicle of Higher Education
   job postings, 316
   website, 315
citation exercises, 119
cite-checking, journal article, 244
civil litigation lawyers, 305
civil procedure, 117, 327
civil wrongs, 116
civ pro. See civil procedure
class
   arguing in, 122
   composite, 337
   legal research, 119
   missing, 121, 123
   number of hours, 122–123
   organization, 120–122
   participation, 159
   sitting in, during school visit, 51
   study aid use in, 125
   typing notes on laptop, 174
classmates
   arguing with, 122
   competition from, 350–351
   gossip, 355
   used to same, 111–112
class rank, in resume,
   213, 267–268
classroom
   diversity, 26
   size of, 151
clerkship
   desirability of, 289–290
   personality traits needed, 290
   salary, 290
   as summer employment, 264
client development, 281,
   287, 288
clinics, 227, 231
clips, 317
cliques, 113

closed-book exams, 195–197
clothing, 271, 337
clubs
   activity, 248
   advocacy, 247
   benefits of, 239
   choosing, 247–248
   outline access for members, 357
   special-interest
      organizations, 248
   student government, 247
code (statutory) courses, 225
collaboration, on papers, 198
collegiality, 281
commercial outlines. See
   study aids
commercial study aids, 183
   hornbooks vs, 186–187
common-law (judge-made law)
   courses, 225
competition
   from classmates, 350–351
   for jobs during winter
      months, 357
computer
   benefits of using, 354–355
   for typing class notes, 174
   use during exams, 202–203
concurring opinion, 158
conditional scholarship, 42
con law. See constitutional law
consideration, contract, 117
constitutional law, 326, 327, 328
   balancing approach of, 119
   cases, 118
Constitutional Law Society, 248
contact information, updating, 90
contact lenses, 100–101
continuing legal education
   (CLE), 311
contracts, 117–118, 326, 327, 328
corporate lawyers, 303
corporation, in-house
   counsel for, 287
corporations course, 221–222

cost
  bar exam, 325
  bar review course, 331
  law school, 41
  of study aids, 184–185
  studying abroad, 234–235
counselor
  career, 339–340
  referrals for, 108
counterarguments, in essay
  answer, 193
courses
  bar-related, 221–222
  case law vs code, 225
  clinics, 227, 231
  directed studies, 229
  discussion, 227
  easy, 225
  expectations,
    discovering, 226–227
  experiential learning
    requirement, 231
  externships for credit, 232
  favorites, identifying, 300
  graduation
    requirements and, 221
  independent research, 229
  lecture vs Socratic
    method, 227–228
  making room for
    interesting, 222–223
  outside law school, 233
  practice-related, 222
  real-world experience, 230–233
  schedule, 220, 223
  school curriculum, selection and
    breadth of, 47–48
  selecting, 220–223, 225
  seminars, 226, 228
  shopping period for, 227
  for solo practitioners, 286
  strategies for selecting, 224–230
  study-aboard, 233–235
  survey, 223
  time of day offered, 230
  variety vs specialization, 224

coursework, in law application
  process, 62
Courthouse New Service (digital
  resources), 317
court simulation, 244
courts of limited jurisdiction, 291
cover letter
  crafting, 266–269
  credible, 268–269
  drop, 270
  format, 269
  importance of, 268
  for judicial clerkship, 291
  researching employers for, 269
  to small and medium-sized law
    firms, 285
  when to send, 260
  writing, 269
credential assembly service
  (CAS), 71–72
Credential Assembly Service
  Authentication and
  Evaluation (CASA&E), 58
criminal law, 117, 327, 328
criminal lawyers, 303–304
criminal procedure course, 222
Crushendo (study aid), 182
Cruz, Jermaine, 309
CSO. See career services office
curriculum, first-year, 18, 115
  civil procedure, 117
  class hours, 122–123
  class pace, 121
  constitutional law, 118–119
  contracts, 117–118
  criminal law, 117
  handling professors, 123–125
  lack of traditional
    homework, 120
  legal research and writing, 119
  one-exam concept, 121–122
  organization, course, 120–122
  property, 118
  syllabus, 120
  torts, 116
cybersecurity lawyers, 304

D

DACA students, loan
  educational funds, 84
data privacy, lawyers, 304
daydreaming, avoiding, 165
debt, 41, 50
defendant, 156–157, 246
defense lawyers, 303–304
deferments, 79–80
degree
  from ABA-approved vs non-ABA
    approved school, 45
  dual/joint degrees, 45–46
  LLM (master of laws), 27, 45, 316
  MLS (master of library
    science), 318
  PhD, 316
degree audit tool, 221
degree granting, 57, 90
Dershowitz, Alan (*Letters to a
  Young Lawyer*), 97
desk/desk chair, 98
desk lamp, 98
dictionary, legal, 122, 148
diplomas, 335, 340
directed studies, 229
directions, to and around law
  school, 109
disabilities, students with, 31–32
discipline, necessity of, 349
discussion courses, 227
dissent, 158
distractions, avoiding, 164
diversity, student, 25–26
  active-duty military members, 34
  age, 27–29
  change in, 27
  disabilities, 31–32
  first-generation students, 30
  full-time/hybrid/part-time/
    evening students, 33
  gender, 27
  LGBTQIA+ students, 30–31
  motivations, 26
  multicultural students, 34–35

exams, law school
  allowable references,
    identifying, 200
  anonymous system, 197
  answering questions in
    order, 202
  blue book use, 190
  brain dump, 196
  closed-book, 195–197
  ensuring
    accommodations, 200–201
  essays, 190–194
  evaluating midterm grades, 199
  exam software, 200
  grading on a curve, 199
  hints from professors, 123
  instructions, importance of
    reading, 201
  issue spotting, 190, 191–192
  library file of previous, 175
  mastering, 189–197
  midterms preparation, 199
  multiple choice, 194
  notify proctors for special
    needs, 203
  one-exam concept,
    121–122, 197, 198
  open-book, 195–197
  open-school, 166, 170, 171, 174
  outline answers, 202
  outline remainder of
    answer, 202
  paper as alternative to, 198
  practice, 175–177
  proctors, 197, 202, 203
  professors suggestion
    for, 201–202
  question order, 202
  reviewing old exams, 199
  review sessions for, 166–168
  schedule, 223
  school system for, 197–199
  short-answer, 194–195
  sleep, importance of, 201
  survival strategies, 200–203

  take-home, 195
  time, keeping track of, 203
  time limits, 201–202
  typing, 202–203
  uniqueness of, 190
  writing legibly, 202–203
exchange programs, 212
exercise, 133
experience, hands-on
  clinics, 227, 231
  externships, 232, 356–357
  gaining, 350
  lack in law school
    curriculum, 350
experiential learning
  requirement, 231
external clinics, 231
externship, 210
  for course credit, 232,
    356–357
  requirements for, 47–48
  as summer job, 262–263
extracurricular activities, 13, 18,
  237–238. See also specific
  activities
  academic writing
    contests, 251–252
  areas of practice, 239
  bar associations, 251
  benefits from, 238–240,
    244, 250
  clubs, 247–248
  impact of, 74–75
  importance, in law school
    admission, 61, 74–75
  law journal, 240–244
  law review, 240–244
  legal work experience, 260
  making new connections, 239
  moot court, 244–246
  for out of college students, 75
  outside of law school,
    251–254
  research assistantships, 249–250
  résumé strengthening with,
    213–214, 240, 266, 268

  for undergrads, 75
  working part time, 252–254
eyeglasses, 100–101

F

face-time, need for, 282
fact patterns, 157, 169
  description, 190–191
  issue-spotting in, 191–192
  multiple-choice questions, 194
  policy question compared,
    192–193
  red herrings in, 191
  size of, 191
facts, cases, 151, 157
faculty. See professors
FAFSA. See Free Application for
  Federal Student Aid
family
  balancing law school and, 29
  electronic wish list for, 101
  involvement, in orientation, 113
  law, 221, 304
  making time for, 135
federal court, 117, 264, 290
the Federalist Society, 248
Federal Rules of Civil Procedure, 117
fee tail, 118, 148
fee waiver program, 74
Feinman, Jay M. (Law School 101:
  Everything You Need to Know
  About American Law), 97
fellowships, 42
financial aid, 42, 81–82, 105. See
  also legal education, financing
  applications, 66–67, 77
  award letters, 82
  for laptop, 96
financial sacrifice, law
  school as, 16
firms. See law firms
first-generation students, 30
first year (1L) curriculum.
  See curriculum, first-year

first year (1L) summer, 211
  academic endeavors, 211–212
  academic support team, 213
  exchange programs, 212
  grades and class rank, reviewing, 213–214
  meeting with professors, 213
  resume updation, 213–214
  study abroad, 211–212
  summer school, sticking around, 212
  transferring to other institutions, 214
  visiting another school, 215
  work during, 215–216
Fischl, Richard Michael (*Getting to Maybe: How to Excel on Law Exams*), 97
fitness review, 330–331
flashcards, 99, 149, 168, 187
flexibility, judicial clerkships, 289–290
Focus Booster (app-based planner), 138
folders, 99
food, 110, 133
"The 4 Best Planners for Law School Students 2025" (article), 138
Free Application for Federal Student Aid (FAFSA), 66–67, 79, 81–82, 85
freelance journalism, 316–317
friends
  electronic wish list for, 101
  making time for, 135
  study groups with, 178
full-time programs, part-time programs vs, 13–14
fun, making time for, 337
future interests, 118

G

gender, diversity in, 27
general exam-strategy programs, 167

generalist, 240
Getting to Maybe: How to Excel on Law Exams (Richard Michael Fischl and Jeremy Paul), 97
Glannon Guides (study aid), 182
global study opportunities, 48–49
goals, study time, 164–165
golden handcuffs dilemma, 282
Google, 303
  Calendar (app-based planner), 139
  Scholar, 272
gossip, 9, 355
governmental organizations
  interviews on campus, 270
  summer jobs at, 261, 262
  working for, 288
grade-point average (GPA), 68, 80, 190, 197
  cumulative, 72
  degree, 72
  easy professors and, 225
  importance in admission process, 62
  résumé inclusion of, 267–268
  school choices and, 38–39
  second semester and, 206
  summer job, effect on landing, 259–260, 263
grades
  class participation effect on, 159
  curve, grading on, 199
  first year, importance of, 207
  importance to employers, 291–292
  interview discussion of, 273
  midterm, evaluating, 199
  reviewing 1L grades, 213–214
grading-on competitions, law journal, 242
Graduate Record Examinations (GRE), 55, 71, 80
graduation
  being unemployed at, 341–343
  career counselor, 339–340
  completing, on time, 336–337

in December, 357
  events, 340
  future career, looking forward, 338–340
  informational interviews, 339
  jitters, 335
  job-advice, 340
  job shadowing, 339
  photo, 337–338
  registrar, meeting with, 336, 337
  requirements, fulfilling, 221, 336
  research careers, 339
  time off after, 339
  unemployed after, 341–343
GRE. *See* Graduate Record Examinations
groceries, 134
group
  peer mentors, 112
  study, 177–179, 354
gunners, 10

H

handwriting, legible, 202–203
Harvard Environmental Law Review, 241
headphones, 96–97
health
  eating well, 133–134
  exercise, 133
  plan, 133
  sleep, 134
health-care lawyers, 304
Health Law Society, 247
HigherEdJobs website, 316
highlighters, office supplies, 98
Hispanic National Bar Association website, 35
hobbies, 127, 131, 132
holdings, court, 158, 166
homework
  lack of traditional, 120
  for orientation, 91
hornbooks, 123, 184

M

managing editor, 314

maps of campus, 109

martindale.com website, 275, 285, 292

Master of Laws (LLM) degree, 27, 45, 316

Master of Library Science (MLS) degree, 318

MBE. *See* Multistate Bar Examination

McCoy, Tajira, 169

medical conditions, productivity and, 164

MEE. *See* Multistate Essay Examination

memorization, value of, 165–166

mens rea, 117

mental filtering, 148

mentors, 130

  judicial clerkships, 264

  law students as, 208

  meeting with, in second semester, 207–208

  for multicultural students, 34–35

merit scholarships, 212

midterms, preparing for, 199

military educational benefits, 83

Miller, Robert H. (*Law School Confidential*), 97

mind-set, attaining the law school, 110, 117

  same classmates, 111–112

  seating charts, 111

Mindset: The New Psychology of Success (Carol S. Dweck), 97

mini-fact patterns, 194

MLS (Master of Library Science) degree, 318

mock trial team, 245. *See also* moot court

monitor, 95–96

moot court, 8, 18

  appellate brief for, 246

  benefits of, 244

  board, 245

  competitions, 246

  intramural, 245–246

  national, 245

motivations, for entering law school, 16–17, 26

moving to law school, planning for, 106–107

MPRE. *See* Multistate Professional Responsibility Examination

MPT. *See* Multistate Performance Test

multicultural students, 34–35

multiple-choice exams, 194

Multistate Bar Examination (MBE), 23, 326, 328–329

Multistate Essay Examination (MEE), 23, 326, 329

Multistate Performance Test (MPT), 23, 326, 329–330

Multistate Professional Responsibility Examination (MPRE), 24, 326, 327–328

Muslim law student association, 248

myHomework Student Planner (app-based planner), 139

N

NALP. *See* National Association for Law Placement

NALP Directory of Legal Employers, 265, 282

naps, 134

National Asian Pacific American Bar Association website, 35

National Association for Law Placement (NALP), 215, 288, 303, 315

  Directory of Legal Employers, 265, 282

  on median starting salaries, 17

  on-campus interview, 270

  website, 50, 265, 282, 314

National Bar Association website, 35

National Conference of Bar Examiners (NCBE), 23, 326

  website, 45, 325, 327

National Jurist, 182

The National Law Journal (digital resources), 317

Natural Resources Defense Council, 262

navigating, to and around campus, 109

NCBE. *See* National Conference of Bar Examiners

need-based scholarships, 212

negotiating, job offer, 294

Nemko, Marty (*Careers For Dummies*), 308

NerdWallet website, 85

networking, for jobs at small and medium sized firms, 285

NextGen bar exam, 23–24, 326, 327

nonlegal jobs, 215–216

nonpaying jobs, 262–263

nonprofit organization

  career with, 288–289

  clerkship at, 264

  summer employment at, 262

nontraditional legal jobs, 313–314

  law librarianship, 317–318

  law school administration, 315

  legal journalism, 316–317

  legal publishing, 314

  teaching law, 315–316

Northen, Kathy, 177

notebooks, 99

notecards, 98

notes, 240

  class, typing on laptop, 174

  law review, 240

  in open-book exams, 166

  thank-you, 278

  writing for law journal, 243

Nutshells (study aid), 182

O

oath/pinning ceremonies, 91–92

offer, contract, 117

office hours, faculty, 124–125

periodical editors, 314

periodical publishing, 314

perpetuities, 118

personal injury lawyers, 305

personal interests, résumé inclusion of, 267

personal items, 99

backpack/book bag, 100

reusable food containers, 100

spare eyeglasses/contact lenses, 100–101

water bottle, 100

personal life, transition to law school and, 104–105

personal statement

law school application and, 64–65

length, 64

prelaw advisor critique, 63

writing, 64–65

perspective, résumé, 267

petitioner, 157

PhD degree, 46, 316

phone interview, 302

photos

graduation, 337–338

for ID card, 90

picture-perfect photo, 337–338

plaintiff, 156–157, 246

planner

apps, 138–139

paper, 138

play and work, balancing, 130–133

policy question, essay, 192–193

politics, as career alternative, 311

portable chargers, 97

portfolio, 275

postgraduation job, searching for, 22

power nap, 134

practice exams

difficulty of, 176

finding, 175–176

purpose of, 175

sample answers, 176

simulated, 332

practice-related courses, 222

preference sheet, law journal, 242

prelaw advisor, 63

prelaw programming, for first-generation student, 30

pre-orientation. *See also* orientation

activities, 87

checking email daily, 88

deadlines for accommodations, 89

final degree granting transcripts, 90

learning disability testing, 89

ongoing duty to disclose, 89–90

programs, 88

submitting photos for ID card, 90

updating contact information, 90

prestige, of judicial clerkship, 289

printer, 96, 268

printing, on exams, 203

priority list, for study session, 164–165

Prisoner Rights (club), 247

private practice

benefits of, 280–281

boutique firms, 287

large firms, 281–283

salaries, 281

small and medium-sized firms, 283–285

solo practice, 286

private school vs state school, 40

private tutor, for bar exam, 333

problem, analyzing, 147

Pro Bono Club (club), 247

procedural posture, 157

procrastinating, 131

proctors, exam, 197, 202, 203

productiveness log, 162

productivity, 162

increasing, methods for, 164–165

problems with, 163–165

study groups, 178–179

professional responsibility exam, 325

professors, 41, 123

on admissions committee, 60

anticipating next move of, 159

career as, 315–316

connecting with, in second semester, 208

easy, 225

important concepts, 124

likes and dislikes, 124

meeting, 1L summer, 213

for multicultural students, 34–35

office hours, 124–125, 356

practice exam availability, 175–177

recommendation letters from, 63, 64

references from, 159, 225–226, 356

relationships with, cultivating, 356

research assistantships with, 249–250

review sessions, 167

seeking help from, 124–125

Socratic method, 149–152

strictness of, 196–197

student-to-faculty ratio, 41

study aids and, 184, 186

suggestions for exams, 201–202

teaching quality, 47

project editor, 314

proofreading

admission application, 65–66

law journal, 244

résumé, 268

writing sample for interview, 272

property, 118, 326, 327, 328

prosecutors, 303–304

public interest, law school commitment to, 48

public sector, working in, 287–289

public speaking

gaining skills in, 347

Socratic method, benefits of, 151

publishing, legal, 314
push points, 159

Q

queries, 317
questions
  bar exam, 326, 328–329
  informational interview, 302
  interview, answering/asking, 272–273, 276
  order of exam, 202
  policy, 192–193
  Socratic method, 10, 149–151
Quimbee (study aid), 182, 183

R

racial diversity, 34–35
rationale, case, 158
rational thinking, 147
reach school, 38
reading
  amount required, 8–9, 120
  assignments, 119
  cases, 153–154
  for class, 146
  extra, 122–123
  keeping up with, 120
real estate lawyers, 305
real-world experience, credit for, 230
  courses outside law school, 233
  experiential learning requirement, 231
  externships, 232
  law clinics, 231
reasonable accommodations, for students with disabilities, 31–32
reasoning, courts, 158
recommendation, letters of. *See also* references
  from employers, 64
  law school application and, 56, 61, 63, 64

LSAC and, 73
  from prelaw advisor, 63
redact, 272
red herrings, spotting in a fact pattern, 191
references
  academic, 315–316
  class participation and, 159
  from clerkship, 264
  from faculty in your field of interest, 225–226
  importance to employers, 292
  research assistantships and, 250
  for teaching positions in law school, 315–316
refund, 90, 105
regional law schools, 43
registrar
  exam number, assigning, 197
  meeting prior to graduation, 336, 337
regulatory and compliance law, 305
rejection
  job offer, 294–295
  of law school application, 79
relationships, law school's effect on personal, 104–105
relaxation time, 131, 135
Remember The Milk (app-based planner), 139
remission, tuition, 83
reorientation, 206
reputation, law school, 42–43
RescueTime (app-based planner), 139
research
  assistant, references and, 226
  careers, 339
  independent, 229
  judicial clerkship positions and, 289, 290
  legal, 119
  paper, for seminar course, 226, 228
  skills, in small and medium-sized firms, 285

research assistantship
  advantages of, 250
  duties of, 249
  finding, 249–250
  value of, 356
researching employers, cover letter, 269
residence requirements, 337
resources. *See also* websites
  books, 97
  job-advice books, 340
  for journalism career, 317
  on nontraditional career options, 309
  study aids, 182–187
  use of bar, for exams, 333
respondent, 157
resume
  for alternative career job search, 319
  career services office and, 266, 270
  crafting, 266–269
  differences from undergraduate, 266
  drop, 266, 270
  important elements in, 267–268
  posting, 271
  size, 267
  to small and medium-sized law firms, 285
  strengthening with extracurricular activities, 240
  successful legal, 266–268
  tailoring to employer, 266–267
  updation of, 213–214
  when to send, 260
reusable food containers, 100
review course, bar
  advantages of, 329, 330–332
  cost, 331
  practice exams, simulated, 332
  schedule, 331
review sessions, 166–168
Rome, Lucy, 138
roommates, 106

About the Author

Tracy L. Simmons, JD, MA, is Associate Dean of Admissions and Student Affairs at Howard University School of Law. She brings more than 25 years of experience in higher education — including leadership in admissions, financial aid, student affairs, and diversity work — and has helped thousands of students navigate the path to and through law school.

A long-standing advocate for access and equity, Simmons has served for over 17 years as a consultant with the Council on Legal Education Opportunity (CLEO) and has held leadership roles with the Association of American Law Schools (AALS), the National Association of Student Financial Aid Administrators (NASFAA), and the Law School Admission Council (LSAC), including service on the LSAC Board of Trustees.

She is also a co-founder of the Womxn of Color Collective for law school professionals; co-chair of the Legal Professions Chapter of NADOHE; an advisor to the CAI Council for Children; a board member of Barrier Breakers, Inc.; and a member of the Board of Advisors for Brother-in-Law at Howard Law.

Simmons holds a JD from Golden Gate University School of Law and an MA in Education from San Diego State University. A proud member of Alpha Kappa Alpha Sorority, Inc., she is deeply committed to mentorship, community-building, and expanding opportunities in the legal profession.

Dedication

To my parents, Edward and Marion Simmons — also known as Papa Simmons and Mama Merge — I hope you are proud. I wouldn't be here without you, literally or figuratively. On my hardest days and my brightest days, even when you drive me a little crazy, you have always had my back.

You pushed me to be better than I believed I could be. You saw things in me long before I saw them myself. I didn't always appreciate it, and I didn't always understand it — but as a grown woman, I now know exactly what you were doing. Though I didn't give you grandchildren, I offer you this gift — our legacy in writing.

As the postcard from *Saints and Sinners* said, you've been my personal Mother Teresa.

I love you both more than words on a page.

To my law school admissions tramily — you are my people. You remind me that this work is heart work. Thank you for the laughter, the venting sessions, the shared mission, and the unwavering commitment to opening doors for others. You've made this journey richer than I could have ever imagined. Your support has carried me through seasons of uncertainty, triumph, and everything in between, and I am forever grateful.

Author's Acknowledgments

First and foremost, I thank God. Without Him, I am nothing. When I was too achy to sit and write, too tired to believe I had anything worth sharing, He reminded me that I am simply the vessel — and that purpose will always find its way to the page.

To my brilliant agent, Tajira McCoy — thank you for believing in me before I believed in myself. Your vision, leadership, and relentless "stick-to-it-ness" (yes, I'm keeping that word!) changed the trajectory of my life. You saw this book when it was only an idea whispered in my brain.

To my editor, Tim Gallan — thank you for stepping in when I felt lost and directionless. With a gentle but steady hand, you guided me back to purpose. Your patience, insight, and unwavering support helped this second edition become what it needed to be.

To Dean Cherie Scricca, Director Cheryl Barnes, and Professor Rod Fong — thank you for taking a chance on me and opening doors others may not have. Your belief and encouragement have shaped my career and this moment.

To the readers — especially the ones who have been told they couldn't do something; those who felt unseen, unheard, or unvalued — this is for you. For the dreamers and the doers. For the advocates and the changemakers. For anyone who dares to give voice to the voiceless and fight the good fight — whether protecting children, strengthening communities, safeguarding artists, or elevating justice for the "big guy" and the "little guy."

One of my favorite songs reminds me, "What you won't do, do for love."

And a favorite truth reminds me, "The first step is often the hardest — and the most important."

Writing this second edition was a step I never thought I'd take. But it was out of my love for the work that I do and the love and joy of seeing so many amazing people finish their race and reach their goal. May it inspire you to take yours.

To everyone who helped bring this book to life — thank you. Your support carried me through every chapter.

Publisher's Acknowledgments

Acquisitions Editor: Alicia Sparrow

Development Editor: Tim Gallan

Copy Editor: Megan Knoll

Senior Managing Editor: Kristie Pyles

Managing Editor: Ajith Kumar

Production Editor: Bharaneedharan Murthy

Cover Image: © S Fanti/peopleimages.com/ stock.adobe.com